ONIONS IN
THE STEW

Other books by Betty MacDonald in
COMMON READER EDITIONS:

The Plague and I

Anybody Can Do Anything

ONIONS IN THE STEW

BY BETTY MacDONALD

A COMMON READER EDITION • THE AKADINE PRESS

For Joan and Jerry and Anne and Bob – our best friends

Onions in the Stew

A COMMON READER EDITION published 1998
by The Akadine Press, Inc., by arrangement with
Joan MacDonald Keil and Anne Elizabeth Canham.

A COMMON READER EDITION and fountain colophon are trademarks
of The Akadine Press, Inc.

ISBN 1-888173-30-0

10 9 8 7 6 5 4

CONTENTS

Where hearts were high and fortunes low,
and onions in the stew.

CHARLES DIVINE

CHAPTER I

NO MONEY AND
NO FURNITURE

FOR twelve years we MacDonalds have been living on an island in Puget Sound. There is no getting away from it, life on an island is different from life in the St. Francis Hotel but you can get used to it, can even grow to like it. *"C'est la guerre,"* we used to say looking wistfully toward the lights of the big comfortable warm city just across the way. Now, as November (or July) settles around the house like a wet sponge, we say placidly to each other, "I love it here. I wouldn't live anywhere else."

I cannot say that everyone should live as we do, but you might be happy on an island if you can face up to the following:

1. Dinner guests are often still with you seven days, weeks, months later and sleeping in the lawn swing is *fun* (I keep telling Don) if you take two sleeping pills and remember that the raccoons are just trying to be *friends*.

2. Any definite appointment, such as childbirth or jury duty, acts as an automatic signal for the ferryboats to stop running.

3. Finding island property is easy, especially up here in the Northwest where most of the time even the *people* are completely surrounded by water. Financing is something

else again. Bankers are urban and everything not visible from a bank is "too far out."

4. A telephone call from a relative beginning "Hello, dear, we've been thinking of you . . ." means you are going to get somebody's children.

5. Any dinner can be stretched by the addition of noodles to something.

6. If you miss the last ferry—the 1:05 A.M.—you have to sit on the dock all night, but the time will come when you will be grateful for that large body of water between you and those thirteen parking tickets.

7. Anyone contemplating island dwelling must be physically strong and it is an added advantage if you aren't too bright.

Our island, discovered in 1792 by Captain Vancouver and named Vashon after his friend Admiral James Vashon, is medium sized as islands go, being approximately fifteen miles from shoulder to calf and five miles around the hips. It is green, the intense green of chopped parsley, plump and curvy, reposes in the icy waters of Puget Sound, runs north and south between the cities of Seattle and Tacoma and is more or less accessible to each by ferryboat.

On the map Vashon Island looks somewhat like a peacock and somewhat like a buzzard. Which depends on the end you choose for the head and how long you have been trapped here. The climate, about ten degrees warmer and wetter than Seattle and vicinity is ideal for primroses, currants, rhododendrons, strawberries, mildew and people with dry skin who like to read. The population is around five thousand *people* and an uncounted number of sniveling cowards who move back to the city for the winter.

Because of its location and the fact that it rises steeply from the water into high plateaus, Vashon Island is plethoric with views. Across the west are the fierce snowy craggy Olympic Mountains and the magnificent untamed Olympic Peninsula, black with timber, alive with game and fish, soggy with lakes and streams, quivering with wildness. Separating Vashon from the Olympic Mountains and Peninsula is the narrow, winding, lovely West Channel of Puget Sound. To the east are the smoky purple Cascade Mountains and Seattle. North are other islands, Bainbridge, Blake, Whidbey and the Olympic Mountains. South of us is Mount Rainier, that magnificent, unbelievably shy mountain who parts her clouds and shows her exquisite face only after she has made sure Uncle Jim and Aunt Helen are really on their way back to Minneapolis. Mount Rainier is 14,408 feet high which is higher than Fujiyama but only half as high as Mount Everest. It has twenty-six glaciers, listed in the encyclopedia as quite an accomplishment, and was also discovered by Captain Vancouver who seems to have spent a great deal of time cruising around this part of the world discovering things. Except in the very early morning or rare summer evenings when the foothills show, Mount Rainier appears to be a mirage floating in clouds, appearing and disappearing (mostly disappearing) just above the horizon.

It is described locally as looking "just like a dish of ice cream"—strawberry or vanilla depending on the time of day. To make the description perfect, the ice cream should have pale blue sauce drooled over it.

Everything on Vashon Island grows with insane vigor and you have the distinct feeling, as you leave the dock and start up the main highway, that you should have hired a native guide or at least brought along a machete. Alder, syringa, maple, elderberry, madroña, pine, salmonberry, willow, wild cucumber, blackberry, fir, laurel and dogwood crowd the edges of the roads turning them into green tunnels and only the assiduous chopping and slashing by the county and the telephone and power companies keeps this jungle from closing up the highways altogether.

From the water Vashon looks like a stout gentleman taking a Sunday nap under a wooly dark green afghan. The afghan, obviously homemade, is fringed on the edges, occasionally lumpy, eked out with odds and ends of paler and darker wools, but very ample so that it falls in thick folds to the water. Against this vast greenness, houses scattered along the shore appear small and forlorn, like discarded paper boxes floated in on the tide. The few hillside houses look half smothered and defeated, like frail invalids in the clutches of a huge feather bed.

The farm land of Vashon—Vashon is famous for its red currants, pie cherries, peaches, strawberries, gooseberries, boysenberries, loganberries, raspberries, chickens, eggs, goat's milk, Croft lilies and orchids—is gently sloping and covered with plump green and brown patchwork fields tucked in around the edges with blanket-stitching fences. Scattered here and there over the landscape are rather dilapidated out-buildings, placid cows and goats stomach-deep in lush pasture, and churches. Churches are everywhere. Vashon was once, perhaps still is, a mecca for the more vigorously religious—Free Methodists, Baptists, and so on. The other milder religions have their small strongholds too. As Vashon still retains a pungent frontier atmosphere the over-all effect is faintly ridiculous—like a man sitting in the parlor in his undershirt, drinking beer and reading the Bible. A tiny white church up to its knees in non-ecclesiastical currant bushes holds a bony arm bearing a small cross high up toward the pale sky. A large hipped white church glares disapprovingly at the movie theatre across the way. A small brown church has its frail back braced against a horde of immense invading alders, its front porch sags wearily under a load of wild cucumber vines. A very old trembly gray church keeps its yard tidy and tries not to notice how its friends have fallen off. In among the churches are houses, mostly old, mostly shapeless and paintless, set in neat green yards, rearing up wild eyed and rickety out of tangles, peering out of thickets, hiding behind orchards or teetering nervously on the edge of bluffs above the water. The newly built, freshly painted houses are either along the main highway or on the beaches. Vashon is not a geranium-planted-in-the-wheelbarrow, wagon-wheel-against-the-fence, Ye Olde Tea Shoppe community.

Our ugliness is rawboned, useful, natural and honest. Our beauty is accidental, untampered with, often breathtaking.

Oval ponds with flat silver surfaces lying in green fields like forgotten handmirrors. White pullets flapping across a green broadloom meadow like scraps of torn paper. A solitary maple tree sitting stolidly in the middle of an empty pasture, its full dark green skirt spread carefully over its thick ankles, a stout lady looking at the mountain. A red water tank spraddle-legged above rows of greenhouses, pale blue and cool like ice cubes. Green dance-hall streamers of boysenberry vines looped from post to post. Scotch broom pouring in over the hills like a flood of melted butter. Currant bushes bleeding red currants down their brown stems. Peach trees with freshly whitewashed trunks and crowded bright pink branches marching through newly plowed orchards like stiff bouquets. Strawberry patches rolling right up to the edge of the sky, the troughs between the plants scalloping the horizon.

Every road on Vashon leads to the water eventually. From almost every inch of the island we can see either the water or Mount Rainier or the Olympics or the Cascades or all four. All the edges of the island are fringed with the black spikes of virgin firs.

There are several very high points, perhaps a thousand feet or more above the water. From these places we can look down at the gray-blue Sound winding among islands dark and hairy with trees. The tides and currents show up in the channels like spilled ink. The ferryboats are white ducks waddling earnestly from shore to shore. The channel directly in front of our house, known as the East Channel, is the test course for the Bremerton Navy Yard. During the war our horizon was crossed by a steady procession of large serious gray vessels. Today we see only occasional battleships, destroyers or aircraft carriers, but every evening dark red and orange freighters glide toward the Strait; their booms fore and aft, picked out by the late sunshine, look like Tinker Toys. Filmy scarves of gray smoke trail behind them, a heavy wake thunders in to shore after they are out of sight. At night or in the early morning we hear the chunk, chunk, chunk of tugs no bigger than chips, huffing and puffing as they drag huge fantails of logs to the mills. Sometimes we see a school of blackfish leaping about in the sunshine like playful submarines. They slap their tails on the water and a glistening spray goes fifty feet in the air.

As I say, almost every inch of Vashon Island has a view, but the gullies, ravines, deep hollows and collars of the highway with no view except gray sky, wet woods and the ferry cars, seem to be the preferred home sites. We have our own school of architecture too—known in our family as a "Halvorsen House." A Halvorsen House, obviously the offspring of the mating of a gas station with a park restroom, is undeniably sturdy, has small high nearsighted windows under the eaves, a narrow brimmed roof jammed low on its forehead, no fireplace, no view, but it is anchored to its land by an enormous full cement basement or cellar. Even in the recent real estate slump Halvorsen Houses sold as fast as they were built.

The town of Vashon, quite a typical western, crossroads settlement, is small, flourishing, friendly, adequate and tacky. It has a bank, library, bakery (that bakes the most delicious bread in the world), two restaurants, shoestore, movie theatre, ice cream store, television shop, radio shop, state liquor store, bowling alley, drugstore, two hardware stores, two grocery stores, beauty parlor, variety shop (combination dry-goods and ten-cent store) two dress shops, two doctors, two dentists, an optician, a community club, several real estate offices, a funeral parlor, three gas stations and car repair shops, a post office, print shop and newspaper office, a bulldozing and heavy-equipment contractor (whose huge machines scoop out dams, cut logs, build roads down cliffs, push back the Sound with sea walls, and clear land), a furniture store, cleaner, barbershop, taxi, beer parlor, florist and of course its generous complement of churches. All the buildings are different. Most of them have high fronts like caps with the visors turned up—some are low and squashed like railway express packages—some have glass bricks set into the wall like clinics—one or two are made of banana-colored stucco—a couple are red brick. Vashon reminds me of a nice girl who doesn't know how to dress. Her pink hat, green dress, brown coat, black shoes, gray stockings, yellow scarf, orange belt and purple gloves will keep out the rain but they'll never get her elected Peach Festival Queen.

The stores of Vashon have nothing in common with the early day, "hay, bacon, gasoline and soft drinks" country store. Our stores are modern, well stocked and obliging—if they don't have it they will get it. Only occasionally do they show signs of naïveté. Once when we first moved here I sent Don to get me some wild rice purposely forgetting to tell him it was $2.25 a package. He came home with eight boxes and after I had stopped screaming he explained defensively, "I only had one but the woman at the checking counter said that as long as they were two for a quarter why didn't I take a couple more, so I did. We can use it, can't we? She said 'Wild rice don't go good in Vashon. It's a slow-mover.' "

Ten years ago a good steak dinner including soup and pie and coffee was forty-five cents—now it is a dollar without the soup. Haircuts used to be thirty-five cents—now are a dollar. Eight years ago half-soles were $1.75—today they are $1.75.

Everybody goes to Vashon on Saturday. The sidewalks overflow with harassed mothers in blue jeans herding parades of lagging children; worried old people talking in low voices as they try to stretch their pensions; Indians lolling against the buildings eating ice cream cones; red-cheeked farmers tossing plump sacks of feed into the back of old trucks; husbands waiting martyred in parked cars; giggling schoolgirls with shifty eyes pushing each other off the sidewalks; small boys making odd buzzing noises as they dart around the shoppers; plump gray-haired women in starched housedresses studying long lists or giving the high school girls cruel eyes; spindly-legged grocery boys staggering under mountainous loads as they search wildly for "that red sedan with the dent in the fender"; men with greasy hair and pants, low on their hips, hanging around the beer parlor; boys with crew cuts and blue jeans, low on their hips, hanging around old cars.

At night from the north end of Vashon we can see the lights of Seattle glittering on the horizon like a lapful of costume jewelry. From the south end the lights of Tacoma twinkle briskly along the water, then blaze up and mingle with the stars. We like this. We say, there just across the water is a city of almost a million—another of a quarter of a million is there. We can go *there* any time. It assures us that we are here by choice.

How is it we moved to Vashon Island in the first place? Well, it was just after Pearl Harbor and my husband, Donald, and I had recently met and married. Up to the time of our marriage I had been living at home with my two children, Anne twelve and Joan eleven, my mother and two of my four sisters, in a brown house in the University District where we had numerous pets, a great deal of fun, hordes of company and hardly any money.

I was working for a contractor who was building something or other, very vital, for the government at terrific expense in Alaska. It seems to me that I have heard that it was a dock and somebody forgot to take the tides into consideration and so most of the times it stands thirty feet above the water. Anyway my title was Chief Clerk which sounds impressive but wasn't, as I spent my days drinking coffee and checking purchase orders for: 500 cans cabbage—#2½—at 16¢ ea. . . . $80.00. I didn't have to check the price or the totals —we had a man for that job (very responsible—required arithmetic). All I had to do was to see that the mimeographing was clear and "cabbage" was spelled right. I was paid $47.50 a week which was never enough but was considered marvelous pay for a woman in those days in Seattle where it is still the prevailing idea that all female employees (bless their little hearts) would really rather be home baking Toll House cookies and any male not down on all fours (this does not include the government where you can be even farther down if political affiliations are okay) is automatically paid twice as much as the brightest female.

Don, who was doing final test at the Boeing Airplane Factory (I don't remember his salary, but it never seemed to be enough either), shared a rather dank, dark hillside duplex just off the campus of the University of Washington with an intellectual pal who read philosophy by candlelight, never shaved, tucked fishbones behind the cushions of the couch and considered a thorough housecleaning the tacking of another Japanese print over another spot of mildew. On stormy evenings, with a fire on the hearth and enough martinis, the apartment seemed rather desirable, but I shuddered when I thought of it in the daylight.

Then Don's roommate suddenly decided to take his fishbones to Algiers and Don asked me to marry him. We spent our weekend honeymoon (all that was allowed defense workers) in the apartment sans the roommate but avec the mildew, an eviction notice from the landlord who was tired of intellectuals, a shutoff notice from the gas company (gas had been roommate's responsibility, Don explained) and an old buddy of Don's who turned up in quite an unsteady condition and couldn't or wouldn't grasp the fact that "good ole Don" was married. I was beginning to wonder if he was, especially as Boeing for a wedding present had transferred him to the graveyard shift, which meant that he would work all night, I would work all day and we would see each other and the children briefly on Sundays. The eviction notice stated firmly that we were to be out of the apartment by the following Monday. From Monday to Friday I visited practically every real estate office in the city (roof-over-head seemed to be this roommate's responsibility) and was told by each that there was nothing to rent, there never had been anything to rent, there never would be anything to rent and "there's a war on!"

Sunday evening Don and Anne and Joan and I were sitting in front of the fire in his apartment feeling like people without passports, when the very charming Japanese professor, who with his wife lived in the top part of the duplex, came down and told us that they were being sent to internment camp and we could have their apartment. We thanked him fervently, but felt like grave snatchers as we piled into the car and raced over to see the landlord who was old and not friendly and brought out a list two miles long of applicants who he said were of *much* longer standing and *much* more desirable and *didn't* have children. Don talked and talked in his quiet voice, I sat up straight and tried to look like a good tenant and the girls explained earnestly to the landlord, who had big tufts of hair in his ears, that they weren't to be considered "children"—that most hated word in landlord language—as they were very old and anyway they were just going to visit until school was out. Finally, grudgingly, the landlord agreed to let us have the apartment but he called after us in a loud voice as we were getting in the car, "I expect you folks to tend to business now. No wild parties and don't let the pipes freeze." Anne and Joan thought this hysterically funny and collapsed in the back seat in giggles. I was furious. I thought the landlord was rude and unfair and I wanted Don to do something manly and retaliative. I demanded it.

Don looked at me quizzically and said, " 'Hope not sunshine ev'ry hour. Fear not clouds will always lour.' " Don is a Scot.

Anne and Joan celebrated our good fortune with a root beer float. Tuesday, Don and I moved in.

The upstairs apartment was light and airy, had a woodburning fireplace, a view of Mount Rainier if you had good eyes, two large friendly gray squirrels who lived in the maple tree outside the bedroom window, and a studio couch in an alcove for Anne and Joan. We were very happy and quite comfortable. Then came warm weather and the normally quiet hillside around us suddenly exploded with shrieking children, barking dogs, yowling cats and yoohooing mothers. Peddlers followed each other up our stairs like ants and when they weren't banging on the back door they were leaning on the front doorbell. Don made a large sign: DEFENSE WORKER SLEEPING—PLEASE DO NOT DISTURB! which I hung on the door when I left in the morning. It didn't help at all. The peddlers pushed it aside and knocked under it. Don grew very pale and much dourer. Each evening when I telephoned the girls they reminded me wistfully that school would be out in a few weeks "and where am I going to keep my bicycle, skis, shell collection?" etc. The man across the street began digging up his vegetable garden. The people next door to him got a puppy. I decided that I had better start looking for a house. Any house big enough for Don and me, Anne and Joan, Mother's dog Tudor, my cat Mrs. Miniver, our several thousand books and records, Joan's dried snakeskin and shell box of pretty rocks, Anne's collection of Sonja Henie pictures and Alma Gluck records, their bicycles, roller skates, ice skates and skis, my office dress, my other dress, Don's college bluebooks, his elk antlers, the brown suit he bought but could never wear because it had quite obviously been fashioned for a chimpanzee as the sleeves of the jacket were longer than the trouser legs, and the Jackie Coogan doll he had won at a carnival in Council Bluffs, Iowa, some twenty-two years before. The only trouble was that in Seattle, where we lived, there weren't any houses for rent and none for sale for nothing, which is what we had. We did like the country, it is true, we still do, but we would have gladly moved into the police station if it had been for rent furnished. You see, in addition to no money, we had no furniture.

CHAPTER II

OWNER DESPERATE

I STRONGLY suspect that most real estate salesmen have diplomas from that charm school whose other graduates are the complaint clerk in the tax assessor's office and all room clerks in large hotels. The charm school whose motto is: "A kick in the groin for everyone—we don't care who you are."

"I would like to rent a furnished house," I said appealingly to Mr. Swanson of the Cozy Homes Realty.

"And I would like a million dollars, ha, ha, ha!" said jolly old Mr. Swanson, his eyes behind his spectacles as merry as cold grease.

"I would like to rent a furnished . . ." I said wistfully to Mrs. Wirts of the Country Homes Realty: Just Ask Us—We Have It.

"Say, don't you know there's a war on?" yelled Mrs. Wirts from her desk across the room—obviously a renter didn't warrant the unwedging of her large tweed behind from the swivel chair.

"I would like to rent . . ." I said faintly to Mr. Evinrude of the Evinrude, Rillets, Wasket and Fester Realty Company: Waterfront Our Specialty.

"Listen, lady," said Mr. Evinrude jumping to his feet and digging the point of his Eversharp pencil into my thorax, "we haven't had a rental in this office for fourteen months and we prob'ly won't for another fourteen months. There's a war on, in case you haven't heard."

"I would like to rent. . . ." I said wearily to Miss Chunk of the Rural Realty Company.

"There's a war on . . . it's Boeing . . . the shipyards . . . Alaska . . . Bremerton Navy Yard. . . ." It sounded reasonable. A war boom equals an influx of war workers equals no houses, but I wasn't convinced then and I'm not now. Because after *that* war was over and *those* war workers had gone home one of my sisters wanted to buy a house with four bedrooms for $20,000. She went to at least fifteen real estate firms and was told over and over again that if she wanted such a *big* house with inside plumbing she would "have to go thirty-thirty-five thousand anyways."

A neighbor of hers had a four-bedroom house with inside plumbing she wanted to sell for $20,000. She was told over and over again that such a *big* house wouldn't sell. That nobody wanted a *big* house. That they would be lucky if they could unload such a *big* house at $7,500. My sister and her neighbor had been to the same real estate agencies but they didn't find it out for four months and then only through their milkman who introduced them and closed the deal.

Having, during the course of the last twelve years, had dealings both as buyer and seller with about one hundred and ninety-seven real estate agents here and in California where everybody is supposed to be super-charged with enthusiasm and loyalty to the climate at least, I have a few simple warnings to post:

1. Be prepared to answer all relevant questions such as: How old are you? How much do you weigh?

2. Do not be misled into thinking food will improve a salesman's attitude. "I never cared much for these rustic joints," Mrs. Morks said frankly. "Say, would it be too much trouble if I had another tuna on white without the pimento, dear? It's a long ways out here, you know."

3. If you say specifically that you want to *rent* a *furnished* house *on the water,* be prepared to spend the next few weeks looking at *unfurnished* houses for *sale* on *dry hills.*

Do not expect even a view of the water in spite of the fact that any salesman connected with any real estate firm in the Pacific Northwest cannot take two steps in any direction without tripping over a lake or an arm of the Sound.

4. Remember that: STATELY WHITE COLONIAL FAMILY HOME merely means painted white no matter how long ago. WIDOW'S PARADISE indicates owned by widow or should be owned by widow—obvious assumption being that all widows are bead brains. TERRITORIAL VIEW is phrase used for sewage disposal plants, walls of other houses, street car tracks, gasoline storage tanks, garbage dumps and telephone poles. It is to be distinguished from MOUNTAIN VIEW—any rise of ground, or FOREST VIEW—one spindly fir with two pickers near the top. RIGHT NEIGHBOR-HOOD FOR KIDDIES describes main highways, gas works, red light district, next door to tavern and all property on condemned water.

In the Pacific Northwest, there are several hundred islands, varying in size from small enough to be cuddled in the crook of your arm to over a hundred miles long. Not one of them, no matter how small, has that discarded floating paper-plate look so often associated with the word "island." These are young, virile, heavily wooded sturdy offspring who have so recently burst from the water they are still shaking the drops out of their high wooded crowns. Five of the larger islands are within commuting distance of Seattle. They are all ringed with beaches both sandy and rocky, and homes, both permanent and summer, some of which might be for rent, we thought. But when I tackled a reasonably intelligent-looking real estate agent and asked him about these islands, he treated me as if I had bounded in and demanded a snap decision as to the exact number of female seals in residence on the Pribilof Islands. "Vashon Island?" he kept repeating incredulously. "Bainbridge? Whidbey? What ever give you the idea to move over there? My gosh, I've lived in Seattle thirty-one years and I never even seen them islands.

Now we gotta little six-on-one dream for sale on Highway 99. . . ."

"We'd better look for ourselves," I told Don after the tenth try.

We investigated Bainbridge Island first because I used to visit there when I was a little girl and had pleasant memories of large, well-furnished houses with inside plumbing, electric lights, even grand pianos, all owned by *darling* people who would undoubtedly not only let us move in but would probably not let us pay any rent. All the houses, I remembered, were delightfully rustic, had orchards with yellow plums, sandy beaches with clams and gardens with bulbs.

Don had also visited on Bainbridge Island. Smiling dreamily he said, "And then we chartered this boat and loaded on the beer, there were about eighteen cases, and for three days Jack's girl sat in the bathtub wearing the captain's hat. We lost Bill overboard I don't remember just where but I'm pretty sure it was near Bainbridge."

I decided to take the children with us because I wanted Don to see how much fun an island could be with a little family, all *decent* people, none in captain's hats. Friday night I told Anne and Joan that the next day we were going to take a *lovely* picnic and go across the *beautiful* Sound on a *funny* old ferryboat and look for a cozy house where we could all be together. My voice oozed out of my mouth like molasses, and because of the sentimental picture of our all being together, I blinked up a few tears.

Anne and Joan looked at each other knowingly, at me suspiciously, at Don belligerently and wailed at Mother, "But we always go to the movie show on Saturday, don't we, Margar? We promised Patsy and Genevieve and anyway we're having macaroni and cheese for dinner, aren't we, Margar?"

Don was frankly relieved, but I was hurt. Not as hurt, of course, as I had been when Anne was in the fourth grade and wouldn't let me come to school on parents' night because she was ashamed of me because I didn't look like Ethel's mother who had the general proportions and texture of a

Sherman tank. Nor as hurt as I had been when Anne and Joan asked me not to walk to church with them because I smoked (though not on the way to church). Or as hurt as I had been when Joan explained sadly that the reason her friend Elma couldn't stay all night was because we played the radio and kept Jesus out of the house.

The big weakness in a working mother is that absence does make the heart grow fonder, even producing in her a half-baked tendency to remember the children as lonely little angels with great big Valentine hearts filled to bursting with goodness and love for Mommy. It was always a shock to be reunited with the truth, which is that a child is a young human whose natural instinct is to get her own way one hundred percent of the time, even if it involves moving the earth off its axis, or Mother off her rocker. My mother comforted me by explaining again and again that "Anne and Joan are *too* normal. All children like to do the same thing every day at the same time."

It was just as well that Don and I did go by ourselves as the day was gray and raw and we finally ate our lunch in the car in a nice warm gas station.

We took the nine o'clock ferry from Colman Dock in Seattle. I told Don we wouldn't bother about breakfast at home because they had such delicious food on the ferry.

"Like what?" he asked suspiciously.

"Like buttermilk hotcakes and little pig sausages," I said, thinking of my happy childhood. "And the ferry ride takes forty-five minutes, so we'll have plenty of time."

The ferry ride did take forty-five minutes, but a clammy doughnut beaded with moisture and a cup of coffee evidently just dipped out of the bilge were the only refreshments offered. When the ferry docked we drove off, and started looking for a real estate office. We found one, not too far from the dock. It was small and white with vines over the doorway and the proprietor, Mr. Haggerty, was so pleasant I had to go out and look again to be sure the office sign did say Real Estate. Not once did Mr. Haggerty say "there's a war on," but only that he didn't have much to rent because of a ship-yard operating on the island. "I'll be delighted to show you what I have, though," he said, getting some big old-fashioned keys out of a drawer.

What he had was one large thin-walled rickety summer house, miles and miles and miles from the ferry, a store, a school or another house. It had no electricity and the bath-room was on the back porch. The house did have a fine view of the Olympic Mountains, a sandy beach, four bed-rooms, adequate lumpy beds and enough sagging wicker fur-niture and it was rent for sixty dollars a month. Don wanted to take it at once. But I, who had lived without elec-tricity or friends and with the toilet outdoors, stood firm. By standing firm I mean that I started out in a well-modu-lated voice to point out the more glaring inconveniences, especially to a working mother, and ended up bawling about the hardships I had endured with my other husband.

Even then Don gave up reluctantly and I really sympa-thized with him because in those days, giving up a furnished house for rent, any house, was like kicking aside a big pack-age of new fifty-dollar bills with an elastic band around it just lying there on the sidewalk with nobody in sight who might have dropped it.

The only other place for rent on Bainbridge, Mr. Hag-gerty told us with unparalleled honesty, was much farther from the ferry, had no lights either and was at the foot of a steep cliff. "It's easy to get to at low tide," he said, laughing. "The rest of the time you'd better be a fish."

"Let's go see it anyway," Don said, assuming a lifetime-lease look. I stiffened and got tears in my eyes and Mr. Hag-gerty winked and said he had forgotten the key.

So then I told him about my happy childhood and the yellow plums and asked about my friends with the grand pianos and chintz couches. He said, "The Garsons? The Garsons. You mean the Garsons at Willow Point. Well, my golly, they haven't even *been* on the island for fifteen years."

"What about the Emersons?" I asked.

"The Emersons? The Emersons who used to live on Shady Beach? Why, Mrs. Emerson died twelve years ago and Mr. Emerson was so broke up he went to California to live." We went through the Hedlunds, the Crawfords, the Wickhams, and the Taylors. If they weren't dead they had all been gone at *least* ten years, more like twenty. So I brushed a few crumbs off my Civil War uniform and we all got in the car and left.

We decided to try Whidbey Island next. This time we *will* take a picnic, I said, and invited Anne and Joan to go. They looked at each other and said, "Sunday? You mean this Sunday?" and I said yes and Anne wailed, "But I promised Marilyn I would go to her house right after Sunday School and try on lipstick with her."

Joan said, "But, Mommy, Johnny and I are fixing up a camp in his basement and anyway his mother's baking cinnamon rolls. Why don't you ever go on Saturday?"

"I've already tried Saturday," I said dryly.

"But that was *last* Saturday," Anne said accusingly.

"Why doesn't Johnny's mother bake on Saturday?" I asked rather sharply.

"Oh, she usually does," Joan said, "but her stove was broken."

So Don and I drove north and took a ferry from an improbable-sounding place named Mukilteo. Whidbey Island is approximately ninety miles long, has hundreds of miles of beautiful sandy beaches, faces the Strait of Juan de Fuca and the Olympic Mountains on the west and Camano Island, Possession Sound and Saratoga Passage on the east. It is revered for getting less rain than Seattle and vicinity, *but*—and this should have loomed large to someone who had to be at her desk at seven-thirty in the morning after getting breakfast, fixing lunches, making the beds, arranging about dinner and perhaps a little mascara—its *southernmost* tip was at least twenty-five miles from Seattle and its most attractive beaches were at the northern ninety-mile end.

But it was spring and the apple trees were sticks of pink

cotton candy, dandelions were flung over the green-velvet fields like gold pieces, meadowlarks paused on fence posts to toss songs into the morning, and the bleakness of winter, with its dreary getting up and going to bed in darkness, seemed a long way off.

Enthusiastically I said to Don, "We just *have* to find a place on Whidbey Island, it is so beautiful."

Just then the car got something caught in its throat and began gagging and coughing in a very last-gasp manner. We turned off the highway and came to a stop under a maple tree newly equipped with pale green shiny oilcloth leaves. Don got out, lifted the hood of the car and began poking around. "The fan seems to be broken," he said finally, sadly. "I guess we had better go home, if we can."

We made it to the Mukilteo dock where with one last belch and shudder the car lost consciousness.

We walked up to a large gray building, about a block away, with GARAGE across the front of its cap, and Don, in his low, quiet voice, told some striped-overall legs sticking out from under a pickup truck what had happened. As Don talked the man hammered vigorously, loudly on something, tap, tap, tap. I didn't think he could hear but he apparently did for after a few hundred taps he came sliding out, stood up, wiped his hands on some waste and walked down to the dock with us. He lifted up the hood of the car, looked at the engine, lifted up the trunk and looked at the two hundred or so books Don kept there and said, "I'd trade her in if I was you."

"All right," said Don amiably. "What do you have?"

"I got a Chrysler sedan that's in awful good shape," the man said. "Come on back to the garage and I'll show it to you."

When we got back to the garage he pointed out a dark blue sedan dozing by the grease rack. "She's a dilly," he said. "Belonged to an old lady who only drove her on Sundays. Runs like a watch."

I, very innocent and not knowing that every used car

on every lot in the United States of America is supposed to
have belonged to either a sea captain or an old lady who
only drove on Sundays, thought the car actually looked like
an old lady. Plump and clean and navy blue and responsible.

Don kicked the tires non-committally.

"Drive her around the block," the garageman said generously. "She's a sweetheart."

We drove "sweetheart" around the block. She was quiet
and sedate and her clock ticked.

I said, "Let's buy her." The car was definitely a she.
Don, who is not given to snap decisions and can take fifteen
minutes to answer "Do you want mustard on your bologna
sandwich?", said nothing. He was considering.

When we got back to the garage the man took us into his
little office where he kept parts, waste, cans of oil, copies of
the *Police Gazette,* empty coffee cups and bills of sale. He
sat down in an old swivel chair and leaned way back. I sat
on a straight chair. Don leaned against a shelf stacked with
cans of anti-freeze which was very scarce at that time. The
garageman began to talk first. He was very very sad about
Don's car. After a while Don began to talk. He was very very
sad about the garageman's car. Finally, suddenly, when I
thought they were both going to cry, they came to terms and
in practically no time at all we were wheeling along the
highway in "sweetheart" who had only two noticeable flaws.
Her trunk was now filled with books and she had no door
handles on the inside. When I asked the garageman about
the door handles he said, "Golly, I don't know—probably took
off because of children. You know how you're always readin'
about kids openin' the door when the car's goin' and fallin'
out in front of a truck?" He implied that we were mighty
lucky that someone had been kind enough to save us from
this tragedy. However, riding in a car without door handles
on the inside made me feel like a canned peach peering out
of its jar at the landscape.

We were invited to spend the next weekend on Vashon

Island. The Havers, whom we visited, had a charming house right on the beach, the tides were perfect for clamming; and Saturday night as Don and I lay in bed on their porch, listening to the slurp, splash, slurp of the waves against the sea wall, and watching the ferry gliding across the moonlit water, we decided that this was the perfect place. The beach was rich with clams and driftwood. The water was filled with salmon, sole, cod and Spanish mackerel. The soil was so fertile that syringa and alder grew twelve feet a season. The climate was warmer than Seattle, the ferry crossing took only fifteen minutes and it was walking distance from the ferry. The next morning, as we dug clams in the hot sunshine, we told George Haver, "We like this place. This exact spot. We want to live here."

George was glad that we liked his beach, but very discouraging about our finding anything to rent. He explained that all the people on that particular beach had been coming over there for thirty-five years and, even though there was no road and they had to walk in by a county trail and bring in all their provisions and possessions by boat or by wife, they were all very attached to their houses and never rented them. We were so downcast by this information that he took us for a boat ride around the point.

In the course of the ride he said, "As long as you're disappointed anyway, I'm going to show you a house that will spoil you for any other beach house."

He steered the boat to shore, pulled it up on a log and we climbed a small winding path to the house.

He had told the truth. It was the most attractive house we had seen and it certainly did spoil us for all the sagging built-by-Grandpa-designed-by-the-cat structures we had seen and were to see. Unfortunately, however, the Hendersons, who were living in it and who had bought it from the doctor who had built it, were very happy there.

"We are going to live here forever," they told us, smugly.

The house, built of hewn fir timbers, was snuggled on the lap of the plump green hillside. The roof was hand-split cedar shakes, each shake at least an inch thick. The rain and the salt air had turned it all a soft pewter color. The kitchen, which was small, had knotty pine walls with a bricked-in electric stove and a trash burner across one corner. Against the windows which looked at Puget Sound and Mount Rainier over an enormous window box filled with pink geraniums, was a Flemish blue drop-leaf table and four stools. The drainboard and insides of the cupboards were the same Flemish blue. The floor was pine planks put down with wooden pegs and calked. The living room, which opened from the kitchen by a swinging pine half-door, was about forty feet long, had the same plank floors (four by twelves), an enormous stone fireplace that went up two stories, a small rustic stairway leading to a balcony from which opened three small knotty pine bedrooms and a bath. At the south end of the balcony was the master bedroom. It had a beamed ceiling, pine walls and a fireplace with a copper hood. In all the rooms were hand-braided rugs and lovely pine furniture made by the doctor. There were two patios, one off the kitchen, one in the angle of the ell formed by the master-bedroom wing and the living room. They were made of rounds of cedar with flowering moss in between. Around the south patio was a rockery filled with heather. Above it on a knoll was a gnarled old apple tree. The ground under the apple tree was carpeted with blue ajuga and yellow tulips. Across the front of the house and available to the living room by French doors was a rustic porch overlooking the water and the sandy beach and facing Mount Rainier.

It was the house everybody dreams of finding. But it definitely wasn't for rent or for sale, so we finished our drinks, patted the dogs and said goodbye to Vashon.

Then my sister Dede found and rented a small beach house on Quartermaster Harbor at the other end of Vashon Island. For the next few weeks each Saturday morning we would load the car with groceries, the children, Tudor the dog, Mother and her sketching things, bathing suits, sun-tan oil and fifty pounds of ice because the house had that kind of an icebox, and go to Vashon.

In spite of having to stop the car every fifteen minutes for Tudor to be sick and so often not making it. In spite of my two dear little daughters acting as if we had put leg irons on them and were dragging them to the stocks because we were interrupting their regular Saturday and Sunday plans. In spite of the fact that the ice always leaked on something not improved by ice water, such as cigarettes or Cornflakes. In spite of the fact that the house was really very inconvenient with remarkably uncomfortable beds and a filthy little coaloil stove that made even the orange juice taste like coal oil —we had a wonderful time. The water was warm for swimming. There were huge silvery piles of driftwood for beach fires. There were the mingled smells of fresh coffee and salt air. And there was sleep refreshing as only a sleep induced by too much sun, too much swimming and too much food, can be.

Don and I became revitalized and renewed our efforts to find a place on Vashon on the water. We went to see George Haver again and he produced a brother-in-law in the real estate business who was affable, knew and didn't care that we had no money, was familiar with every inch of Vashon Island and told the truth. He said, "Why don't you just look at *everything* for sale or rent?" So we did.

We looked at houses at the bottom of cliffs. We looked at crumbling houses furnished in sagging wicker and discarded pottery. We discovered that beach houses, no matter how attractive they are on the outside, are usually the catchalls for things not quite up to snuff or down to St. Vincent de Paul. With unrelieved regularity we saw lamp shades of pleated black chiffon over pink, black iron spears supporting faded brocade draperies, mahjong sets, large wicker trays with tassels, framed Maxfield Parrishes, frayed faded American oriental rugs, bulging Morris chairs, mostly with broken back controls, and wine jugs made into lamps. To say nothing of the entire sets of clear green glass dishes—the plates divided into stalls to keep three items of food from touching—the wooden candelabra with imitation gold wax dripped down the sides and the bunches and bunches of gilded cattails mixed with magenta everlasting flowers. Don and I got so that we could tell by the kind of fern in the abalone-shell hanging basket whether the rugs would be ragged Wilton or faded oriental.

Still we kept on. After we had finished Vashon we went to Camano Island. We looked at Manchester on the Olympic Peninsula. We drove to Tacoma and Everett and even went clear up to the San Juan Islands, an archipelago of 172 islands lying between Vancouver Island and the mainland in the Strait of Georgia. The San Juans are about seventy-five miles north of Seattle but we told each other wistfully, "If we do find the place in the San Juans, perhaps we can manage with Mother until the war and our jobs are over."

Then one morning I was in a restaurant drinking coffee and dispiritedly leafing through the "For Sale—Waterfront" section of the paper when I saw what appeared to be an advertisement of the Henderson house on Vashon. The ad said: Lodge-type log house, huge stone fireplace, 400′ of sandy beach—for sale $7000 furnished.

I called Mrs. Henderson at the office where she worked and she told me that it was their house. That her husband had been offered a wonderful job in California and they thought he should take it. I asked her why she hadn't called me and she said, "Oh, I thought of course you had found a house by this time." I choked back an impulse to say, "Oh, sure and while I was at it I worked out a plan for world peace and a cure for cancer." Instead, I made arrangements to go over the next weekend. My hands were shaking as I hung up the phone.

The next Saturday, as Don and I swung along the trail leading from the dock to the Hendersons' house, carrying our share of the groceries and liquor for the weekend (unwritten law of beach Mrs. Henderson had said, but one obviously repealed the day we moved in) I said excitedly, "Don,

I just know we are going to get this house. I feel it was meant to be. Won't living over here be wonderful for the girls?"

Don, who is a pure Scot on both sides of his family, is not exactly an optimist. In fact, if I were to be absolutely truthful, and I wouldn't dare because we are so happily married, I would say that Don is a charter member, perhaps the founder, of that old Scottish brotherhood sworn always to bring bad news home even if it means mounting a rabid camel and riding naked over the Himalayas in winter.

As we admired the huge virgin firs against the blue sky, breathed deeply of the fresh salty air—Vashon air is really so pure and clean that even coming from Seattle, which is also supposed to have good air, seems like stepping from a coal mine into an oxygen tent—and listened to the shrill happy summer sounds coming from the houses below us on the shore, I said again, "Don't you have that feeling, Don? That this house was *meant* for us?"

Don said, "I'd have more of that feeling if we had any money. There certainly is plenty of erosion along here."

But the house *was* for sale and the Hendersons had gotten it from the doctor who built it *with no down payment* because the doctor had to go in the Navy, and they were willing, really eager, to sell it to us the same way. We were to pay $150 a month until we had established a down payment, then we would go into the bank and have it refinanced. We were all terribly casual and gay, made more so by the fact that none of us had any money, didn't want the others to find it out and I kept my hand over Don's truthful mouth practically all day Sunday.

We made arrangements to come out the next weekend with two payments (which we intended to borrow) and the house would be ours.

"You see," I said to Don as we stood on the upper deck of the ferry on our way home. "It *was* meant to be."

Don pointed at the cars bouncing onto the ferry, each one denting its exhaust pipe because the deckhand hadn't lowered the ramp far enough, which he still doesn't, and remarked gloomily, "That ramp isn't down far enough."

CHAPTER III

TWO MILLION IF BY SEA

I GUESS that all of us have said at some time or another, "I will never allow *things* to dominate my life. I will keep my possessions down to a minimum." If, like me, you have nurtured the idea that you have kept your possessions down to Deargrandmother's Satsuma tea set and a few first editions, then you should move to an island. Try mixing that minimum with water and see what you get. Deargrandmother's Satsuma tea set turned out to be three old trunks minus handles, filled with clothes and/or ingots, eight barrels of vases and dishes, stuff out of ten medicine cabinets, assorted boxes of canned goods, records, elk antlers, photographs, pillows, pots and pans, record players, bamboo rakes, skirt hangers, lamp shades, ironing boards and dog beds. My few first editions, supplemented by the contents of the trunk of Don's car, were mistakenly left to rise in the moving van overnight and when we unloaded them at Vashon they had swelled into eighty-seven cartons filled with lead.

This was October after an entire summer spent with the fluctuating Hendersons who would sell one weekend, the next greeted us with tears in their eyes and said they couldn't bear to leave. My sisters Dede and Madge had married and moved into small apartments, Mother was to stay with my sister Mary while her husband was overseas, so I got the washing machine, the *Encyclopaedia Britannica,* Mother's portrait

and the Christmas tree ornaments. There was also a gentlemen's agreement that I would take my children, Mother's
dog and my cat if Mary would take the assorted turtles, gold-
fish and canaries belonging to the household. The first step
was to move out of our apartment into Mother's house. This
was accomplished easily. We simply kept dumping things in
the car and driving them to Mother's until the apartment
was empty. I packed. Don carried and drove. I started out
very methodically. "Books—reference" I marked on the outside of a carton. "Sheets—towels" I marked on another.
"Silverware" another. When Don attempted to help I said
kindly but firmly, "You had better let me do it, dear. I know
exactly what I am doing and I want things to be orderly."

"Living room draperies" I wrote on a neat newspaper
bundle. "Candles, vases, bric-a-brac" I marked a carton.
Then somehow I began running out of enough of the same
thing to fill a box—also out of boxes and newspapers—also
out of strength. By the end of the day I was rolling a jar of
mayonnaise, a heel of salami and a half-filled bottle of Guer-
lain's Blue Hour perfume in my tweed skirt and not even
stamping the bundle "Perishable."

Next came getting the things to Vashon, which was easy
too. Alison's husband borrowed a moving van, someone
else solicited an unemployed musician to drive it, Don and
the children and I loaded it and the car and we were off.
One last sentimental look at the old brown house revealed
that we had left Mother's portrait, the skis, and Tudor the
dog, who didn't care for cars and kept oozing in one side and
out the other. The rearranging to get these things in took
just the right amount of time for us to miss the ferry and
wait an hour on the dock. Also, just as we turned onto the
West Seattle Viaduct, Tudor reared up, put his paws on
Don's shoulders and threw up down the back of his blue
cashmere sweater. Don groaned and looked accusingly at
me. He couldn't do much else because the traffic is always
very heavy on the viaduct and a sudden stop or swerve might
mean being squashed by a Standard Oil truck, and I for one

certainly didn't want gasoline all over my clean jeans, I told the girls gaily. Crowded in the front seat with Don and me were the two girls, the portrait, the elk antlers, and a lot of strained silence. When we got to the dock at last, I carefully maneuvered the sweater and T-shirt over Don's head and substituted the red sweatshirt still warm from Mrs. Miniver, the cat. Tudor watched the operation reproachfully, the girls giggled behind their hands and Don's expression, to put the kindliest interpretation upon it, was rage suffused with despair spread thinly over a boiling caldron of desire to commit wificide and dogicide.

Things weren't really going too badly, however, we kept saying loudly, hollowly. We *had* intended to get the ten-o'clock ferry, but, as is usually the case with expeditions of this kind, we weren't even packed by ten. The ferry we had just missed was the two-thirty. Of course everybody was starving and the little store on the dock had only a gum-ball machine and a few O'Henry bars so stale the chocolate had turned to silver and the peanuts tasted like peach pits, but we ate them with gusto, even Tudor who the girls felt should be rewarded.

"For what?" Don asked grimly.

Harris, the musician, was sleeping in the van so we didn't bother him.

The day was lovely—hazy with a sun like a marigold. The tide was going out and the wet sand by the dock steamed faintly and gave off a nice seaweedy smell. "Wood will certainly be no problem anyway," I said cheerfully, pointing out logs in huge jackstraw heaps along the shores on either side of the dock.

"I like wood that is already sawed," Don said, unenthusiastically.

"Over at Marilyn's summer home we gathered bark," Anne said. "Even when it is soaking wet it burns keen."

"Remember those creosote logs we got at Dede's?" Joan said. "There's a nice little fat one. They weigh a lot but they certainly make a hot fire. Let's get it, Don."

Don said sternly, "One of the first laws of the beach is that anything on your property belongs to you. The man who lives in that green house is probably counting on that nice fat little log for his fire tonight."

"Darn!" Joan said. "It's just the right size."

"If there are creosotes on this side there are probably some on the other," Don said.

"But the tide will be high on our side," Joan said.

So Don explained about the tides and he apparently knew what he was talking about because he used words such as "lunar," "barometric pressure," "coastal configuration" and "tidal bore," but I only half listened as I am very well satisfied with my conception of the tide situation, which is that every twelve hours somebody, perhaps the man in the moon, pulls the plug and lets out some of the ocean. After a while he turns on the faucet and fills it up again. If he is in a hurry we have a tidal wave.

The wash from an aircraft carrier suddenly began pounding the shore. Because the tide was out, the waves slapped the flat beach with a tremendous noise like giant handclapping. The splintery old dock trembled and Tudor barked. Anne and Joan laughed and shouted and the day lost a little of its grimness and took on more of a holiday aspect.

Then the ferry came in and Don bought our first commuter's ticket: car and driver ten rides for $3.70; passengers, ten cents each. Today the fare is ninety cents for a car and driver; twenty-five cents for a passenger—a commuter's ticket is slightly less.

Hamburgers in the little lunchroom on the ferry revived us all still further—even Harris, who told us proudly he had drunk a pint of gin while driving the van through the traffic.

Our new beautiful pewter-colored dream house had no road. This tiny flaw in its perfection, at first candidly spoken of and looked upon as a flaw but so insignificant compared to things like a salt water beach and hand-braided rugs, had during the summer of fluctuation and persuasion somehow emerged as a blessing. No road meant no bores, the Hendersons said. No road meant privacy. No road meant nothing to run over the children and animals. "We don't want a road," our neighbors said and are still saying, only each year more faintly, with less conviction. "We don't want a road, either," we said bravely that summer when we were negotiating. Then came the day of reckoning and we were faced with the uncomfortable fact that walking the mile and a half from the ferry on a beautiful trail along the water carrying a pound of bacon and a quart of gin is one thing. Hauling in a van load of furniture and possessions is unquestionably another.

Thank God the civilization-ridden neighbors on the south side of us did have a road. They had a road that was steep and rutted and ended at least two hundred feet from the beach, but they generously offered to let us use it. They also let us use three rowboats and an outboard motor. Don and Harris tied all the boats together and we all loaded them. Harris insisted on steering the lead boat, which was unfortunate, as he seemed possessed with the idea (perhaps because of the pint of gin) that we were moving *from* Vashon *to* Seattle and kept heading out to sea, chairs, books and pillows spilling in his wake.

Harris, though confused, was eager and strong and by nightfall we had most of the stuff on our sea wall, a few things in the house and the washing machine in one of the boats. I invited Harris to dinner, but he pointed out that he had only six inches of beach left before high tide, so Don paid him and he slithered off, the girls waving wildly at his narrow back.

Then we all staggered wearily up the path to our beautiful new house, which was as cold as a crypt and piled high with junk. While Don and Joanie built roaring, quick-dying carton fires in the kitchen trash burner and the fireplaces, Anne and I pawed feverishly through boxes looking for the food. The night before, feeling just like Mamsie Pepper, I had baked a ham and a pot of beans and had wrapped the stuff for salad in a damp dishtowel, "so that everything will be ready and cozy for moving day," I told Don. But where were they? They certainly were not in this old box of pictures—or this one of vases or this . . . After almost an hour of fruitless search we decided that they might still be on the sea wall. I took Tudor and a flashlight and went down. Even though my neck, my back, my arms, my legs and my palms ached and with each step on the path little jagged pains ran down my earlobes, I still experienced a wonderful feeling of security as I realized that this was *our* path and I was going down to look for *our* ham on *our* sea wall.

When I got down to the sea wall I had another surge of emotion as I listened to the waves slopping against the wooden pilings and realized that the tide was in and so these were *our* waves because Mr. Henderson had explained that we owned the tidelands too.

I flashed the light over the heaps of boxes and trunks piled higgledy-piggledy all over the sea wall, hoping against hope that I had marked the box of food or that, if I hadn't, in some mysterious way the ham would make its presence known. I hadn't and it didn't, so I called Tudor.

"Here, boy," I said kindly. "Here, Tudor, boy." As I have said Tudor was my mother's dog and as I had heard my mother, who is a dog lover and a better-than-average veterinary, say a million times that a dog should be well trained, that it is not fair to the *dog*, and, as I hadn't been around Tudor too much, I presumed that I might get a little co-operation from him. A little of the man's best friend, old dog Tray stuff. I called again with even more kindness.

"Here, Tudor, old boy." Tudor, who was busy sniffing a rock, absolutely ignored me. "Tudor," I said rather sharply. Instantly he flattened himself on the ground, buried his head in his paws and awaited a blow.

I sweetened my voice again. "Tudor, old boy," I said, trying to speak just loud enough to be heard over the waves but not loud enough to frighten the little stinker. "Tudor, old boy, food! Good food! Find it, boy!" I patted the piles of boxes and trunks enthusiastically. Tudor raised his head, gave me a long disdainful look, then ran up the path to the house.

Tudor was no help but he had given me an idea. I began to sniff the boxes myself. It was not easy to get a true scent over and above the salt water and the rich rotten cabbage smell of the Tacoma pulp mill which occasionally rides in on the south wind, but I finally found the ham. It was under "Books—reference" and on top of "Living room draperies."

I insisted on setting the big pine table in the north corner of the living room and lighting the candles, but we ate clustered crossly around the fire. October nights on the salt water are penetratingly chilly.

After dinner while Anne and Joan washed the dishes in *our* new sink, which fact did not seem to lift their low opinion of this drudgery, Don and I made up the beds. When we went to find the blankets and sheets I thanked God for that short-lived spurt of efficiency—the boxes were clearly marked: "Blankets—raspberry jam—bathing suits—bed linen."

A fireplace in a bedroom is a very luxurious item. Even poking tired feet down into the icy reaches of clean sheets—"Teach me to live, that I may dread the grave as little as my bed"—is not so painful when at the same time you are looking into a merrily crackling fire.

After we had turned out the lights, Don and I watched the leaping shadows on the pine ceiling and listened to Anne and Joan's childish trebles murmuring insults to each other through the walls of their adjoining bedrooms. The wind had freshened and was making small plaintive noises in the eaves. The bed was very comfortable. I sighed deeply, contentedly, and closed my eyes. Then suddenly I was aware that in addition to the crackle of *our* fire, the slosh of *our* waves, the moan of the wind under *our* eaves, the haggling of *our* children, I was listening to *rain* on our roof.

Fumbling for the bedlight I said wearily to Don, "Do you hear that? It's raining."

Don said, "Swhat?"

I said, "Rain. Listen, it's raining and the books and records are still down on the sea wall."

Sighing heavily, Don sat up and reached for his bathrobe. I got up and put mine on. Hearing sounds of activity from our bedroom the girls called out in the owlish way of children, "Who? What? Who? Where? Who? Who? Who?"

I explained over my shoulder as I ran down the stairs and out onto the porch where we had dumped the tarpaulins. Snatching up a couple I started down the path—Don followed with the flashlight. The rain was brisk and wet. After we had tucked the tarpaulins over and around the boxes and trunks, Don flashed the light on the washing machine defiantly spraddled in the rowboat. The waves were almost washing over the stern. "Come on," he said without enthusiasm, "we'll have to try and pull the boat up the steps." I jerked on the rope and he jerked on the washing machine and we managed finally to get the prow onto the top step, the stern in the water, the washing machine veering dangerously toward the south. Grimly tying the painter to a slender maple tree Don said, " 'An' lea'e us nought but grief and pain, for promis'd joy.' "

Busy threading my bathrobe cord through the oarlocks and then over and under the wringer in the vain hope that I could keep the washing machine in the rowboat but knowing very well it was like trying to restrain a wounded buffalo with a piece of thread, I snarled and said, "And I used to wonder why they sold the house furnished."

By the time we got back to bed, the crackling fire in the fireplace had burned to coals, but it was still comforting and a delight after the chilly interlude on the sea wall in the rain.

From far across the water a freighter tooted. The rain on the roof sounded like millions of birds' feet. I said to

Don, "Well, here we are, all together at last in our own house."

Don said, "Unk." He was very tired. With a snap the last piece of wood broke apart. The glow from the fireplace was very faint now. The noise of the Sound less of the slurp, slop, splash and more of a rhythmic thrummmmmm, like a drum roll, showed that the little waves had matured to good-sized swells. "A heavenly sound," I thought sleepily.

Then above the wind, the rain and the surf I thought I detected a heavy groaning scraping noise.

"The washing machine," Don said suddenly, loudly, in my ear. "The little bastard is still trying to get away."

CHAPTER IV

LIFE AS USUAL IN A VERY

UNUSUAL SETTING

ANY change as drastic as moving from the city to an island should be accomplished gradually, like reducing. But there was old La Guerre as well as time and tide, which were no longer merely figures of speech, and suddenly we were up to our chins in a new life and with *one* day to adjust.

To make the move, Don and I had taken Friday and Monday off, and in addition I had begged and been grudgingly granted a special dispensation from the "big boss" to eat my lunch in half an hour and not be at my desk until eight instead of regular wartime seven-thirty. Don having finally finished his stint on the night shift, now had to be at work at the enchanting hour of six-thirty A. M. The children kept assuring us that they could stay away from school for months, even years—"Everybody does when they move," but Don and I callously advised them that as long as we had to go back to work, we were enrolling them in school on Monday. "Yes, Monday! This Monday. Because we want you to learn something. Because people who don't go to school are dummies. Of course, I don't think Abraham Lincoln was a dummy," and so on, and so on.

We had moved Saturday. That gave us Sunday to unpack, put away, look around, plan ahead and get wood.

Sunday morning when I got up later, tireder and nastier than I had planned, I found that the washing machine had gotten away after all. Joan and Don with their irritating early-morning cheerfulness and 20-20 vision had spotted it riding the waves halfway to Three Tree Point, directly across from us.

"See," they told Anne and me after they had dragged us out on the porch, "there it is, right there by that white streak."

"I'm cold," Anne said. "Let's go in the house and start the fire."

Joan said, "Can't you even see the rowboat?"

"No," Anne said, huddling her arms around her.

"You're not trying," Joan said. "Now look right across the Sound at that bare place on the hill."

Don said cheerfully, "The water's awfully rough out there. I can see huge whitecaps. Let's row out now before breakfast."

"I'm not going any place until I have a cup of coffee," I said crossly.

"I'm not either," Anne said. "Only I'm going to have cocoa. Let's start the fire."

"Ah, come on, Mommy," Joan said. "A boat ride before breakfast would be fun."

"Why don't you and Joan go," I said to Don, "and Anne and I will get breakfast."

"Yes," Anne said eagerly to Joan. "You and Don go and Mommy and I will have breakfast all ready when you get back."

"We'll all have to go," Don said. "Towing that washing machine in that rough water is going to be very ticklish business."

So we had breakfast first and after my second cup of coffee I became mildly enthusiastic about the boat trip. "Hurry with your cocoa, Andy," I said brightly. "We're going for our very first boat ride."

"Does Don know how to row?" Anne said suspiciously.

44

"Of course," I said. "Don't you, Don?"

"Well, I haven't had too much experience with boats," Don said truthfully, "but I can manage, I guess."

"Can you swim?" I asked him.

"I would be able to," he said, "if my bones weren't so heavy. I always sink."

I looked out at the Sound again. The water in the middle looked much rougher and several large dark clouds grumbled menacingly as they shoved and pushed each other around directly overhead. I poured myself another cup of coffee.

"Oh, Mommy," Joan said, "we'll *never* get started."

"This may be the last cup of coffee I'll ever have," I said, "and I intend to enjoy it."

"You may as well pour me one too," Don said, sighing resignedly.

"Well, I'm going down and get the boat in the water," Joan said.

"Go ahead," Anne said. "I'm going to make myself another piece of cinnamon toast."

"Why don't you get one of the neighbors to help you?" I said, peering past the pink geraniums in the window box toward the horizon. "If that speck I see out there is the rowboat with the washing machine in it, it's halfway to Alaska."

"Oh, nonsense," Don said. "People row across the Sound all the time. It won't take us long."

"I wish we had life jackets," I said.

"Oh, Betty," Anne said, suddenly switching loyalty in the irritating way children do, "don't be silly. Joan and I are wonderful swimmers. We could probably swim across the Sound. Anyway Don can handle the boat. Come on, let's go before it starts to rain again. I'll eat my toast in the boat."

When we got to the beach Joan had the big rowboat in the water and was splashily rowing up and down in front of the sea wall. We called to her to come in and after Don had pulled the boat on to the beach with a tremendous jerk that sent Joan, who was about to stand up, sprawling and lost an oar overboard, we all climbed in and began arguing about who was to sit where.

There was a great deal of unnecessary talk about my tremendous weight and how if I sat on one side with only one of the girls' meager flyweight to balance me, the boat would tip over. This could have been easily solved by my sitting in the prow but that was a favorite spot and both girls wanted it. They finally agreed to take turns, so that when we were in the middle of the Sound in rough water, they vigorously crowded past Don and the oars, rocked the boat dangerously and kicked me in the ankles while they changed seats.

Don was not very adept at the oars. He blamed it on "these damned old oars which keep slipping out of the oarlocks," but Joan informed him tactlessly that he didn't hold the blades straight, he should dip deeper, he was rowing too hard with his right oar and he was getting everybody wet. She had learned *everything* about rowing at Aunty Dede's and she would be glad to help him.

Anne announced that she had learned *everything* about rowing on Lake Washington where she and Marilyn rowed the dinghy of Marilyn's father's "enormous speedy cruiser." She told Don he was dipping too deep, he was holding the blades too straight, but it was all right for him to row so hard with his right oar because it would turn us around and we could see where we were going. I, who had been rowing since I was five years old and, in addition, had seen all the Washington crew races, and really did know everything about rowing, kept my mouth shut because I have never cared for this sport and was not anxious to take the oars. With set lips, Don continued to dip and pull and splash toward the washing machine, which finally even Anne and I could see.

Like a stout gray lady on an excursion boat, it had slid up and wedged itself in the prow of the rowboat, from which position it stolidly watched our maneuvers to ease alongside and get the painter. This was not too easy as the water was very choppy and the painter was tangled around the washing machine's legs. In his attempt to lift the washing machine and untangle the rope, Don leaned so hard on the side of our boat we dipped water.

Anne immediately began to shriek, "We're tipping over! We're sinking! Help! Help!"

Joan stood up and shouted, "Watch out, everybody, I'm going to get in the other boat!"

I yelled, "Don't get in the other boat, Joan! Shut up, Anne! Don, be careful!" and Don said, "EVERYBODY BE QUIET!" just as the black clouds above us released large wet raindrops, which began splatting on our heads.

Joan said, "Please, Mommy, let me get in the other boat. I can hand you the rope."

Don said, "Okay, Joanie, but wait until I steady the boat."

I said, "Don, *don't* let her! The washing machine will come loose and squash her and what if we can't get the rope and she drifts away?"

"Don't be silly," Don said. "Okay, Joanie, here you go." Nimbly Joan jumped into the stern of the other boat which was clear up out of the water owing to the weight of the washing machine, skipped down to the prow, crawled *under* the washing machine and fed the painter out the small opening between the wringer and the point of the prow. I grabbed the rope and yelled at her to "get out from under that washing machine right now!" She did, announcing unconcernedly as she jumped back into our boat, "It was caught on that faucet on the side and here's your bathrobe cord."

As soon as we started rowing back toward home, the washing machine became unwedged and slid down and leaned over the starboard side, thus making it as difficult as possible to tow. Of course Joan wanted to get back in the boat and try to push it into the prow again, but even Don vetoed this. We finally reached shore, the washing machine defiant and unco-operative all the way, and when we tried to maneuver it up the narrow trail to the house, it weighed just as much as possible and kept flinging its wringer around its head like a billy club.

When we had it comfortably installed in the service room, the girls insisted that I test it out. I filled it with water, threw in some dishtowels and turned it on and it swirled and swished very efficiently.

Joan said, "I'm certainly glad it works because I didn't pack anything but dirty clothes."

"How perfectly disgusting!" Anne said.

Don said, "I wonder if you'd rinse out a few pairs of my sun-tans."

Anne said, "Of course, all *my* clothes are clean, but I think I'll wash all my summer clothes again and put them away."

Joan said, "Can you wash coats in washing machines? My school coat has mustard and a lot of hamburger juice on it."

I said, "Before we get too enthusiastic about washing, let's see if the wringer works." I turned off the washing part and turned on the wringer. The rollers began turning smoothly against each other, neatly pressing the water out of a piece of seaweed picked up on the trip.

"Okay," I said to Don and the girls. "Everything's working fine. Bring on your dirty clothes."

Then I reached in to get one of the dishtowels and the next thing I knew I was across the room, crumpled against the cement wall, and Anne and Joan were bending over me wailing, "Mommy, Mommy, are you hurt?", and Don, who understands electricity was saying soothingly from across the room, "Probably sand in the brushes."

Don finished the washing though, with Anne and Joan and me crouched in the doorway waiting for him to be electrocuted. Nothing happened except that he took all the buttons off Joan's blouses with a popping sound like shelling peas. Afterward he took the washing machine all apart, removed some seaweed and the sand from the brushes and a

clamshell or two from the tub, oiled it and said he could
not understand what had happened as he could find nothing
basically wrong. He intimated that it must have been some
careless action on my part. However, as long as we had it,
that washing machine had those occasional rebellious spells,
shooting sparks from the water, grinding things up in the
wringer, secreting a red sock in its bowels so it could turn
everything pink, even knocking down a devout Christian
Scientist who had no fear.

After Don had finished the washing and we had all had
some more coffee and cocoa, we began the unpacking, the
melding of our things with the already established, the taking
down of the flower prints and trying to find the right spots
for our pictures. While I worked I handed down rapid fair
decisions on vital questions such as: "Isn't this my blouse,
Mommy, you can tell by the ink stain on the collar, see?"—
"It's my blouse, Betty, you know perfectly well it is. Don't
you remember, it is the one Madge bought but it was too
small so she gave it to Alison and you took it because Alison
had taken your checked one and you gave it to me?" and
"Betty, are you going to let the girls wear all my sweaters?"
(That was the year for girls to wear men's sweaters.) "They
have already taken all my sweatshirts." The last was wailed
plaintively at me from the bedroom where Don was rapidly
filling up all the drawers with *his* things. I still keep my
underwear, stockings, girdles, gloves, jewelry, diary, night-
gowns, and scarves in the two little drawers in my bedside
table. My sweaters and shorts share a blanket drawer under
one of the bunks with the bathing suits.

Those pictures in movie magazines of the star's bedroom with a separate closet for purses and another separate closet for fur coats, make me drool with envy. Not that
I would have anything to put in them but it would be so
wonderful, when wishing to change purses, not to have to
stand on the hamper and fish around in the top closet at the
end of the bathtub, where I also keep eight hundred clean

flour sacks (remains of chicken-farming days—second attempt —different husband) and suitcases.

The next problem was getting our food to fit into the medium-sized icebox. All refrigerators seem to be designed for people who buy half a turkey, and as I am the type of shopper who makes butchers call out, "Here comes Betty, Al—better get out that big new side of beef," I ended up, as I always shall, with a large carton of green vegetables outside on the umbrella table, and the icebox stuffed to the point where I had to sneak the door open and even then the tomatoes delicately balanced on top of the milk bottles bounced into the woodbox. The ham was as big as Tudor and required an unconscionable amount of room.

"Oh, well," I said comfortingly to myself as I rammed the refrigerator door shut against it, "we can have ham and eggs for breakfast, cold ham and potato salad for supper, ham sandwiches, ham omelettes, ham and lima beans, split pea soup—we won't have to buy anything for weeks and weeks!"

Then we sat down to supper and Don said with disbelief, "Ham? Again?"

Anne said, "Marilyn's family always goes to a restaurant on Sunday."

Joan said, "Johnny's mother makes fried chicken every Sunday. She bakes her own bread too."

Anne said, "Marilyn's mother certainly is a lot of fun, huh, Joanie?"

Taking a minute sliver of ham on his fork and staring at it without enthusiasm, Don said, "Isn't that my yellow sweater you're wearing, Anne?"

"You mean this sweater?" asked Anne in absolute amazement. "This yellow one?"

"Yes, that one," said Don levelly.

Carefully cutting off a piece of ham the size of a grain of rice Anne said with elaborate unconcern, "I'm positive this is Uncle Cleve's sweater. I can tell by the way the cuffs turn back."

Joan who was fixing herself an enormous ham sandwich, an operation usually forbidden at the table but now abetted by approving nods and smiles from me, remarked in a pleasant conversational tone, "That's a lie. I saw you get that sweater out of Don's drawer over at the apartment yesterday."

"What a sneak!" Anne said furiously. "What a nasty little double-crossing sneak. All you ever do is spy and tattle and get-in-good-with-the-company. I just loathe you. . . ."

"That will do," I said hopefully.

"Who took my navy blue sweatshirt?" Don asked. "It is the only one I have that is really big enough for me."

"Navy blue? Sweatshirt?" Joan asked innocently.

"I have just a few things" (twelve drawers—two cupboards—three shelves and he was not nearly unpacked), Don said plaintively, "and I would like to keep them."

Her eyes brimming with hurt, Anne said, "I thought this was Uncle Cleve's sweater but if you're going to be so terribly disagreeable I'll take it off right now." She flounced to her feet and I shouted, "Sit down and eat your ham."

Joan said, "Does your navy blue sweatshirt have long sleeves and some white paint on the shoulder?"

"Yes," Don said.

"I haven't seen it," Joan said.

"Well, now who's a liar?" Anne warbled.

"More ham, anyone?" I said my voice trembling with emotion. "Please have some more ham!"

Then came getting the girls ready for school. Joan's approach to the problem was very simple. She merely asked me forty-two times if I had put *three whole sandwiches* in her lunch. I said I had and she said what about an apple—I said yes and she said cookies? Yes. She was ready.

Anne's preparation involved first going through and despising all her clothes, then choosing the least loathsome things and ironing them, even things as smooth as mirrors. She wouldn't allow me to iron them—too careless; or Joan

—too stupid. She was halfway through her third blouse—first one turned out to be "absolutely filthy"—tiny speck on part that tucked into the skirt—the second—"entirely rotted under arms from perspiration. How I loathe hand-me-downs! How I wish we were rich. How I despise living in the country. Why do we always have to change schools every five minutes" (this was the first change to my knowledge). I showed her that the "entirely rotted" was merely a small wrinkle from being packed. This brought tears to her eyes so I let her alone, and went out to put breakfast on the table. She called to me excitedly. I put down my spatula and went into the living room, steeled to combat rot and filth.

She was standing by the ironing board, her face sparkling with excitement and delight. "Look, Mommy, isn't he adorable?" she said pointing at a large buck standing on the porch peering in the window. "Just imagine, a real live deer on *our* porch. Oh, I love living in the country! It's so romantic!"

So we enrolled the children in school. Joan in the seventh grade of the Vashon Grade School, a comfortable brown-shingled building about three miles from us; and Anne as a freshman in the Vashon High School, a large modern brick edifice about seven miles away. To get the school bus the girls had two choices. If the tide was low they could walk to the Sanders' (the neighbors with the road) and go up their road. If the tide was high they had to walk the county trail and get on the bus down by the store at the dock. Joan liked her school and seemed to get along very well, only occasionally bringing me tales of hiding the lids to the inkwells, breaking a window in the gym, eating somebody else's lunch, for which misdemeanors she was, very unfairly, I thought, kept after school, which meant she had to walk the three miles home, usually in the rain. The first time this happened I threatened heatedly to go up to school and *do something*. Anne and Joan were delighted.

Joan said, "Yes, and you just tell Miss Harwood that the *doctor* said I *have* to chew gum."

Anne said, "Be sure and wear your gray suit and explain to her that we are from the *city*."

Don told me not to be hasty and produced from his past several valiant incidents having to do with his plowing through blizzards on cardboard soles carrying mush sandwiches, he was so *eager* to get an education.

Because of my job or weakness or both, I never did get up to school until the night of the Christmas entertainment, which was absolutely charming with Joanie singing a solo and a wonderful simplicity of spirit which could be found only in a country school. Even I didn't have enough of the Hun in me to inject an old complaint into such an atmosphere. So on occasion, as long as she attended Vashon Grade School and as long as she indulged in climbing out of windows and throwing chalk, and so on, Joan was kept after school and had to walk home. Actually, now that I think about it, it was a very healthy punishment.

Anne immediately loathed her school because: *a.* It was a school. *b.* "They sing hymns at noon instead of dancing." *c.* "All the teachers are missionaries." *d.* It was in the country. So, many evenings when I came home from work, I would learn that Anne had stayed home with some mysterious ailment. Aching toenails—non-focusing eyes—pains in her heels. On such evenings I would be greeted with a sparkling, clean house, stuffed pork chops and hot apple pie for dinner, all the ironing done, the beds made. The temptation to keep this little homebody home was almost overpowering. But my conscience told me that I must force her to continue with book learning, especially in view of the fact that she was reputed to have a terrific I.Q. 170 or -2—all she apparently wanted was to learn to card wool and make biscuits. Even when I stopped work the following February, I had only a little better luck getting Anne all the way to school. If I did get her on board the school bus, with her books and the assurance that her hot lunch was paid for (sandwiches from home were so vulgar), I had no guarantee that she wouldn't go into a decline on the way to school and have to spend the day lying on a couch in the nurse's room. Also she either did no work or work they couldn't understand. How well I remember the day I was summoned to school and presented, via trembling hand, one of Anne's compositions entitled, "I Don't Believe in God and Neither Does My Uncle Frank."

Joan's way was so much easier. Explaining her A's and B's, she said, "Well, all you have to do is to get a man teacher and be nice to him and then he makes you a checker and checkers don't have to take tests."

As soon as we had the children in school and were reasonably sure they knew where to catch the bus according to the tides, Don and I went back to work. Don had to catch (and that is the right word) the five-fifteen ferry in order to be at Boeing's Renton plant, about twenty miles from the dock, at six-thirty.

Our schedule then was: up at four-thirty (I fear if I have five husbands I'll always manage to find one that gets up at some ungodly hour)—Don make fire in the trash burner —turn on oven to defrost the kitchen—Betty make coffee and Don's lunch ("Try to always use that homemade mayonnaise that melts and makes the sandwiches like wet washrags," Don said bitterly). I usually set the table and laid out everything the night before. After he had dressed, Don unhurriedly drank his coffee and orange juice, ate his poached eggs, and leisurely lit a cigarette. After the third drag, he would suddenly stare unbelievingly at the clock, leap out of his chair, grab his raincoat, hurl himself through the door into the rain and blackness. I would pour myself a cup of coffee and heave a sigh of relief just as Don, having forgotten to put new batteries in his flashlight or to take his lunch, would come bursting in again. While he did either or both of these things, I went out on the porch and tried to check by sound, whether the tide was in or out. If it was out we were glad because he could go by the beach. If it was in he had to take a tiny slippery overgrown footpath through the woods to the Sanders'. He was gone again. The clock said one minute of five. Don allowed sixteen minutes to run up the beach, get in his car, start the motor and drive the mile and a half to the ferry. He always made it unless the car wouldn't start, there was a log across the road, the ferry left early or he was out of gas.

At five-thirty I'd fix the girls' breakfast—at least set their places at the table and get out the bread and the toaster and the peanut butter and the cocoa—then I'd go through the icy living room, down a dank passageway to the dark, cold little service room where the shower was. This location of the shower, so handy for swimmers, had seemed adorable to me in the summer. In the winter it seemed like something overlooked by the Marquis de Sade. After I'd checked the floor, the bathmat and the inside of the shower curtain for slugs, spiders, centipedes and wood lice, I would turn on the shower full force hot and let it heat up the room while I ran up and made our bed. About this time I was not spilling over with wild enthusiasm for life on an island. Fortunately, five minutes under the hot shower restored my spirits to normal, or is it?

At six-thirty I awakened the girls, refereed their morning quarrels over underwear, skirts, sweaters, bobby pins, ironing, socks, who did the most work the day before and who was my favorite child, decided with Anne, who was and is a wonderful cook, what we would have for dinner, reminded Joanie, who wasn't but is now a wonderful cook, to be sure and bring up wood when she got home from school and checked them both for lunch money and my perfume.

Then I kissed them, grabbed my flashlight and left. It was always seven o'clock and my ferry left at seven-twenty and I should have left at six-fifty and now I would have to run the last quarter of a mile. I wore loafers and woolen socks over my silk stockings, carried my office shoes along with my lunch, purse, current book and grocery list in a large green felt bag.

The county trail connecting our beach with the rest of the world, begins at a cluster of mailboxes down by the dock, meanders along the steep southeast face of the island about fifty feet above the shore, and ends at our house. Years ago when the passenger boat used to stop at the dock just south of us, the trail began there and went north, probably ending about where it begins today. Now all that is left of this part of the county trail is a slender overgrown path through the woods—a path that leads over huge fallen logs, through head-high nettles, into a stream and right up the face of a blue clay bluff. From the ferry dock to Dolphin Point the present county trail is quite respectable, with occasional rustic bridges over steep ravines, wooden flumes to carry off winter torrents, even small scattered pockets of gravel, all evidence that the trail has at some time or other been given at least a cursory glance by the county. From Dolphin Point to our house, it is little more than a cow path, narrow, gar-landed with wild blackberry, syringa, elderberry, salmon-berry and wild cucumber. In the spring and summer it is treacherous with the nettles which seem to spring up even while they are being slashed, and crowd the sensitive traveler from both sides. In the fall the trail is slippery and lacy with spiderwebs stretched trustingly every night from elder-berry to syringa about face high. I used to try to catch these spiderwebs by swinging my green felt bag ahead of me as I walked, but if it was dark when I left the house (and it usually was) I often missed and ran the rest of the way to the ferry clawing wildly at an invisible veil complete, I was afraid, with a dot that was alive.

When I reached the "big tree," an old growth fir almost twelve feet in diameter, and about a quarter of a mile from the dock, I could see whether the ferry was in, really in or going out again.

It was from the "big tree" that I always had to start running.

According to a testimonial I read recently by a man who had lost thirty-six pounds eating nothing but steak (typical male reducing diet—wife no doubt expected to accomplish similar results on soup meat and mineral oil mayonnaise), during the final twenty minutes of a half-hour walk while the stomach is empty, one pint of bile is drained and this greatly retards hardening of the arteries. Just feel my arteries, they are like velvet.

This boisterous early morning activity also started my blood circulating, churning, really, and by the time I got to work I was not only bileless, I was boiling hot and it was very disheartening to step into an office heated to eighty degrees, blue with cigar smoke and filled with bloodless co-workers who shrank away from even the tiny draught of the swinging door and threatened to go straight to the "big boss" if I didn't "close that transom right now!"

Why did I put up with so many hardships? Why didn't I quit? Because when we bought the house we had counted on our both working for at least six months. Also there was a war and all able-bodied Americans were supposed to work. Also we needed the money. This brings me to an interesting observation on false pride. Why is admitting that you work because you need the money a shameful thing, like snoring? Has age anything to do with this? Has it anything to do with inflation? It seems to me that every day I run into another "false pride" who says about her job, "I'm not really working" (little laugh) "I just got bored staying home and I love people. I think people are so interesting and one sees so many people in my work. Honestly, Betty, you could write a book about the people I see, though of course we do get an awfully nice class of people but actually even *poor* people are interesting. I just love to study people."

I have friends "studying people" in drugstores, dress shops (I. Magnin's excluded, because to People Studiers even working at Magnin's is grand), department stores, and insurance offices. All People Studiers are shifty-eyed, smoke cork-tipped cigarettes and have crumpled faces. They range in age from thirteen to seventy-five and are predominantly female.

My first morning of walking the trail I had plenty of time. I had left the house at a quarter of seven and, when I got to the "big tree," the ferry was just leaving the dock at Harper, a small settlement on the Olympic Peninsula and the ferry's only other stop. I made my way to the dock in a leisurely fashion and leaned on the splintery old railing. A sea gull swooped down and lit beside me. He had part of one toe missing, his vest was dirty and he had a face like a Hollywood producer, but I was grateful for his friendliness.

Together we examined the morning. In the east the Cascade Range, including Mt. Ranier and all of its foothills, was a purple cutout pasted on a pale green sky. Across the west the Olympic Mountains were a white-crested wave. The water, a rippleless sheet of foil, reflected a single late-blooming star. The fat little ferry, head high above the water, swam steadily toward Blake Island, a plump lonely little place without a single light or inhabitant.

It was nearly seven-fifteen and rosy-faced people began hurrying past me along the dock. Their feet made nice hollow purposeful clumps on the boardwalk. All the women carried bags containing town shoes. I wondered if I should change my shoes then or wait and do it in a genteel fashion in the ladies' lounge on the ferry. I glanced down at my feet and there, lying between my two brown loafers, was a five-dollar bill.

"It is an omen of good luck," I told Don and the children that night as I stuffed it in the teapot, traditional place for Mother, even carefree working variety, to stuff money. It was too.

CHAPTER V

GOD IS THE BOSS

IN THE city, as I remember, weather was a topic passed around with the salted peanuts and not expected to hang around much past the introductions. In the country, weather is as important as food and sometimes means the difference between life and death. Discussions of it can branch out into all sorts of interesting directions, such as Mrs. Exeter's baby which was almost born on the beach because of the storm that took out the dolphins (those bruised bunches of pilings at the end of docks without which the ferries cannot nuzzle into the slip) so the ferry couldn't land, and a call to the Coast Guard delayed because of a prune upside-down-cake recipe dictated over an eighteen-party telephone line, or that summer we didn't have any rain from May until September.

In the twelve years since we moved to Vashon Island we have experienced the most rain, the driest summer (that wonderful one), the coldest winter, the most snow, the severest earthquake, the worst slides, the highest tide, the lowest tide, the strongest winds, the longest unceasing period of rain, the densest fog, the hottest day, the earliest spring, the latest spring, the coldest summer, the warmest fall, the dreariest winter (this one), the wettest Christmas, in addition to a total eclipse of the moon, a total eclipse of the sun, and a flying saucer on the Oregon coast.

We have also come to expect, in times of great emergency, no co-operation from the elements.

There was that time, after weeks of agonized waiting (which included withering looks if we dared to use the telephone in the evening for fear "he" might want to call), when Anne was finally asked to the Junior Prom (attended by even freshmen on Vashon) by the right boy. She had a beautiful pale blue net party dress (borrowed from friend of Aunt Alison) and Roger, *the* boy, worked after school in Beall's Greenhouses (here on Vashon and the third largest orchid growers in the United States) and he had promised her an orchid, her first. He assured her it would be "still good." Everything was wonderful! With a tremendous sigh of relief the family settled back to normalcy, at least our version of it. There were a few tense moments the night of the prom when Anne couldn't decide whether to hide Don and me and pretend she and Joan lived on the beach alone or whether, in tuxedo and formal, we were to be just lounging around in the background, ready to run down to the beach and get a log or two if the fire got low.

Finally Joan, always realistic, said, "I don't know where you get such dumb ideas, Anne. Why should *we* dress up for Roger? *We're* not going out with him. Say, there's a girl in school, Betty, who gets all her clothes off the city dump. Last week she got a keen pleated skirt with only a few moth holes in it." Anne told her not to be disgusting, *if* she could help it. Anne's last admonition when she went to dress was, "Now, when I come downstairs, *don't* tell me I look nice."

"We won't have to because you won't," Joan said.

"You shut up!" Anne shrieked.

"You make me sick, old false pride," Joan said.

"Can't we ever have any peace?" Don said. So I turned up the radio.

Anne did look beautiful. The pale blue was perfect for her red hair and turquoise-blue eyes, but we all kept a stony silence as she stamped down the stairs, walked over and jerked the orchid away from Roger who, for such a "big wheel," seemed unusually frail and apprehensive. After they had gone Joan got out her homework (mere gesture) and I got out the ironing board. Then they were back, Anne bawling, Roger looking miserable.

"The tide!" Anne wailed. "It's high! Roger got his shoes all wet just *getting* here. Can't you do *something?*"

"Why don't you walk the trail?" Joan asked.

"You mind your own business," Anne screamed, because for some strange adolescent reason walking the trail was a shameful thing to her, like picking up coal off the railroad tracks.

Finally we quieted her and she wore her loafers and carried her shoes and Roger borrowed a pair of Don's shoes (mine would have been a better fit, but pride, both Roger's and mine, prevented my suggesting it) and carried his own and they waded through the tide. Anne had a wonderful time at the prom, but she said that she despised living on an island and how would I feel if I was going to the Junior Prom and a ship went by and got my party dress all wet and seaweedy.

Then came Halloween. Anne and Joan were invited to a party at the Falcon's Nest, a very grand place (since burned down) reputed to have been built by a Chicago millionaire for his daughter. It was a massive house with iron gates and stone pillars. The fireplace was so enormous the andirons let down and the eight-foot logs were rolled in with a peavey. There was a balcony, festooned with real leopard, tiger, puma and zebra skins, that went all around the eighty-foot living room. The bathrooms were supplied with *salt* and fresh water, and the living room chandelier was a real Indian canoe, full size, with light bulbs around the edge and a petrified Indian paddling it. The Falcon's Nest was on the hill back of us within easy walking distance.

"Oh, you *are* lucky!" I told the girls. "I'd love to see that house. I hear the garage in the basement will hold *thirty* cars."

Anne said, "I wish we didn't have to walk though. Do you think we'll ever have a Cadillac?"

Joan said, "Everybody walks on Halloween, dopey. Don't you remember last year we trick-and-treated for twenty-two blocks?"

"I wish we were back in the city," Anne said. "I wish we still lived with Margar."

I said, "Look at that beautiful moon, girls. It's just perfect for Halloween."

Joan said, "Oh, boy, tomorrow night's Halloween!"

Anne said, "Moonlight on the water makes me feel lonely."

I said heartily, "Halloween in the country will be *wonderful!*"

When we woke up the next morning we were having one of our better storms. Winds of fifty miles an hour, drenching rains, enormous waves that thundered on the beach like big guns. As I fixed Don's lunch and set the table I watched the rain beading the kitchen windows and the wind knocking the geraniums around in the window box, and my heart ached. This was not too unusual, as I have never been exactly hilarious in the early hours, often going through an entire divorce and marrying Howard Hughes while I am waiting for the coffee to boil. But this morning my sorrow was for my children. My poor little disappointed children so cruelly imprisoned on this desolate island by my hardhearted husband.

Old Hard Heart came whistling in at that point and said cheerfully, "Another hot day, I see."

I said, "I could just cry for Anne and Joan. Tonight's Halloween and they are invited to a party at the Falcon's Nest."

Looking out the window, Don said, "They'll sure have to wear their raincoats."

"That isn't the point," I said furiously. "It's walking the trail in the rain and their costumes getting all soggy and oh, just everything!" I glared out the window at the storm.

Don said, "Betty, you're a sentimentalist. Children are

realists. Anne and Joan probably won't be nearly as disappointed in the weather as you are."

"But they will," I said. "They were counting on the moonlight."

"And it's raining and it can't be helped, so they will have to face it," Don said, lighting a cigarette. "Have you ever heard of anybody who amounted to anything who didn't have a few hardships in his life?"

This brings up a point. All books on "Child—the Training of," "Home—Making It Happy," and so on, agree that the parents should *always* be in *absolute accord* on matters of discipline. This is a lovely thought and would certainly make any home happier, but from my experience and observation it could only be possible if the mother and father were deaf mutes or identical twins. Take Don and me, for instance. We loved the children. We loved each other. But when a crisis involving discipline arose in our happy little home and it was necessary for us, as reasonable understanding parents, to hark back to our childhoods and try to recall how we felt about the same situation at the same age so we could be fair, we were as far apart as an Eskimo and a Maori.

Don comes from a stern, unrelenting Scotch (both mother and father MacDonalds), Free Methodist ("free" certainly misnomer) family of twelve children. The stories of his childhood had to do with oatmeal, working twelve hours a day for Western Union when he was ten or perhaps it was seven years old, hauling ashes to earn school clothes, church five days a week and hour-long prayers on bony knees every single night. Up to the time of my father's death when I was twelve, my three sisters, my brother and I had experienced discipline of a sort. I say "of a sort" because Daddy, though very strict when he was home, was a mining engineer and away most of the time and when he was gone Mother was her usual fun-loving, easygoing self and we did as we pleased. After Daddy died we really did as we pleased. Exactly. If we didn't want to go to school we didn't (we usually did though and a couple of us even had

4. averages)—if we felt like studying we did, if we didn't, we didn't—if we wanted to stay with friends for two or three weeks we did, sometimes not even calling up to give our whereabouts—if we wanted to spend our Sunday School (Episcopal) money for candy, we did. About the only laws of behavior, aside from nice manners, laid down by Mother were that we couldn't sulk and we were expected to tell the truth, no matter how appalling. Also, even when Daddy was alive we were encouraged to bring all of our friends home with us, as many as we liked for as long as we liked.

Don wanted to be "notified" well in advance of guests. He never got used to the nocturnal shrieks and giggles and trips to the icebox and lending of *his* pajamas occasioned by Millie's or Ruthie's or Jeanie's or Molly's staying all night. He just was not used to adolescents, but is anybody?

So the girls, bundled up in yellow slickers, sou'westers and galoshes, went to the Halloween party. The tide was high so we escorted them along the trail but Don did promise to come and get them in the car at eleven-thirty. We thought the tide would be out a little by then. There was a tree down across the trail, a big alder, and the water in the flume by the "big tree" sounded like a waterfall. It was a wild night. We left Anne and Joan at the gate to the Falcon's Nest at Anne's request, even though the drive was about a mile long. Don wanted to start back right away but I insisted on waiting until I could see Anne and Joan's bobbing flashlights up by the door. Through the lashing trees the house, lighted from top to bottom, looked like something out of *Jane Eyre*.

When Don and I got home we built up the fire, put *Pinafore* on the record player and had a Scotch and soda. At eleven-thirty I thought we should go up and get them. Don told me to relax and he'd play some Burl Ives. At midnight Anne called. She said not to come for them for a half an hour as they were eating and having a *wonderful* time. "She sounded excited and happy," I told Don almost tearfully.

He said, "Why shouldn't she have a good time—it's a party," which remark of course opened such an enormous chasm between us that I didn't even see any point in attempting to bridge it with conversation. Especially as it involved the basic difference between men and women and goes way back to date of birth when the doctor (male) informs the father (male) that he has a son (male), and the passing out of cigars and rejoicing can be heard for sixty miles. Then if it is a girl there is a great deal of smiling *anyway,* of being a good sport and talking about next time.

Thanksgiving was fun. Most of my family came out. There were fifteen of us, we had two turkeys (one provided by Mary) and the day was beautiful and everybody loved our house and thought we were so lucky to live on an island that my sister Alison and her husband bought a big old house with five acres and the roof on backward (owner-built) within easy commuting of us if you happened to be a goat, and my brother Cleve bought a small old house with three acres and the icebox on the back porch (local carpenter) within easy commuting if you happened to be a goat with a car.

Then came Christmas. Oh, I was *glad* we lived in the country where we wouldn't run any risks of being tainted by the gross commercialism so rampant in the city. We were going to have a real Christmas, pure in spirit, old-fashioned in execution.

"We will make *all* of our presents and we will have the *biggest* Christmas tree we have ever had and we will cut it on *our own* property," I told my noticeably unenthusiastic little family. As I spoke I could hear the ringing of the axe in the crisp winter air, could see the children standing by, eyes shining, faces wreathed with old-fashioned smiles, while I perhaps hummed a carol or two. Mentally I added popcorn balls, strings of cranberries and gilded walnuts to the festivities.

Anne wailed, "Oh, aren't we going to the city for Christmas? I told everybody at school we were."

Joan said, "What do you mean, make our own presents? You mean like those ugly little calendars we used to make in the third grade?"

"*I* certainly don't want one," Anne said.

Don said, "Are you dead set on getting our Christmas tree on our own property?"

"I certainly am," I said. "That's one of the *main* advantages in living in the country. I'd feel like a fool telling any of the people at the office that we *bought* our Christmas tree."

"Well, then you'd better get busy on some ideas for decorating a leafless alder," Don said.

"What about those great big firs right up there?" I said pointing up back of the house.

"Four feet in diameter is a little big even for your taste, isn't it?" Don said.

"Oh, I don't mean using one of them for the tree," I said. "I mean, aren't there some seedlings around. Up on the Olympic Peninsula all the trees had little trees by the millions."

"But those weren't virgin trees," Don said. Both girls laughed loudly.

I said, "I'll bet you five dollars I can find a pretty Christmas tree on our own property."

"By flashlight?" Joan asked. "It's dark when you leave and dark when you get home."

"I'll look on weekends," I said.

The next weekend it rained. Also the next. But as Christmas was the following Friday we went out anyway. We walked along the beach until we could see Tacoma. We found miles and miles of vacant property all solidly overgrown with alder, madroña, blackberries, syringa, buddleia, elderberry and maple. Sometimes firs or cedars loomed black against the sky but, sans a helicopter, we couldn't get at them. Sunday we tried the hillsides near us. We found a few fir trees but they were anaemic sallow little things jammed in between alders, syringa, elderberry, madroñas and maples.

"Now are you satisfied?" Don asked, as we stumbled along in the dark and rain toward home.

Anne said, "Marilyn's mother always has a blue Christmas tree with pink balls. Last Christmas she got a mink coat and Marilyn got a blue peignoir."

"Painwar! What's that?" Joan asked.

"Something much too old for Marilyn," I said crossly.

"You mean like Kotex?" Joan asked.

From the Sanders' sea wall Don called out, "Tide's high." It seemed to me he sounded glad.

Monday morning, Mr. Harvey, a banker who lived around the point from us and with whom I sometimes got a ride to town, if he was early and I was late and I saw him on the ferry, asked me if we had gotten our Christmas tree yet. I told him in amusing detail, but leaving out most of the fighting and all my crabbiness, of our fruitless search. Whereupon he told me that he had some enormous balsam firs on his place, all perfectly symmetrical, and he would be delighted to let us have one. I said that Don and I would be down that night after work. He said he would have the tree ready for us. He did, cut and packaged. It was perfectly beautiful with cones on its thick branches, thirty-one feet tall (the distance I had told him it was from our living room floor to the peak of the roof—I was only about ten feet off), and the largest tree in the history of the family. We floated it home.

A ferry acquaintance of Don's, who had been a high rigger in the logging camps, helped us put it up. The family Christmas tree ornaments which I had inherited were not quite sufficient, especially after Don had decorated the upper branches by balancing on one of the beams, snagging a branch with the poker, attaching an ornament and letting the branch snap back and smash the ornament against the wall. We strung popcorn, made stars out of tinfoil, gilded walnuts, added three more strings of lights and two dozen of the largest candy canes (Vashon purchase) and the tree was lovely.

Christmas eve we went in to my sister Mary's as we always do. It was raining hard, but we were very gay with our carload of presents (mostly bought at the Vashon drugstore)—anyway in the city rain is merely shiny black pavement, blurry street lights and using the windshield swipes.

The entire family was at Mary's—at that time only eighteen—now thirty-two and rapidly increasing. Mary's house looked beautiful and very Christmasy and there was a delicious supper and magnificent Christmas spirit. We had a wonderful time. Then as we sang "Silent Night" for the last time Don announced suddenly that we had only twenty-seven minutes to get the last ferry.

By taking back streets and going through Chinatown, we made it and the next thing we knew we were on the Sanders' sea wall looking down at the tide which was slapping playfully at the *top* step. The trail was dark with an impenetrable darkness like oily smoke, wet and very slippery. By the time we got home it was two-thirty and our Christmas presents and our spirits (even mine so homemade and old-fashioned) were like yesterday's dumplings.

Don cheerfully built the fires while I put Christmas carols on the record player and made oyster stew. The girls' reaction was tepid.

Christmas morning, rain was still lashing the windows and gurgling in the downspouts, but we managed a semblance of gaiety as we opened our partially dried-out presents in front of a roaring fire. The sagging atmosphere was leavened still further by the girls' getting just what they wanted (I believe it was men's sweaters, deep purple lipstick and a reasonable facsimile of a peignoir that year) *and* Mother and Alison and her husband, who had been invited to dinner, loyally appearing.

Then came January and the big snow. We are not used to snow in this country, are never prepared for it and, even when it is actually flittering down and lying on the ground and the sky is leaden and the weatherman predicts twelve inches, we keep talking gamely about those winters when the nasturtiums bloomed straight through.

I remember how surprised I was at ten o'clock that morning when I left my office building to go across the street for coffee and found that it was snowing hard—small dry flakes that powdered my hair and were still unmelted when I looked in the mirror behind the coffee urns.

By noon the snow was three or four inches deep on the downtown sidewalks and the radio reported six inches and more in the residential districts. Everyone in the office began calling home and excitedly relaying reports of six, eight, even twelve inches of snow, stuck cars, and no bus service. I tried to call the Russells, the only other year-rounders on the beach, to ask them to look out for Anne and Joan and keep them at their house until Don got home at four or thereabouts. The operator said the lines to Vashon were temporarily out of order. Every once in a while I went to the window and looked out. In spite of the wind, a thick white curtain of Lux flakes had turned the early afternoon into dusk and made the street lights wan and ineffectual. The roofs of the parked cars on the street below were heaped with snow which was pulled by the wind into peaks like seven-minute icing.

About three o'clock the "big boss" announced reluctantly that he was closing the office. He said that most of the city busses had stopped running and many of us would have to walk. There was a portentous germ-warfare atmosphere about the place. Even those most ardent "get-in-good-with-the-companys" (the ones who had *asked* to work on Thanksgiving) were hustling into their coats and hurrying out. I tried to call Vashon again but the lines were still out. I put on my raincoat (white poplin and stylish but no warmer than cellophane) and galoshes and started for the Vashon bus stop five blocks away. The wind, apparently fresh off a glacier, had gathered great momentum on the north-and-south streets and came whining down between the buildings with an armload of snow that made each crossing a little nightmare of streaming eyes and frozen legs. Everybody was walking huddled with their heads down, their coats pulled around them like bathrobes.

When I got to the Vashon bus stop, an unprotected corner by a furniture store, I found most of the commuters already there. Apparently every office in Seattle had closed early. While we crowded in the small doorway waiting for the bus, I heard that the lights always went off on Vashon during a snow—the telephone was already out and probably would be for weeks—the ferries probably wouldn't be running—this looked like a *big snow*—big snows always caused terrible slides—a wind like this would certainly take out a lot of sea walls—they hoped the local grocers (five all told—two very small) had plenty of food on hand because it certainly looked as if we were going to be marooned for a long time.

I became almost frantic with worry. What if I couldn't get to the island? Poor little Anne and Joan would be there all alone. I tried to inventory the supplies we had on hand. All I could accurately remember was a new case of Frisky dog food, part of a case of Puss'n Boots cat food, and three cartons of Camels. I remembered stories Gammy, my grandmother, had told us when we were children and wouldn't eat something she had cooked (wise precaution), of the starving Armenian children who were grateful for willow twigs and cow dung. I thought of pictures I had seen of Swiss people digging the bodies of their loved ones out of avalanches. I wondered if smoking was really harmful for children. All those cigarettes and nothing to do day after long dark day. I wondered where Don was. I thought of our huge virgin firs, so black and majestic against a summer sky, now loaded with snow, leaning, leaning and finally crashing down on the house where two tiny matchstick figures shivered by a fire made out of the last chair.

Then the bus came. We all squeezed on board and drove to the dock, where we were informed the ferry, in the clutches of the wild north wind, had crashed into the dolphins and knocked them down. The ferry was now leaving from another dock in downtown Seattle. We drove back to Seattle and down onto the dock. There was a long line of waiting cars, but the bus had priority and went right to the front. There was no Vashon ferry in the slip nor in sight on the troubled waters. I got out of the bus and walked up and down the line of cars, talking to people I knew and even ones I didn't know because disaster does much to break down the barriers of reticence.

Going from car to car I learned that the lights always went off on Vashon during a snow—the telephone was already out and probably would be for weeks—the ferries probably wouldn't be running after this trip *if* they made it—this looked like a *big snow*—big snows always caused terrible slides—a wind like this would certainly take out a lot of sea walls—they hoped the local grocers had plenty of food on hand because it certainly looked as if we were going to be marooned for a *long long* time—had I seen the size of the waves—they were *enormous* and would be much much *more enormous* out in the middle of the passage—certainly made a person wonder if these boats were really seaworthy—after all they were old to begin with—had been discarded by San Francisco. . . .

The ferry finally left at eight o'clock. The waves *were* enormous, the ferry creaked and groaned and writhed in pain. In the restaurant where I sat out the trip, the coffee cups slid off the counter and one quite sensible-looking woman pushed away her apple pie and sobbed, "We'll never make it. We'll all be drowned!"

We landed at the Vashon dock about nine-thirty. At the store, Bob Russell and I were told the trail was impassable and we would have to go by the beach. The tide, for some strange co-operative reason, was out. We started out. The wind was at our backs, but the rocky beach was like walking on frosty billiard balls and our flashlights were futile against the driving snow. It took us almost an hour to reach the point where Bob lived. He wanted me to come in and warm

71

up a little before going on, but I was too worried about the children. I stumped on. My nylon-clad legs were numb. My face felt as if it had been sandpapered. I recognized our sea wall, but the path from the beach to the house was completely obliterated.

On my hands and knees I crawled where I thought the path should be. I reached the kitchen door just as Don and the children came down the steps. They helped me to my feet, dragged me into the kitchen and gave me a big drink of whisky by candlelight.

"The lights are off, the telephone won't work, and the pipes are all frozen," Don told me cheerfully.

"The school's closed," Anne caroled. "It'll probably be closed all winter."

"Isn't this snow keen?" Joan said.

We were snowed in for two weeks. At first I was happy because I couldn't go to work and could be with my family. Anne was hysterical because of no school, Joan loved the snow and Don was very cheerful about hauling water from the spring and wood from the beach.

Then came the *second* day and cooking on the trash burner without an oven, by candlelight, lost a little of its hilarity; Don didn't leap to his feet eagerly when I called WOOD, and the girls began quarreling the minute they opened their eyes. At night I dozed off to something murmured by Joan and answered by Anne's shriek, "Mommy, Joan's caught a mouse" (or a fly or a spider) "and she's going to put it in my room! Stop her!"—to Don's, "Peace! All I want is a little peace! Do something, Betty!"

By the sixth day I began to wonder what all those delightful things were that I had been planning to do when I stopped working. By delightful I didn't mean cooking, washing dishes, scrubbing, washing clothes, mending, making beds, refereeing quarrels, carrying wood or sweeping. I had faint recollections of dreams of long country evenings spent in front of a roaring fire reading Shakespeare, each of us taking a part, the way we used to do when Daddy was alive, listening to symphonies on the record player, braiding rugs.

Of course, the first drawback was the fire and Don's attitude toward the woodpile which had become that of a mother puma guarding her young. If I had more than two matches and a sliver going at once, I had to listen to moans about waste and lectures on not looking ahead. Naturally, during this period the beach was as clean as a plate—the tide didn't even bring in seaweed.

Another thing was the matter of light. We had one kerosene lamp and one kerosene lantern but we had no kerosene. We had quite a few candles but we learned that a wick is a wick even if a candle is three feet tall and bayberry. We couldn't play the record player because it was electric—I hadn't learned how to braid rugs—the Shakespeare was in one of the hundreds of boxes in the back hall (the house had only three small bookcases) and the last thing I wanted to do was to look for it.

We played bridge—this was not too much fun for me as I was the only one who knew how and my pupils refused to take my word for anything, one of them kept falling asleep and the other two slapped across the table. Finally our life boiled down to reading, eating, sleeping, getting wood and getting on each other's nerves. Even eating lacked its customary fillip, and when I was asked what I was fixing for lunch or dinner and I told them, I was almost certain to hear at least one "Ugh!" This was partly induced by ennui and partly by the fact that our only really ample supplies were the dog food, the cat food and noodles, of which we seemed to have about a thousand pounds.

One bleak morning toward the end of the siege, I was shuffling around the kitchen contemplating a casserole of noodles, Puss'n Boots and candle stubs, when Don announced, "My God, we have run out of *whisky!*" and offered to mush up to Vashon and get some supplies.

I said I would make a list, but he told me not to bother as he knew what we needed and he was the judge of what his knapsack would hold and what his tired bony shoulders could carry. Of course at this point the girls rushed in with demands for absolutely vital things such as hormone cream, movie magazines, Firecracker Red nail polish and bobby pins. After a great deal of discussion and a few tears, Don said firmly he would not forget the kerosene. He *would* get some candy and gum. He *would* get bobby pins. He would *not* get movie magazines, hormone cream or nail polish. He *would* get the mail. He would *not* forget the matches.

We bundled him up and waved him off and, as he crunched down the beach past the spring which was a frozen waterfall and the big logs in their white fur scarves, I could almost hear the enclosing howl of the wolves and smell the cow dung burning in our sod hut.

While Don was gone there was a fine bark tide and for hours and hours Anne and Joan and I filled gunny sacks with bark, dragged them along the beach and heaved them up onto the sea wall. Then we each hauled one sackful up the path to the house. When the fire in the fireplace was burning hot and bright, the way only bark soaked in salt water can burn, I made a pot of coffee and we each had a cup.

While we drank our coffee, Joan told (with noticeable envy) of her friend Evelyn who got her clothes off the city dump and had dirt floors in her house which *never* had to be swept, and Anne described in exact detail her next formal which she thought should be of black velvet, strapless and very tight.

Joan said that Evelyn's father used to have a very good job but he didn't agree with the policy of any company so he couldn't work any more. Anne said that two of the girls in her class at school smoked. Joan said that Evelyn's Indian girlfriend, who came down from Canada every summer to pick fruit, had a baby in the Swansons' chicken house, a darling little boy. Wasn't she lucky? Anne said that she thought that thirteen was really old enough to smoke if you used a holder. I asked her if she would like a cigarette and she accepted eagerly, as did Joan. They coughed and choked their way through two apiece. I noted with interest that Joan was by far the more experienced smoker of the two.

When the last tear had been wiped away and the last stub crushed out, Mamsie Pepper MacDonald said to her little daughters, "Now, girls, if you feel that you must smoke, please smoke in front of me."

"Why?" Joan asked. "Do you like to watch us?"

"It's not that," I said hurriedly. "It's just that I want you to discuss things like smoking with Don and me. I really don't think you are old enough to smoke, but if you must try it, and I guess all girls do" (I did my early smoking behind the greenhouse in Volunteer Park when I was eleven—Benedarettes silk-tipped which tasted like burning gunny sacks—but were the only thing available at Jane's house) "I'd prefer to have you do it in front of us. I don't want you to feel you have to sneak."

Whereupon both girls looked so sneaky I was embarrassed for them and left the room.

Don came back at dusk with the kerosene, several cans of beef stew, very heavy and tasting like dog food, candy, gum, movie magazines, nail polish, mail, whisky, steaks, bacon, eggs, canned milk, matches, lettuce, coffee and noodles.

He brought the noodles, he said, because, although I hadn't said anything, he noticed the supply was getting low. He had been driven both to and from Vashon by an Army jeep—the Army had also brought oil to Beall's Greenhouses and saved several million dollars' worth of orchids. The reason he had taken so long was because the liquor store, filled with customers, was locked. The real proprietor was home sick and a very well-oiled friend had taken over and decided for some well-oiled reason that the customers were unruly and should be locked *in* the store. He wouldn't let anybody in or out for several hours.

"A liquor store wouldn't be a bad place to be locked in during a big snow," Don said dreamily.

Anne said, "It says right here in *Photoplay* that Lana Turner didn't go to college and *she's* certainly successful."

CHAPTER VI

WE MADE IT OURSELVES

THERE were times during that first long, dreary, wet, dark winter when I wondered what I had ever seen in this nasty little island. When I longed to pitch a tent in, say, the lobby of a downtown movie theatre—a stifling hot downtown movie theatre.

The fireplace in our living room is very large. Its maw will hold, without crowding, eight large logs or three sacks of bark or ten big cartons squashed or three orange crates whole or sixty-two big magazines rolled up. Before we moved in, when we were just visiting, I noticed that the Hendersons had tiny fires in only one corner of this great friendly fireplace. I thought this niggardly and uncozy of the Hendersons and I called any little fire an "Emmy fire" after Mrs. Henderson. That was when we first moved in, before we realized that *wood,* the getting and burning of, was going to dominate our entire existence.

At first, getting wood seemed fun. An excursion. A gay family enterprise. And it was free. No fourteen dollars a cord any more. All we had to do was to go down to the beach in front of the house and pick it up, or go to the woods in back of the house and roll it down. We had alder and fir and cedar just for the cutting or picking up and we were lavish with it. We kept great big eight-log MacDonald fires burning in both fireplaces and the stove (no "Emmy fires" for us) from early morning until late at night and the house became warmed all the way through. If we had been less enthusiastic and more observant we might have noticed the cracking and snapping of the pine walls and beams warning us that such heat was unaccustomed.

But we were so happy in our new life and it was still October and there were many bright days and many bark tides and we considered a six-by-twelve-foot woodpile on the sea wall a big supply and kept the fires roaring until the chimneys were hot and we could eat in comfort at the dining room table with only one sweater and without heating the plates until they had to be passed with tongs. Then the days began getting shorter. At the same time the bark tides were fewer and the weather wetter and colder. Don and Joan, our wood-getters, began to speak of Emmy Henderson as a pretty smart little lady. Three toothpicks, a broomstraw and a rolled-up copy of *Quick* centered on one firebrick became their idea of a dinner fire. Anne and I took to heating the dinner plates until they turned brown and the food sizzled on them. We all wore two or three or four sweaters all the time. We filled hot water bottles with boiling water right out of the teakettle and put them in our beds before dinner. We never had colds, but we didn't have much fun either. It was like living in a mine. Dark and damp and cold when we got up. Dark and damp and cold when we went to bed. We let the animals sleep on all the couches and chairs because they warmed them.

Then one morning it was spring. The willows blew in the sunshine like freshly washed golden hair. The white hyacinths bloomed. The cherry trees were frothy with blossoms. We had our first steamed clams and fell in love with Vashon all over again.

Digging clams on your own beach is a special thing. An unexpected dividend, like having a beautiful daughter who can also divine water. I remember that first Saturday morning in April when we were awakened by the sun pouring in the window and lying on our bedroom floor in golden pools.

I remember the sea gulls playing tag against a delphinium-blue sky and the Sound glittering in the sun like a broken mirror. The tide was far out, past the eel grass, and the sand steamed in the sunlight and was warm on our bare feet.

"Wait until they squirt," Don cautioned Anne and me, but we couldn't. We dug huge holes in the wrong places and found only cockles or "Indian clams" as they are called around here. Don and Joan wisely waited for squirts and got big sweet butter clams. Dotting the sand at intervals like open mouths were sea anemones which obligingly sprayed our feet when we stepped on them but infuriated us by pretending to be clams.

Occasionally, while I was digging and Anne was picking up, long worms hunched their way out of the sand. Some of these were cream colored, flat and corrugated like grosgrain ribbon; some were thin and springy and red like copper wire; some were pale and smooth and slimy and almost three feet long like intestines. Don and Joan thought they were interesting and callously picked them up and examined them, Anne shrieked and shuddered and covered her eyes and I gulped and turned away. Some of them, I believe the clam worm is one, leave their delicate little white lime houses like stems of clay pipes, behind them on the sand. Over the years Don and Joan tried these worms for fishing but said they weren't very satisfactory.

While we were digging the butter clams we found a few jackknife clams which are the exact size and shape of a jackknife and have a smooth shell covered with a firm, glistening golden brown skin like tortoise shell; also several enormous horse clams, one of them weighing about three pounds. We discarded these because we wanted the jackknife clams to multiply and we knew from experience the horse clams were slimy and strong. When we had our bucket half full of butter clams we walked down past the old dock where the beach is rocky and the Little Neck clams flourish.

The main difference in appearance between the butter

or Washington clam and the Little Neck is the marking on the shell. The butter clam's thick heavy shell is pale and smooth except for the circular ridges of growth. The shell of the Little Neck clam is smaller and thinner, is dark gray or brown, and has in addition to the growth ridges, distinct grooves that radiate from the beak of the shell. The meat of the butter clam is thick and pink and slightly tough. The Little Neck is small and plump and white and tender. Little necks are near the surface and close to the tide line. To get at them we had first to move several tons of surface rocks, then with a potato hook, claw among the buried rocks. Each time we lifted a rock we exposed a nest of little purple shore crabs who panicked in the sunlight and ran around in circles and into each other like people during an earthquake.

After we had removed the crabs and Joan had picked up one and chased Anne with it and Anne had obligingly shrieked, we scratched in the rocks until we uncovered the Little Necks which seemed to grow in clusters of four and five. For steaming we preferred them small so we reburied any larger than an inch and a half.

One of the troubles with clam digging is that you can't stop. There is always one more place you must try. When we had our bucket full Joanie said, "Before we go let's try just one dig over by that big rock." So we filled our pockets. Then Andy wanted to try down close to the water "just once." Then Don saw a lot of squirts right by the dock and pretty soon we had not only the bucket but a small wooden box full and were so tired we had to rest on a log before starting home.

That's another thing about clam digging. In the excitement of the chase you usually dig up more territory than if you were spading up a large vegetable garden, to say nothing of lifting tons of rocks. The tiredness doesn't really set in until you start the walk home carrying the clams, then you feel as if you had forgotten to take off your diving shoes.

I believe that steamed clams should be served hot with

melted butter and only melted butter. The flavor of freshly dug clams is very delicate and is ruined by the addition of Worcestershire Sauce, garlic or vinegar. With steamed clams we like only hot buttered toast and adults. It takes an almost fanatical affection for children or clams to put up with the "What's this little green thing, Mommy? Do we eat this ugly black part? Do you think this is a worm?" that always accompanies any child's eating of clams. In addition to the company of adults we advocate plenty of clams—at least half a gallon per person.

By the way, the way to get the sand out of clams is to let them stand in sea water for an hour or so. For years I was told to "put them in fresh water and cornmeal." All clams have ever done for me in this concoction is to stick out their tongues and hold on to all their sand.

A good recipe for a quick delicious *Clam Chowder* which we have evolved over the years is:

At least four cups of butter clams cut out of the shell and washed thoroughly.

Grind with the clams:

> 1 green pepper
> 1 bunch green onions
> 6 slices of bacon
> 2 large peeled potatoes
> 1 bunch parsley

Put everything in a large kettle, add one cube of butter and enough water to cover. Cook slowly until the potatoes are done. Add two or three large cans of milk, salt and coarse ground pepper to taste. Serve, as soon as the milk is hot, with buttered toast.

Another good thing to do with clams, especially butter clams is—*Clam Fritters*:

Peel and grate and let soak in cold water overnight—3 large potatoes. The next morning drain the potatoes, put in a large bowl and add:

3 well beaten eggs
4 tbsps flour—more if they don't hold together—a lot depends on the potatoes
1 grated onion
½ tsp or so of salt
coarse ground pepper
2 cups ground clams
½ cup finely chopped parsley

Cook on a griddle in bacon fat. Serve with butter and crisp bacon.

We were proud that we had the best clam beach in this small community and were delighted to share it with our neighbors, even with occasional strangers. One summer morning two prim little old maiden ladies, carrying a shoe-box lunch, knocked on the kitchen door, explained shyly that they had walked the trail from the dock and asked permission to have a picnic on our beach. "We won't leave a scrap of rubbish," they promised. "We don't smoke or drink and we will not start a fire." A little later one of them knocked again and said that she had seen some clams squirting and would I allow her to buy three if she dug them. I told her we would love to give her the clams and loaned her a bucket and a shovel. Some hours later she and her friend, quite red-faced and wet around the hems, proudly showed us the eight clams they had dug.

The next day on the ferry I was telling a man who lives at the other end of the island about these quaint old ladies. He said, "By God, nobody is going to dig clams on *my* beach. I bought the property and I pay taxes on it and I've got a shotgun to protect it. Last Sunday they had some sort of church picnic next door and the kids kept coming over on *my* beach and, by God, I went up to the house and got my gun and I said, 'This is *my* property and I'll shoot any trespassers!' Believe me those kids got off in a hurry."

I said, "But I feel so sorry for people who live in the city and don't have a beach and clams."

"Sorry nothing," he said. "If they're so crazy about the

beach, let them buy a piece of property. I bought mine and I pay taxes. . . ."

I am happy to say that I have met very few islanders with this man's miserable viewpoint. He belongs to a small coterie who at one time made an abortive attempt to keep Vashon Island a "rich man's paradise," which term has always seemed to my poverty-ridden ears to be extremely paradoxical.

During the time when the ferry company was raising the rates every half hour or so and we were all complaining, another member of this public-spirited group said, "Glad to see the rates going up. Hope they make it so damned expensive all the rabble will have to move off." By rabble I assumed he meant us unfortunates with mortgages and without Cadillacs.

In addition to clams, our beach offers us on occasion geoducks, sea cucumbers, squid, crabs, piddocks, cockles and mussels. There are also scallops and shrimps but they are so far out it is easier to buy them from the scallop and shrimp boats for a dollar a bucket. Geoducks are found only at the lowest tide, are scarce, and digging them requires quick action and enormous tenacity. There is a game limit on geoducks—so many per person per season—I don't know what it is but I'm no more worried about exceeding it than I am about getting too many dinosaurs.

One June morning during the lowest tides of the year, Anne and Joan and Don and I were moseying along the edge of the water looking for Mossy Chitons—funny little things about the size of and color of field mice, that cling to rocks and with dorsal plates shaped like butterflies and in wonderful colors of turquoise-blue, pale yellow, chestnut-brown and white—and Giant Chitons which are bright red, look like apples, used to be eaten by the Indians and Don wanted to try one. Suddenly Joanie who was in the lead yelled, "Geoduck! Hurry!"

We ran, but on tiptoe so as not to warn the geoduck who had his huge siphon or neck sticking out of the sand like a periscope. As soon as we reached the spot, Joanie knelt down and got a good grip on the geoduck's neck, Don and I started digging with our hands and Anne ran home for the shovel. The geoduck was close to the edge of the water and the sand was mushy and not too difficult to dig with bare hands if you discount the fact that our fingernails were up to our wrists by the time Anne brought the shovel. You can't ever rest when you are digging a geoduck so Anne relieved Joan at the neck, Don began to dig with the shovel and Joan and I with our hands, followed the neck down into the sand and water digging with our fingers as we tried to find the shell.

The hole in which Joan and Anne and I were kneeling was about six feet in diameter, at least three feet deep and filled with water, when I finally felt the edge of the shell. I shouted at Don who rushed to my side, slipped his hand along the siphon which the geoduck had been drawing farther and farther down into the sand, until he felt the shell, then he took up where I had left off. My job then was to shovel as fast as I could around the edge of the hole while Anne held on to the neck. Joan bailed with an old coffee can and the tide hurried in with billions of gallons more water. We were all fully dressed in jeans and sweatshirts and all wet to our armpits, and covered with mud and sand. Some neighbor children came by in a rowboat, saw that we were working on a geoduck and spread the word along the beach. People began coming up to watch, until we had an audience of fifteen or so. We spoke but didn't dare stop because of the tide. We kept taking turns holding on to the neck. The hole was the size of a crater and it was almost noon when at last with a terrific sucking noise, Don pulled out the geoduck.

It was a big one. The oblong shell, covered with a dirty, yellow, wrinkled skin, was about seven inches long and five inches wide. It must have weighed at least five pounds. After everyone in our audience had examined it and told us how they cooked geoduck, how their Aunt Eunice cooked geoduck, why they didn't like geoduck, etc., we took it home, cut it out of the shell, skinned the neck and removed the stomach. Then I put the geoduck meat along with a dozen soda crackers and a handful of parsley through the food chopper using the fine blade, added a couple of well-beaten eggs and some coarse ground pepper and made the result into patties which I sautéed in butter. They were heavenly, with a sweet nutty flavor somewhere between scallop and abalone.

I speak very lightly of squid being part of our obtainable sea food. Actually the only squid I have eaten have been bought in the Farmer's Market in Seattle. Several times when we were down by the old dock trolling for perch we hooked small octopus and squid (the difference is that the octopus has eight arms and the squid ten) but nobody including Don ever had the sadistic impulse to bring it into the boat with me. When I buy squid they have already been peeled and gutted and are limp and white. Sautéed in butter for not more than one minute on each side, they are tender and have a delicate flavor akin to a scallop. Cooked too long they assume the exact flavor and texture of a sautéed rubber glove.

In spite of having heard several sea-food fanatics claim they are "absolutely divine," no one in our family has ever eaten sea cucumbers. Our trouble seems to be that we can't hurdle their appearance which is *not* like a cucumber, but is like an enormous red spiny slug.

Piddocks are clams with some sort of neurosis that makes them afraid to face life. Instead they burrow into the hard clay or sandstone along our shores. As the deeply imbedded anterior end of their shell is larger than the posterior (copied from the clam book), once in they are entombed for life unless some innocent armed with a mattock happens along and thinks he has found a geoduck the way Don and the girls and I did. We chipped for hours in the hot June sun before we finally unearthed the piddock, medium-sized and smashed. We were so disappointed we didn't even bring it home. Don's opinion is that if they tasted like a combination of truffles and hundred-year-old brandy, piddocks could not be worth the effort.

Crabs are plentiful and good-sized but our crab traps

either get bogged down with starfish or, having been set by glackity adolescents who don't know how to tie knots, are carried away by the tide. In the middle of the summer, the medium-sized crabs come close enough to shore to be netted from a rowboat, but we only do this for fun, because eating them is too much like putting mayonnaise on a spider for my taste.

I believe that we are the only ones on this beach who eat the delicious cockles. Mussels are abundant but like mushrooms, *some* are poisonous and *some* are not, and I'm not enough of a zoologist or sport to take a chance.

Our local shrimps are small and tough and in no way compare to either Alaska or Gulf shrimp. Our scallops are smaller than the eastern variety but are very delicious and certainly much cheaper.

By going out in the rowboat we get sole, blackmouth (baby King salmon), silver salmon, cod, Spanish mackerel, red snapper and perch. In the fall for a dollar, or sometimes two if they are very large, we can row out and buy big salmon from the fishing boats.

When we first moved here we were told by some expert fisherman that by spinning on the incoming tide, we could catch silvers. What with one thing and another we didn't get around to testing this theory until a year or so ago when I was having some publicity pictures taken. As usual, we were vainly trying to think of some pose a little more arresting than the usual arms grasping opposite elbows and toothy smile so dear to the book jackets of female authors, when I remembered about spinning for silvers. The photographer was overjoyed but Don said, "It's no use. The tide is going out and they won't bite."

I said, "Oh, what difference does that make! The fact that I'm casting is the important thing."

Don said, "You'll just look ridiculous because it will be obvious to everybody that the tide is going out." Also that I don't know how to cast.

But the photographer, who was tired, said he didn't

think it mattered that much, so we went down to the beach and I made one cast and caught a silver about twelve inches long. Since then we have spun and spun (if that is the expression) at exactly the moment when the tide is changing, but we have never had a bite.

Also edible, and for nothing, on our own property are blackberries, salmon berries, huckleberries, both blue and red, watercress, Chinese pheasants and mushrooms. The mushrooms, the delicious, easily identified Shaggy-Manes, are plentiful, but one time I decided to try a new kind. The new kind, also plentiful, were a soft innocent gray, bell-shaped, thick and meaty. I gathered a big basket of them, carefully choosing one of each stage of development from tiny button to rotting adult, brought them up to the house, sat down with our mushroom book and attempted to match them to the book's vacillating descriptions and uncolored indistinct photographs.

After several hours of research I was at least reasonably sure that I had neither the Death Cup (*Amanita phalloides*): "There is no known antidote," or Fly Amanita (*Amanita muscaria*): "It is said that it is cooked and eaten by the Russians yet is known to have caused much sickness and many deaths." But without colored plates I couldn't decide whether I had the Inky Coprinus (*Coprinus atramentarius*), "edible"; or the Dog Cortinarius (*Cortinarius caninus*) on the deadlines or edibility of which the book disdained to comment.

Being in a reckless mood I put an iron skillet on the fire, tossed in a big lump of butter and began washing and slicing the mushrooms. They had a nice even firm texture and a pleasant unpoisonous smell so I filled the skillet full. When I thought they were done I heaped some invitingly on crisp toast and offered them to Anne and Joan and Don who were sitting at the kitchen table contentedly eating vegetable soup and, as Don said, "Not at all enthusiastic about changing to poisonous mushrooms, no matter how crisp the toast." I told them they were being pretty ridiculous and reminded them how well Daddy had trained his children in mushroom gathering. Don said, "No doubt," and continued with his soup.

Rather defiantly I ate all the mushrooms, even flouncing up and getting a second helping. They tasted a tiny bit like Shaggy-Manes and a great deal like cardboard soaked in Mercurochrome. I said to Don and the girls, "The flavor is not exciting but it is so mild and inoffensive and the mushrooms are so plentiful and keep their shape so beautifully when cooked, that I'm going to use nothing else from now on. I'm not even going to bother to pick the Shaggy-Manes."

"Do you want a piece of fresh applesauce cake?" Anne asked.

"Oh, no," I said coolly, "the mushrooms were very filling."

I was drinking my second cup of coffee when suddenly without any warning at all, everything went black. I said, "Oh, my God, the mushrooms!" and tried vainly to remember whether mushroom poisoning is acid or alkali and what the drugstore calendar had said to do in either case. All that I could dredge up was that peat moss is acid—wood ashes are alkali.

Anne said, calmly, "Stick your finger down your throat."

Don said, "Drink olive oil but don't do anything until I call the doctor." He rushed to the phone which is ever a futile gesture as the line is always in use, then rushed back to the kitchen and asked anxiously, "How do you feel?"

"Like somebody is holding a black pillow over my face," I said. "What about drinking mustard and water?"

"Stick your finger down your throat," Joan said.

"Drink olive oil," Don said.

So I drank the olive oil and then stuck my finger down my throat and immediately felt quite well. Don tried to call the doctor again, but the phone was still busy. Three rooted camellia cuttings and one recipe for icebox cookies later, he got the line and the doctor, who told him to bring me up to his office. Once on the way up to the office things got very dark gray and perspiration ran into my eyes.

The doctor kept me waiting an hour, then looked at my eyes, took my blood pressure and gave me a lecture on the dangers of gathering your own mushrooms. As I went out the door he called out gaily, "If you lose consciousness within the next eight hours, call me, but it will probably be too late."

The druggist told me that I should have drunk mineral oil as olive oil is absorbed by the system and mineral oil isn't.

An Italian farmer friend of Don's whom we met in the hardware store said, "Them mushrooms wasn't poison. Fall mushrooms are never poison. It's in the spring you gotta watch out. My wife almost die from mushrooms, two, three times but always in the spring. Now before she eats mushrooms she drink big glass of olive oil. Never has any more trouble."

In addition to the food which grows naturally on our place, we get occasional bonanzas by beachcombing. The best was that first winter during the war when coffee was the big problem and cigarettes were often unobtainable.

We had had a fierce storm with high waves, driving winds and lashing rain. The morning after the storm, being Sunday, we all went down to the beach to, as Don always says, "see what God hath wrought." There, scattered along the tide line, were at least a dozen wooden boxes. We gathered them up and stacked them on the sea wall. When pried open they revealed army rations of several kinds—a sort of hash which tasted just like Pard and made us feel even sorrier for our boys overseas; hard tack which we fed to the ducks and sea gulls; and cans containing a few pieces of hard candy, three cigarettes, some powdered lemon juice, and a little can of powdered coffee. We heard that families farther down the beach got hams and sacks of flour, none the worse for the ducking. We didn't know whether this was true or just one of those instances where people have to make their story the best.

We often get rowboats but honesty, the knowledge that ours also occasionally goes adrift, and large printed license numbers on the side, prevent our keeping them. However, there is an unwritten agreement that finders are keepers on pike poles, rafts, shovels, toy boats, buckets, and so on.

Beachcombing is fun even when your only reward is a pretty piece of driftwood or an agate. Going down to the beach after a storm is the only time in my adult life when I experience that wonderful, joyous, childhood feeling of expectancy. "After all," I used to tell Anne and Joan (referring only occasionally to the encyclopaedia) "the Pacific Ocean stretches from the Arctic to the Antarctic, covers approximately seventy million square miles, and is as old as the earth. It might bring us *anything!*"

Don and I have a strong feeling that residents should, as far as they are able, patronize the island's industries. For most of us this means the Saturday shopping spree in the village of Vashon, supplemented by the milkman, the laundryman, the telephone shopping service of the big Seattle department stores and occasional jaunts to buy eggs or chickens from a farmer. That first October I made inquiries at the store about a place to buy fresh eggs and was told about a small chicken farm close by. The next Saturday afternoon, Anne and Joan and Don and I walked up there. It was a nice, neat little place with a white picket fence and a small white house. I knocked and the door was opened by a pleasant-looking woman in a clean blue-and-white-checked apron. I said, "We would like to buy some eggs."

She said, "Who are you?"

I said, "We are the MacDonalds."

She said, "MacDonalds? Then you must have bought Dr. Morrow's house."

I said, "We did buy Dr. Morrow's house."

She said, "Then you must be the MacDonalds."

I said, "We are the MacDonalds."

She said, "But the MacDonalds bought Dr. Morrow's house."

I said, "We did. We bought Dr. Morrow's house. We are the MacDonalds. We live at Dolphin Point."

She said, "Well, come right in."

I said, "We came to buy eggs. Do you have any?"

She said, "I only sell to my neighbors."

I said, "We are your neighbors. We bought Dr. Morrow's house on the beach."

She said, "But I thought the MacDonalds bought Dr. Morrow's house."

We gave up and bought our eggs from the store.

For a long time we bought butter from the mother of a friend of Don's at Boeing. It was dark yellow and tasted like cheese, but she left it in the mailbox which was convenient for Don and sometimes she *gave* me a quart of sour cream.

From his Italian farmer friend Don got, for three dollars a gallon, first pressing California olive oil marked, "Extra, extra virgin"; big boxes of red currants, each currant the size of a marble and the color of blood; gooseberries like fat green grapes; and faba, the big flat horse beans which cooked Italian style with olive oil and pepper, taste almost but not exactly like Ivory soap boiled in quinine.

From a friend of a friend of the man who put new rings in our car, we bought for our freezer what he referred to many many times as "a springer" but which turned out to be old, tough, strong, resentful ram that managed to triumph over stewing in basil and garlic or any marinade. We also bought a local pig which was white, as big as a cow and tasted like human flesh even when smoked. Sometimes in desperation because of unexpected company, I would bring out a package of "humey," but even in split pea soup it was unmistakable and Anne and Joan said it made them feel as if they should have rings in their noses and be dancing around the stove.

After a while we bought ten acres on the hill above us and raised our own pigs, lambs, turkeys, geese, cows, chickens, milk, eggs, steers, peaches, cherries and mallard ducks. Our livestock was all beset by strange parasites and impulses which required hundreds of gallons of sulpha and many calls to the veterinary. One cow ate nuts and bolts and baling wire and had to have all four of her stomachs opened up. One of our pigs ate all of her babies. One of our steers breathed in most of a sack of calf meal and exploded. All of our turkeys died every year and the raccoons always ate the baby ducks. And Don bought me a churn. He said, "You always complain so much about Mrs. Evinlips' butter, I thought you'd like to make your own."

"I certainly would," I told him. "From now on we will have some *good* butter."

The butter making went very rapidly and I made a great deal. But after a day or so it turned dark yellow and tasted like cheese. Secretly, I sent for the government bulletin on making butter. The government bulletin, when it finally came, said, in effect, "Some people make better butter than others." So I bought a farm magazine with an article on butter making and it said, "Some people make better butter than others." I made inquiries of neighbors, local farmers, former farmers, gentlemen farmers and learned that some people make butter out of sweet cream and some people make butter out of sour cream but some people make better butter than others.

I tried both sweet and sour. I washed my butter so much I almost wore it out. I changed the temperature of the cream about twenty times and I switched churns three times. For a few days after I made it the butter was fine. Then it turned dark yellow and tasted like cheese. Now I buy my butter from my milkman and it is always pale yellow and sweet.

Either some people do make better butter than others or this *is* the age of plastics.

CHAPTER VII

THE PROBLEM IS
TO HOLD IT BACK

Sometime in early November during my lunch half hour, I happened into a ten cent store to buy some pot holders and came across a display of bulbs marked SPECIAL TODAY—89¢ PER DOZEN. There were bins and bins and bins full. Clipped to the top of each bin was a large lavishly colored picture of what the bulbs would produce. Daffodils with magnificent golden trumpets like Gabriel's Horn, tulips with stiff Kelly green stems supporting blossoms larger than brandy snifters, hyacinths the size and shape of bridesmaids' muffs, ranunculus like cabbages.

Quickly I took out my wallet and counted the grocery money. That night when I came in the door with two shopping bags, the girls said, "Hooray, apples at last!" I said no. They said "Cokes?" I said no. Don said hopefully, "I thought you said you wouldn't have time to go to the cheese stall in the public market?" I said, "There's no use guessing. I've got something perfectly wonderful for all of us and it's a surprise but I'm not going to show you until after dinner."

After dinner while the girls were argumentatively washing and chipping the dishes, I spread newspapers on the dining room table and dumped out the shopping bags. The bulbs were in small brown paper sacks rather illegibly marked "Hycth-bl—Dfdl-emp—Chndxa," etc. I called to the family to come and see Mommy's surprise.

After carefully balancing a greasy skillet on top of a glass, then adding some soapy silverware and a muffin tin with half of a wet muffin still in it (it was her night to wash), Joan came to the kitchen door, looked at the heaps of little paper bags and said brightly, "Oh, boy, dried apricots?"

"Guess again," I said.

Anne picked up "Chndxa," spelled it out loud and said accusingly, "You've been to that health store again!"

Don put down *Time,* picked up "Ran-gnt" and said. "You know I never *could* read your writing."

I said, "I didn't write that."

Rather gingerly he opened the bag and took out what looked like a tiny brown withered hand. With a cry of delight, he said, "Italian mushrooms!"

I grabbed the bag away from him, studied "Ran-gnt" for a minute or two fruitlessly, then said, "You're all pigs. All you think about is food. Thank goodness for *me,* with *my* love for beauty. These are bulbs! I bought them in the ten cent store this noon. They were on sale for almost nothing. There are hyacinths and daffodils and tulips and all kinds of beautiful things." I studied "Ran-gnt" again.

Joan said, "Gosh, I wish you'd *ever* remember to get some dried apricots."

Anne said, "Mommy, look at the way Joan is washing the dishes. The water is ice cold and greasy and the dishes are filthy."

Joan said, "Oh, you're just mad because it's my week to wash."

Anne said, "And she's got Tudor's pan and the cat's dish in with our dishes and she never rinses anything. Look at this muffin pan she expects me to dry. It's got almost a whole muffin in it."

By the time I had given Joan her ten thousandth lesson in correct dishwashing, had explained to Anne for the billionth time why she should study Latin, why I studied Latin, why Don studied Latin, why Joan was going to study Latin, had rinsed out a petticoat, ironed a blouse and put up my hair, it was time for the ten o'clock news. While we listened to the news, I brushed the little bags of bulbs back into the shopping bag. Then Don said, "I think we should plant all those bulbs in the woods and let them naturalize. I don't like gardens that look planted. I think all flowers should grow naturally."

I said, "I like flowers to look natural too, but not so natural that they are all eaten by slugs and killed by nettles and wild cucumber. I plan to put the tulips and daffodils at the top of the rockery in the big patio, the other things in the rockeries, the ranunculuses in that bed by the kitchen and crocuses in the moss between the cedar blocks in the patios."

Don said, "You'd better not dig in that moss, you might kill it. I'll put the crocuses and daffodils in the woods by the spring. They'll look more natural."

I said, "What pleasure would we get out of flowers growing way up by the spring, we never go up there."

Don said, "It wouldn't take much work to widen that trail."

I said, "Well you widen the trail and then we'll see about planting bulbs, only it should be iris because they like water."

"Iris," Don said. "That's what I was thinking of. Did you get any?"

"No," I said.

"What about bluebells?"

"You mean scillas?"

"No, I mean bluebells. My grandmother used to have them in her orchard. They grew under the trees in big masses. They looked so natural."

We were in bed reading and smoking one last cigarette when Don suddenly thrust the *House Beautiful* under my nose and said, "See, that's what I mean." He had the magazine folded back to a colored plate of a forty-room stone house surrounded by gigantic oak trees and at least one hundred and fifty acres of lawn. Flowing from oak tree to oak tree and on off into the distance was a golden river of daffodils, about eight billion of them. "Naturalized," Don said. "That's the way all bulbs should be planted."

Even though we weren't able to reach a compromise as to where the bulbs should be planted, we decided that we would do something about them that weekend, perhaps divide them equally between us.

But Friday afternoon Anne's and Joan's friends Marilyn and Joanne arrived to stay until Sunday night and Saturday morning early Don and I were awakened by the four little girls standing at the foot of our bed, making gagging noises and holding their noses.

"Sobethig sbells awful!" Joan said.

"Sobethig has died under the house," Anne said.

"We are all gettig sick," Joan said. "Hurry ad get up, it's awful."

Anne wailed, "Why does sobethig like this always have to happed whed we have company?" (Especially Marilyn whose mother had a green Cadillac and a Filipino houseboy but whose little girl I was pleased to note had a very dirty neck and no buttons on her pajamas.)

So Don spent all day Saturday and all day Sunday easing himself headfirst over the hot water tank which had been carefully set up in the only entrance to the underneath part of the house, then crawling unenthusiastically around in the dirt, rubble and extra building materials trying to find the rat. I held the flashlight and handed him the poker and helped him move the lumber, while the girls said, "Ugh, it smells awful! Haven't you found it yet? Haven't you found it yet?"

In between times I cooked, tidied up, washed, ironed, made fudge, listened to long recitals of "then I said and she said and he said and the dumb teacher said," refereed quarrels, gave my opinions on the subjects of Betty Grable, Tyrone Power, Lana Turner, Van Johnson, Frank Sinatra, pink lipstick, purple toenail polish, peignoirs, speed boats, trips to Florida and smoking, and withheld my opinion on the subject of Marilyn's beautiful mother and her strapless dresses and green Cadillac, about whom we heard far too much.

The more I heard about Marilyn's beautiful, luxury-saturated mother the more I noticed how thin—well, really emaciated—Marilyn her only child was; how her little gray petticoat straps were fastened with rusty safety pins; how much tartar she had on her crooked little teeth.

Finally it was Sunday night. Marilyn and Joanne had been driven to the ferry; Don had located the rat in the motor of the refrigerator right by the fan; nobody had been able to find Joan's geography book; I was washing my hair with cake soap because of having such a strong sense of beauty and substituting Anem-St. Brg. for shampoo, Don was helping Anne with a theme on "My Happy Weekend"; the bulbs were still in their little bags.

"We'll plant the bulbs next weekend for sure," I told Don later as he mournfully brushed his teeth with salt and soda because I had spent the money for Psdnt-wht or Chndxa-bl.

The next weekend we had a terrific storm. The sort of storm where the wind grabbed the cedar tree (diameter of trunk one foot) right outside the kitchen window and bent it over like a croquet wicket, made the great virgin firs back of the house describe such tremendous arcs that Don and I took turns nervously trying to measure them from the living room window, and tossed big branches with cones on them over the countryside like bouquets. The Sound, whipped into muddy waves fifteen feet high, thundered against the shore with so much fury and power the whole island trembled. It was not raining in the conventional drop or pitter-patter sense. Water was just dumped on us like someone emptying a hot water bottle. The eaves, troughs and gutters were completely defeated and water ran from the edges of the roof in shiny isinglass sheets.

Don and Joan put on oilskins and sou'westers and went

down to the sea wall and brought up creosote logs which made such a fierce fire we had to move the furniture to the ends of the living room, and even then there was a strong smell of hot varnish. We had a cozy time though popping corn, reading aloud and making records of the girls singing "Tangerine" in high nervous voices and Don singing "Rock of Ages" confidently off key, but the bulbs stayed in the little bags.

Then it was February and I had been fired from my job and was staying home and one day the sun came out and it was warm and I began working in the garden and saw small green spikes and humps where there were almost small green spikes and I remembered about the bulbs still in their little sacks marked "Tlps-Ctge-pnk." Being entirely inexperienced and to date a very unsuccessful gardener, I called Mother and asked her if I could plant the bulbs anyway or did I have to wait until next year.

Mother said, "Stick them in. They will be late but it can't be helped. Be sure and put some bone meal under each bulb."

I also told her about the green spikes and asked her to identify them.

She said, "Daffodils and narcissus, probably. I'll come out one of these days and take a look. I love to poke around in an old garden and see what is coming up."

So I planted the bulbs in masses and in spite of the fact that every place I dug I ran into other bulbs and morning-glory roots and planted the ranunculuses upside down, they all grew, were almost as big as the pictures and, for the first time in my life, I could pick an armful of blue hyacinths.

I learned that first spring that gardening is for very small children and adults. The inbetweeners', especially young females', only interest in the garden is picking flowers for their hair. From the day of the first camellia, which was some time in January, Anne and Joan left for school looking from the front like natives about to attend a fiesta, from the back, with their dishtowel bandannas, wooden shoes and long boy's coats, like sad old peasants going out to gather faggots.

After the hyacinths had finished blooming, Don, who is under the illusion that he knows more about gardening than Burbank but actually doesn't know a *Pachysandra terminalis* from an aspirin tablet, strode out one Sunday morning in a spurt of neatness, clipped off all the hyacinth leaves close to the ground and tossed them on the compost heap. The next year where I had had my masses of hyacinths, I had only two or three spindly little stalks with a few scattered blooms like scillas.

I also learned that first spring how riotously things grow here on Vashon. We cleared land in January and by June it was a jungle again. I sent away for a dwarf white buddleia because it was unconditionally guaranteed not to exceed thirty inches, stuck it in what we considered a very poor spot at the top of the rockery in the white garden and it grew ten feet that first year and bore blossoms eight inches long. Right now it is twenty feet high and I cut it to the ground every time I go past it. There are also millions of little dwarf (hah) white buddleias flourishing around the mother plant for a radius of one hundred feet. The blossoms are a pure white, lilac-shaped and lovely if you can see them without tipping over backwards.

Then there are the Empress trees I bought that first spring. "Very rare!" the nurseryman told me, pretending in the crafty sure-fire way all nurserymen do that he didn't really want to sell them, that he was only letting me buy them because his wife was at her sister Cora's. As he dug me up *five* he told me that they were so terribly rare, "Sacred tree of the Empress of China," that there were only two in Seattle. Don and I planted the Empress trees and I hovered over them and stroked them and was awed by their rareness and wondered how they were going to display it.

They then started to grow. Wow! The one by the kitchen door is over forty feet high and by Empress tree standards is still only a little tiny baby. Empress trees have lovely, sweet-scented, periwinkle-blue blossoms in spikes like foxglove. The buds, formed at the ends of the branches in the fall, stand up against the winter sky like brown velvet buttons unless Don happens along with his pruning saw and decides to "shape the trees" by cutting off a limb four inches in diameter.

Empress trees have enormous, loosely attached leaves which drop off all summer long and lie around on the patios and flower beds like palm-leaf fans. We have found that the best, well really the only, way to enjoy the Empress tree blossoms is to go out in the rowboat and look in at them against the sky.

That is really the best way to view all of my gardening. One hundred yards from shore in the rowboat it looks marvelous. Up close there is the embarrassing sight of horsetail, wild morning-glory, dock, wild cucumber, blackberries and nettles, busily choking out the tender planted things.

I suppose our original mistake was in trying to take in the entire seven acres with only Mother as gardener. I mean true gardener, the kind who goes quietly along day after day, transplanting, spraying, pruning, weeding, picking, a little here, a little there. I rush out seasonally and put in long hours for a short time. Don waits until the wild cucumbers are shamelessly bearing little cucumbers right in front of us on the paths, then takes a sharp scythe and goes out to "clear things up," which in my language means slashing off azaleas, ripping out blue ball thistles, mowing down heathers and other acts of vandalism.

Don always prunes things that should never be pruned, digs tiny holes and rams in huge balls of roots, divides by brute force and lifts with a yank. It is very irritating to have the things he plants so mannishly, grow.

The best vegetable garden we ever had was our first, planted in an old cesspool. An old cesspool that didn't work exactly right, the Hendersons told us with a chuckle, intimating that the not working was a temporary thing like rheumatism caused by the damp weather but would clear up in the spring.

When spring came it was not necessary for us to go down to the sea wall to see how the old cesspool was not working. We could tell by just opening any door. Joan said with some pride, "Gosh, you can smell our cesspool clear up at the bus stop." So one Saturday morning Don and I went purposefully down and began poking around. It took us about five minutes to deduce that for years and years the cesspool had not been emptying into the sump, or whatever was planned, but had been viciously seeping into an area about fifty feet long and fifteen feet wide along the sea wall. Don drilled drainage holes in the sea wall, cleaned out the intake and outgo pipes, remarking bitterly that standing in an old cesspool was not his idea of a day off, dug up the sump when the tide was right and he could get at it, and finally had the whole system working again.

Though all the seepage had been drained off and that part of the sea wall smelled better, it looked forsaken and untidy. Don suggested buying clover seed and scattering it around, but as this is his stock remedy for anything not curable by whisky in hot milk, I decided instead to plant a vegetable garden there. I cleared out all the syringa and horsetail and wild blackberry vines, Don dug up the ground and, as it was pure clay, I drafted the girls into helping us scoop up and dump on about fifty (they still say a thousand) buckets of beach sand. For the next two weeks I raked and smashed clay lumps until my hands were reduced to flapping blisters with fingers but I had a fairly friable soil.

I made neat, short, north-and-south rows and we all planted radishes, romaine, carrots, ruby Swiss chard, New Zealand spinach, salsify, cucumbers, summer squash, zucchini, garlic, onions and tomatoes. I marked all the rows carefully with the seed packages stuck on little sticks, but I needn't have bothered. Those vegetables shot out of the ground like rockets and grew so enormous that even nearsighted Anne and I could look north from the old dock and tell our salsify from our carrots.

Because of the fast growth, some of the things were hollow like gourds, but we had enough for the whole Northwest. I was terribly proud and planned on sharing, until the afternoon when Anne and Joan came breathlessly in and told me with relish that the whole beach was talking about my garden and waiting hopefully for us all to get hookworm or Shigella. "Does hookworm start with a sort of pain in your ribs?" Joan asked.

"No," I said shortly, "that is the direct result of seven peanut butter sandwiches and three Cokes before lunch and not making your bed."

Then I called Mary's husband who is a doctor and asked him if we were doing a dangerous thing. He said wistfully that he certainly wished he had some of that fine fertilizer for his garden. He had gone in strongly for coffee grounds that year. In fact had commandeered the entire output from the Naval Hospital and was dumping them on their vegetable garden to loosen the clay soil. The results had not been too satisfactory. Really more like a giant percolator than a garden and certainly did not compare to clay loosened with beach sand and cess.

I planted the tomato plants the Italian way of bending up three or four inches at the top for the plant and burying the rest. I also kept them pruned to one stalk. They grew into small trees and bore bushels of tomatoes. That was the same year I lined all the sea wall with parsley and for the first time in my life had enough.

Heady with the success of that first small garden which I cared for, Don read aloud to me an article from the Gardener's Monthly entitled "Weeding Is a Waste of Time." The big liar who wrote it (a man) said that he spaded up his very large garden, planted his seeds and that was that until harvesttime. "Nature does not expect us to weed—weeds provide the plants with much needed oxygen"—and so on, and so on.

I noticed that there were no pictures of the man's garden, no record of his crop, nor any comments from his wife.

The upshot of this was that the next spring Don had a five acre field, on the farm above us, plowed just a little, bought his seeds by the pound and left the rest up to God and old Weeding-is-a-waste-of-time. We raised about six spindly carrots, a few wrinkled peas which the pheasants ate and the biggest crop of quack grass this side of Wyoming.

Don loves trees—I suspect sometimes that he had a dryad ancestor, because he will never willingly part with any tree and suffers actual physical pain when I chop one down— even the wild cherry that was choking out his favorite weeping pussy-willow. When we began landscaping he rushed feverishly to town and bought out the entire evergreen output of a small nursery. It was fine when they were itty-bitty. Now they have taken hold and though Mother and I secretly slash them back all the time, it doesn't even show and you should see the Sequoias which were about six inches high when Don brought them home. "Zowie!" they said, after he had turned them out of their tiny pots and tucked them into our black leaf mold. "This is a place we like!" and they began beating their chests and springing toward heaven in dark green leaps and bounds.

It is satisfactory, though, to plant things and have them thrive. To celebrate our first Valentine's Day on Vashon, Anne and Joan brought me a pale pink single camellia in a little pink pot. It was a sallow trembly little thing about four inches high with one bloom. I stuck it in the bed with the espaliered apricot tree, even then apparently dedicated to pushing in the south wall of the house. The little camellia grew very well and the next year had four blossoms. After a while we put in a gas furnace. "The exhaust has to come out here" (right by the camellia), the furnaceman said sternly. I was worried. "Shall I move it?" I asked Mother.

"Move that damn wisteria first," Mother said. She hates wisteria because it is vigorous and heedless and its little clutching hands had choked the life out of a rare French lilac before it had time to settle its roots or learn the English for "Cut that out!"

So I moved the wisteria over by the guesthouse where there were no foreigners and where we wanted it to clutch and choke, and forgot about the camellia. I just went out and looked at it to make sure I was not dreaming and the camellia is taller than I am, five feet, six and three-quarters inches in my stocking feet and I have on shoes (just for a lark, of course), it is well branched and loaded with blossoms. Either it likes gas fumes or this is Shangrila.

One of the plants or rather shrubs we bought for the rockery by the small patio is called *Pittosporum tobira,* honestly that is the only name it has. It has shiny evergreen leaves, small waxy white blossoms that look like orange blossoms and smell like hyacinths and are supposed to appear only in semi-tropical climates. I bought it because of its delightful fragrance, because it was small and compact and seemed such a *little* evergreen for the rockery, and also of course because the nurseryman said he didn't really want to sell it but as long as his wife was at her sister Ethel's. . . . When I showed it to several of my gardening friends they liked it because it had such a hard name but shook their heads sadly and said, "You won't have it long. It will never survive our winters." Well, it is now as big around as our umbrella table, about four feet tall and Mother and I have been pruning it for three years.

All this vigor has nothing at all to do with me. Mother can take as much credit as she wants but I was really a very unsuccessful gardener until we moved to Vashon. Here we have an unbeatable combination of salt air, the Japanese Current, continual rain, hundreds of years of leaf mold washed down every winter, and cool summers. This is the perfect climate for rhododendrons, camellias and azaleas, not so good for people. My Fabia rhododendrons, which have tubular orange-apricot blossoms and are labeled by the garden book, "rare and delicate," bloom in May and again in September. Butterfly, a pale yellow hybrid, noted for being both sulky and leggy, has a blossom on every branchlet and has the contours of a teapot. This morning, just for fun, I counted the blossoms on one of our Unknown Warrior rhododendrons—the one the nurseryman said was so spindly we could have it for half price—it has seventy-eight blossoms. The blossoms average seven inches in diameter—the individual flowerets three inches. Mother was worried about these rhododendrons because they began showing color in December and some of the blossoms were frozen.

I should really stop right here while you have the impression that we are living in the Du Pont conservatories. But honesty demands that I go on and say that it is not to be overlooked that such remarkable climatic and soil conditions affect weeds the way they affect non-weeds. What do you think of horsetail that pushes its head right through asphalt paving? What about seedling alders that invade the rockery en masse and grow four feet a season—wild cucumber that climbs to the top of maples—docks with roots two feet long rammed straight down into the ground like spikes, but spikes cemented in—syringa and elderberry that completely healed the raw wound of a landslide down the beach in one season—wild morning-glory sneaking across the guesthouse porch, in the door and around the leg of the Benjamin Franklin stove during the week we were painting?

There is also the little matter of things taking hold—ajuga, for instance—I love its true blue blossoms and lovely copper-colored leaves and it is a good groundcover so I put a clump here and there in the rockeries—on banks—along the road. Before I could say "atropurpurea" it was pushing the lithospermum and perennial candytuft out of the rockery and into the kitchen, had completely obliterated the guesthouse path, killed all the rock roses, and was spitting on its hands getting ready to rip the shakes off the roof. Mother and I yanked it out and moved it clear up into the deep woods, about ten acres away. Yesterday Don took me up to show me the exact location of a surveyor's stake (usual vital last-minute information before leaving on a trip—he had already explained the difference between heavy duty and light duty wiring—how to lower cutting blade on lawn mower) and I was attracted by a brilliant patch of blue at the edge of the wood's road. It was the ajuga in full brilliant battle dress, standing tall, heads erect, marching toward home. I noticed also that it has made a full recovery in the rockeries and is fighting it out with the coral bells for possession of the azaleas.

Another slight disadvantage observed by gardeners in this mild damp country is the size and ferocity of the slugs. We have black, red, yellow, olive-green and gray slugs. We have them up to six inches long, impervious to all baits and fond of Frisky dog food. One time I climbed laboriously down the face of a bank to pick some lovely apricot-colored broom. I had gathered a large armload and was almost up to the house with it before I noticed that on all the branches black slugs were hanging like Bing cherries.

We also have tent caterpillars—worse some years than others. Last summer, a bad year, we had all of our property sprayed but, because of no road, the rest of the beach sprayed only their gardens and didn't do anything about the hills back of them. In the evening when we ate dinner in the patio we had the cozy accompaniment of millions of caterpillars crunching their way through millions of alder leaves. It was a crisp noise like walking in spilled sugar. Very penetrating.

We have no aphis, Japanese beetles or ordinary biting mosquitoes, but when the tent caterpillars hatch we have millions of moths that flutter around the porch and patio lights like torn paper. We have tried all kinds of moth-catching devices, all of which always make a worse mess than the moths and get my windows dirty. That first summer Don rigged up a powerful spotlight focused into a bucket of water with kerosene in it. The moths swarmed around the light, took dips in the kerosene and then insane and dripping, hurled themselves against the living room and kitchen windows, then on to the patios. Moths are heedless fools with fat juicy bodies and I don't relish them batting around but I was never prepared for the girls' hysterical outbursts. We would be peacefully eating dinner when suddenly one (or both) of them would leap to her feet, usually knocking over her milk and her chair, and rush from the table shrieking. If they had company, which they usually did, this would be a signal for them all to begin to yelp and shudder and tip over things.

Even worse than moths are the WooWoos, those mosquito-like creatures with a wing spread of about four inches, a body like a B-29 and inside my nightgown their goal. It has always distressed Don, who is a peaceful man of studied actions, to be suddenly interrupted in his reading of some morbid atomic bit in *Time* by a bloodcurdling shriek and me diving under the covers down by his feet. Each time, after he has disposed of the attacker and is settling himself, he says, "You know, I hate those hysterical outbursts of yours, Betty. If you would only warn me."

And I reply, "But the WooWoo didn't warn *me*."

"That's because you insist on having the window open."

That goes back to our long-enduring argument about night air. Don has always insisted we get enough air from the fireplace. I like a gale blowing in the window. We have compromised on the windows open, screens down, the draperies drawn, which trick is old stuff to the moths and WooWoos who don't like night air either and long ago got hold of the plans of the house and took note of every flaw and crack between screen and windowsill. This year I am thinking of one of those huge tropical mosquito nets soaked in DDT and draped from the ceiling like a tent over me.

In spite of the slugs, moths and WooWoos, I have found nothing that gives me such a sense of accomplishment or peace as gardening—no matter how vigorously I attack it. I'm sure I couldn't have survived either literary success or Anne and Joan's adolescence without it. My favorite time to garden is in early April during one of the feathery warm spring rains when weeds are easy to uproot and the earth has a rich leafy mushroomy smell.

Of course the minute I showed interest in gardening I ran into the Garden-Club-Latin-Namers. "Gosh, what pretty red nasturtiums," I said.

"Oh, you must mean my *Tropaeoleum majus?*" the Latin-Namer answered with a condescending little laugh.

The secret thing I have found out about the Latin-Namers is that very few of them have gardens. "Too busy with my Garden Clubs," one told me last spring when she came up to borrow some flowers for their meeting.

CHAPTER VIII

CIRRIPEDS NOT WANTED

BEFORE embarking on it, my conception of life on an island was much the same as my conception of life in a submarine. I imagined that everybody did everything together all the time. I had visions of jelly-making bees, community suppers, wild blackberry expeditions, sharing the woodcutting and so on. All erroneous. At least for us year-rounders. The summer people, those mothlike creatures with their unreal attitude toward winter and their urban love of urban pursuits, such as having fun, are exceptions. They see a great deal of each other; in fact, as one woman put it, "are in each other's armpits twenty-four hours a day." The rest of us go along for weeks, months, even years, thinking of each other, intending to get together but not quite making it unless we happen to board the same ferry.

The other day I ran into what I consider a close friend on the ferry. I said, "Oh, and you have the new baby with you. I've been dying to see her," and she said, "You must mean Marilyn, Betty. She started to school yesterday. This is Johnny and I guess you missed Larry altogether. Too bad I left him home with Mother." She knew that I have been busy and obviously she has too.

This is not due to any unfriendliness at all. It is due to unseen forces such as the bark tide which kept Don and me from making our semi-yearly visit to the house of charming neighbors who live way down the beach—nine houses. Boiling over with friendliness and good intentions we left the house one sunny October afternoon.

"I understand that Julia's chrysanthemums are simply magnificent this year," I said to Don as we started down the path. "I wonder how George is coming with his gold mine," Don said. George had begun on the mine six years before and it never occurred to either of us that the vein could have run out since we had seen him last. Anyway we got as far as the sea wall, then we saw it. The most magnificent bark tide of the year. From Dolphin Point clear past the old dock, huge brown slabs of bark lay along the water's edge in the sunshine, like seals. Even people invited to dinner don't pass up bark tides like that one, so we rushed back to the house for our canvas bark bags and gloves and got to work. Hours later our beach was clean, the sea wall was piled high and we were too tired to go anywhere but home. However, as we worked we did stop occasionally to wave at our neighbors who like sandpipers could be seen darting around on their beaches gathering up the bonanza. A doctor, an insurance man, a lawyer, a shipbuilder, a banker, a newspaper publisher, all enjoying for an hour or two the same goal.

Vashon Island's population is spread over its surface in small clusters like fly eggs. Each small community has a name, Robinwood Beach, Tahlequah, Burton, Dilworth Point, Cove, Paradise Cove, Shawnee, Magnolia Beach, Portage, Glen Acres, Ellisport, Lisabeula, Colvos, Vashon Heights, Paradise Valley, Luana Beach, Sylvan Beach, Bethel Park, Klahanie Beach, Docton, Sunrise Ridge, Cedarhurst, Dolphin Point (ours), Scales Corner (all I can remember at this time) and the town of Vashon itself. Quite naturally each community believes that its residents are the most refined, most intelligent, most desirable, its beach the finest, its view of Mount Rainier or the Olympics the most spectacular, its clams the sweetest. Such illusions sponsor contentment, are harmless and will no doubt persist until the floating bridge from Seattle is built and the whole world can see that

Dolphin Point is the loveliest spot on Vashon Island, which explains why it has been settled by such a brilliant, talented, enchanting group of people.

For the first few years after we moved to the beach, we had only one year-round neighbor, the Russells. They bought their house the same year we did, and also, as we did, worked and commuted. During those first years we were drawn together by mutual hardships—the snow, no lights, no road, the terrible telephone service, getting enough wood, storms, walking the trail—and mutual enjoyments—Anne and Joan (they have no children), gardening, cooking, eating, the beach, clams, knitting, driftwood, reading, and living on an island.

The Russells were neighbors in the true, old-fashioned, almost forgotten, calf's-foot-jelly sense of the word. A plate never returned empty. Tea and cucumber sandwiches in the afternoon. Half of a fresh cake left on the kitchen table. Hand-knitted Angora socks for the girls. Help with a creosote log, chicken broth for the ailing. "I'm rowing to the store, what can I get you?" It is a sad thing that the pace of today's living has done so much to eliminate this graceful way of life. To us the word "neighbor" is a warm tangible thing instead of merely nomenclature for the house next door.

As time went on and their children finished school, other summer people girded up their loins and became year-rounders. Now, even on the stormiest nights, nights when the wind grabs the giant firs and shakes them until their cones rattle on the roof like pebbles, the clouds explode with rain and the waves attack the sea walls like charging bulls, we can look along our curve of beach and count seven lighted houses, seven beacons of friendship.

As I have said, it takes a certain native hardiness to enjoy living on an island. This hardiness is not always evident but comes to the surface during crises. Take the case of our neighbor with four large grown married sons. She is small and dainty and looks younger than her daughters-in-law but has been known to move a half-ton rock or haul manure three miles when necessary for her garden. She is also noted for not resorting to the barrel of a shotgun in her mouth or any other coward's way out, that time during the war and rationing when her youngest son brought the entire high school football team out for the weekend, supplemented only by a box of candy which they immediately ate. And what do you think of a woman who can entertain an entire Campfire Group for a long rainy weekend in a small servantless house and somebody left the bag containing the weenies and marshmallows on the dock? This same woman, who is my favorite neighbor, asked for and got six grandchildren under six years old for two weeks. Her magic formula for dealing with children is ignoring all faults and accenting tiny virtues. She says, "Instead of telling Tommy day in and day out that he is the naughtiest boy in the United States of America, which could very well be true, take an aspirin and comment on his neatly tied shoes. Almost anybody would rather be known for expert shoe-tying than for kicking the cat." She always tells whiners how charming they are—bullies how brave—bad sports how good—sneaks how honest! This formula also works on husbands but often requires in addition to the blind eye something stronger than aspirin.

For several summers our beach rang with the laughter and other noises of twenty-eight children under twelve. Now most of those are grown but a large new generation is gaining ground rapidly. Next summer in this house alone we should have six under five, and by adding nephews and nieces, ten or eleven of which I can produce at the drop of a hat or the bars, it is a certainty we can hold up our end.

Down by the point there is a fine big family with nine children, most of whom are married and have children of their own. The fourth from the top or from the bottom, I am not sure which, with her husband and three children has recently become a year-rounder. She has deep dimples and many talents, not the least of which is the ability to smile when thirty-eight relatives with children arrive for the weekend.

Island men are really hardier than island women, especially those enduring the daily grind of commuting, supplemented by walking a small narrow slippery trail in the rain. On occasion, particularly after an earthquake or wild storm, walking the trail is an adventure. Sometimes when you round a curve you find the trail has slid off the face of the hill and is crouched at the bottom of a ravine twenty or thirty feet below, and you have to make your precarious way across the face of an oozing clay bank. Other times you suddenly come on mudslides, collapsed bridges or big trees across the path. Once when I was working in town and running the trail in the early morning, an enormous alder fell between me and a neighbor about ten feet ahead of me. We might both have been killed. I remember feeling only surprise because, though it was raining, a fine misty rain, there wasn't a breath of wind. I also remember that the tree, which was over two feet in diameter at the butt, didn't make a sound until it hit the ground. Then it merely sighed and rustled like a rheumatic old lady stretching out on the couch.

On weekends an island man cuts wood, goes fishing, paints his name on his sea wall, mends the downspouts, shoots at bottles, gathers bark, prunes the apple trees, baits the rat traps, tends the outboard motor, calks the rowboat, puts out the crab trap, makes a pitcher of martinis, sits in his car in front of the grocery store reading *Popular Mechanics* while his wife does the weekly shopping, gets a haircut, discusses politics and the weather. The percentage who do nothing but get drunk and hit their wives is slightly smaller than in Seattle across the way. This is attributable to the invigorating yet sobering effect of salt air.

We didn't meet all of the regular inhabitants of our beach for several years as all the boys, one of the girls, and many of the men were in the service. During this period some of the houses were rented. Most of the renters were transient, both in location, occupation and attitude, and though we were moderately friendly, I cannot easily recall their faces or their names. I remember a few scattered incidents.

The time Joan and Anne baby-sat for a woman with three small children and she called me, sobbing hysterically, and said they had eaten up thirteen red points. When grilled they admitted to cocoa, Spam sandwiches with sweet pickles and a plate of fudge. Their defense was that they were hungry, had shared this bacchanalia with Mrs. Hemingway's children, and she had only given them twenty-five cents for hours and hours of tremendous physical labor—carrying those sandwiches to and from the couch. I replaced the Spam, butter, sweet pickles, cocoa, sugar, chocolate and nuts, and contemplated also giving Mrs. Hemingway, obviously a virgin in this respect, a few facts of life regarding baby-sitters. But as she was rather ungracious about the supplies, I held back on the baby-sitting advice, reasoning that she deserved to learn the hard way that all baby-sitters are part boa constrictor and anything you don't want eaten should be studded with mouse traps or locked up.

I also remember beautiful little dark-eyed Mary who lived (well, really rested) on the beach for a month or two. She was frail, she said, and her chest hurt if she carried anything heavy. One rainy evening she and her husband, Wesley, and Don and I came home on the same ferry. We stopped at the store, and I bought two *enormous* shopping bags of groceries. In addition we picked up the laundry, the mail, which was filled with stout magazines, and the milk. I had a shopping bag which must have weighed fifty pounds, my green office bag, the mail, and a bundle of laundry. Don had the other heavier shopping bag, his lunch box and the milk. Wesley had a shopping bag, his lunch bucket and their milk. Mary had her purse and a small loaf of white bread, sliced. When we stopped to rest at the "big tree," my hands, which were a deep purple, wouldn't let go of my bags and Don had to pry them loose, like separating a suicide from his pistol.

When we had all had a cigarette and were ready to go

again, Mary said, "Wesley, honey, you'll have to carry my purse and the bread, my chest hurts."

Wesley said, "I can't, honey, my hands are full."

Then Don said, and his voice oozed concern and tenderness, "Here let *me* take your stuff. I'll put it in *my* shopping bag."

I said, "My chest hurts too and so do my hands and my legs and my stomach and my head."

Mary and Wesley laughed but Don gave me a disappointed look, which just goes to show that the hurty chests of this world are the smart ones and us good sports deserve the big shopping bags we always get.

When I say I cannot remember the war renters I am excepting Lesley Arnold, who, in addition to a husband in the Navy and thirty-one coats, including one lined with real leopard and a full-back wild mink, had large purple eyes which she seemed to keep focused on Don.

It was our first spring on the island I was painting the porch furniture and humming and being happy and trying not to care that I worked harder than anyone in the whole world and was apparently also going to be buried in my tan knitted suit. I love to do things like painting porch furniture on a spring day, or licking bookplates on a rainy day. I am a true homebody, a domestic woman who will fight like a tiger for her children, her man or the last leg of lamb in the butcher shop. My favorite song is "You're Mine, You."

I had just made the discovery that the word "folding," stamped on the bottom of the captain's chairs I was painting, meant "with a hammer" when Anne and Joan came bounding in and announced breathlessly that some new people named Arnold had moved to Vashon and "Mrs. Arnold is about your age only *awfully pretty* with *beautiful* clothes," Anne said. "She gave us a Coke and they are just moving and her husband is in California so I invited her to dinner. Her name is Lesley and she said we could call her it. She's adorable, Betty, and she's brown and has a perfect figure."

A strange chilly premonition, like one of those small unexplained riffles on smooth water, swept over me. However, I said, "How nice. What time did you tell her to come?"

"I didn't tell her any time," Anne said. "I just said dinner. What smells so awful, dinner?"

"Turpentine," I said. "I'll call Mrs. Arnold."

A gust of wind slipped under the newspapers I had spread on the porch, lifted them up and began folding them around the freshly painted chairs like wrappings. "Oh, damn!" I said, slapping furiously at the papers.

"You've got white paint in your hair," Joan said.

Anne said, "What are you going to wear tonight, Mommy?"

"I hadn't thought," I said. "But undoubtedly my tan knitted suit."

"What are we going to have to eat?" Joan asked.

"Oxtails," I said. "I've already got them in."

"Oxtails!" Anne wailed. "Why don't we have fried chicken? Marilyn's mother always has fried chicken when she has company."

"Because," I said rather crossly, "I've got oxtails already in the oven. Anyway, they are delicious and I cook them better than anybody."

"But oxtails sound so *cheap*," Anne said. "And they're so gluey."

"That's the best part," Joan said.

"What else are we going to have?" Anne asked.

"I was planning on having oxtails with carrots and mushrooms, mashed potatoes because the gravy is so good, green salad with olive oil and lemon juice and that fruit stuff made with bananas and oranges and pineapple and coconut."

"I'll make an angel food cake," Anne said.

"You can't. Not enough eggs," I said. "Anyway we won't need cake. Oxtails are filling and fruit is all we will want for dessert."

"Please, Betty, let me make a cake," Anne said.

"Go on, Betty, let her," Joan said. "Only make a devil's food with four layers, Anne."

"If you want to cook, why don't you bake some oatmeal cookies," I said to Anne. "I think we have both raisins and nuts."

"Sure," Joan said. "I'll help."

"Eat them, you mean," Anne said.

"What time is it?" I asked. "Joanie, run in and look at the kitchen clock."

From the kitchen Joan called out, "Quarter to five."

I stood up and stretched. Anne said, "Maybe I'd better just fix the fruit. I wish we had a *fresh* pineapple and a *real* coconut."

"It'll be just as good without," I said. "Put some fresh mint in it. I'm going in and call Mrs. Arnold."

Lesley Arnold's voice was husky to that fascinating point just short of asthma. She was easy and absolutely sure of herself. She said she'd love to come to dinner and couldn't she come early and help. With that tiny laugh with which women indicate that they are so well organized they have had everything done since four that morning, I said no, but to come early and have a martini.

She said, "Anne and Joan are so adorable. I do hope they'll be home."

"They will," I said. "They think you are beautiful and glamorous and can hardly wait to see you."

"The lambs," she said. "I'll be over in a while."

I went upstairs, took a bath, mostly with turpentine to get the white paint off my legs and arms and hair and neck, put on my tan knitted suit, lots of perfume, heavy gold jewelry and heavy makeup. When I came into the kitchen Joan said, "Wow, your eyebrows are dark!"

Anne said, "I think you look glamorous but I wish you'd wear more eyeshadow. *Charm* magazine says that everybody should wear eyeshadow even in the daytime."

"Even on the beach?" I asked.

"Of course," Anne said. "I'm going to wear eyeshadow with my bathing suit this summer."

"I'm not," Joan said.

"No, you'll probably wear filth and blackberry stains," Anne said.

I said quickly, "Joanie, you set the table, while I make the martinis."

Anne said, "I'll set the table; Joan, you make the living room fire."

"Oh, sure," Joan said, " 'I'll light the candles; Joanie, you carry up a thousand-pound log.' "

"What's all this loose talk about logs?" Don said from the doorway.

Lesley Arnold was so beautiful she made me slightly sick at my stomach. She had large purple, really purple, eyes, small regular features, glistening white teeth, and hair, the color of unbleached muslin, pulled severely back and held with a large tortoise-shell barrette. Her skin was the color of good bourbon. She had on a goldy brown, sleeveless, glazed-chintz dress, cut very low, a gold cashmere sweater, huge topaz-and-diamond earrings and three heavy topaz-and-diamond bracelets. Her slender brown feet were wrapped in natural leather thongs. She made me feel just like a hygiene teacher. A hot hygiene teacher in an ugly tan knitted suit, the wrong shoes and no husband.

Don, my honest, blunt Scotsman, was so dashing (drooling?) that even the girls were impressed. After dinner some of the beach people came up and we drank highballs, played records, recorded our own squeaky voices and were terribly gay until after three o'clock. Lesley was certainly very very attractive. At least I thought so until she pushed me up against the icebox and said, "I've asked your big handsome husband to walk me home—do you mind?"

"Help yourself—take two," I said, my eyes on the dripping ice tray I was holding.

"Can I have a kiss, too?" she said.

"Why don't you ask *him?*" I said.

By the time Don got home I had washed the dishes, emptied all the ashtrays, even vacuumed. (I didn't want any-

117

body getting up in court and saying I hadn't done my share.) Don said, "I hurried as fast as I could."

"Those things take time," I said.

"What things?" he asked.

"Things like kissing Lesley," I said.

"Oh, that," Don said. "She asked me to kiss her so I pecked her on the cheek."

We were all supposed to go to Lesley's for breakfast the next morning and then to someone else's house for sandwiches. But somehow or another I was making clam fritters at eleven in the morning and hamburgers at four in the afternoon and, in between, Lesley took everybody, especially the men, down to her house while I cleaned up the mess and made things attractive again. I was spreading relish on a bun when they came back the second time, Don carrying a bottle of Scotch which Lesley said was a consolation prize for me. I may have been a little curt because she said, "Why, Betty, I believe you're jealous."

"Jealous?" I said. "Of course I'm not."

Anne, who had been helping me said, "But she is jealous. She's mad because you asked Don to kiss you and Joan and I are too." Her eyes were blazing.

Lesley put her arm around Anne and said, "Why, baby, Betty and I were just joking. She's not jealous of me. You and Joanie bring your hamburgers and come sit by me." And lucky old unjealous Mommy got to cook them.

Then there is the night Anne and Joan were staying all night in town and Don and I planned to have dinner at the Alibi, the Vashon restaurant, and go to the Vashon movie show. We were sitting in the kitchen having an old-fashioned and discussing this fabulous outing when Lesley called and said she was all alone and wouldn't we come down. I said that we were going out to dinner. She said come down for a drink then as she was all alone. I said we were already having a drink. She said she was all alone and Johnny wasn't coming home until the next Wednesday and wouldn't we please. It was a nasty rainy night and I felt sorry for her all alone so, like a fool, I asked her to have dinner and go to the show with us. She said she would, but only if we would come down to her house and have a drink. So we went and she had on black velvet slacks and a black cashmere sweater and diamonds and French perfume and the minute we walked in she told Don how tired he looked, how terribly tired, how absolutely worn out. Of course Don was glad to lie down on the couch, especially when she put a bottle of House of Lords Scotch within easy reach. This time she made me feel like a great big botany teacher in tweeds and without a husband.

After she had been gay, Don had been tired and I'd been uncomfortable for about an hour, I said, "Come on, let's go. I'm starving and the show starts at eight-ten."

"Show?" Lesley said. "What show?"

"The movie show at Vashon," I said. "I told you on the phone we were going."

She said, "But, Betty, it's a terrible night and Don is *so* tired."

I said, "Don promised to take me to the show."

"What's playing?" she asked.

"I don't know," I said sulkily.

"Now, Betty," she said, "be reasonable. Don is *tired, terribly* tired. You don't want to drag him out into the rain and cold just to see any old movie."

"I do too," I said.

Lesley laughed and said, "Oh, Betty, you're priceless." Then she got up and went out into the kitchen.

Old Dead Tired was gazing into the fire.

I went upstairs and splashed cold water on my forehead until I was reasonably sure I wouldn't have a stroke. When I came down Lesley in a ruffledy puffledy apron was setting up a cardtable in front of the fire.

I said, "We're going out to dinner."

She said, "You have another drink and relax. I've got dinner all ready."

She brought in one of those revolting ripe olive, macaroni, Brussels sprouts, chestnut casseroles so dear to the heart of the bum cook. However, if it had been English Lark in Madeira I couldn't have eaten a bite, I was so furious.

Don managed to dredge up enough strength to sit at the table, but I could tell he wasn't too enthusiastic about either the casserole or the raisin-stuffed prune salad. At least he still preferred my cooking.

When we were walking up the beach on our way home I said, "Don, how could you let her do that to me?"

"Do what?" Don asked. "Didn't you have a good time?"

I said, "We planned to go out and she didn't want to go, so we didn't." Out there on the beach it sounded senseless.

Don said, "Look, the stars are out. We might have a clear day for a change. Say, you'd better teach Lesley how to cook."

"I couldn't teach that woman *anything*," I said through gritted teeth.

And so the summer went on and on and on and on and on. Lesley took sun baths all day and wore different real jewels and a different new dress (all cut to the navel) every night. Every afternoon at about five-thirty she would call to have Don help her pull up her boat, open her whisky, carry her groceries, saw up her logs (this sounds like one of those songs—"He threads my needle and he chops my wood"), fix her stove, check her wiring and she was clever enough to make it sound natural.

Don liked her and Anne and Joan still adored her and they all made me feel like Typhoid Mary if I criticized her even the tiniest bit. I had terrible dreams of frustration every night and woke up every morning even nastier than usual.

"Lesley has me on the head of a pin and she is enjoying every minute of it," I told Don.

He said, "Why are you so stinking about Lesley? She's a nice gal and she's lonely."

"Yes, lonely for *my* husband," I said.

"You're being ridiculous," Don said, but I think we

were both relieved when she moved to San Francisco in October. Anne and Joan were inconsolable.

"She had thirty-one coats," Anne told one of her friends, "and three Dior dresses."

"And real diamonds and rubies," Joan said.

"And she had a perfect figure, thirty-six-inch bust, twenty-four-inch waist and thirty-four-inch hips," Anne said.

"And she had a gold-color convertible and fourteen cashmere sweaters," Joan said.

"Gosh, she was beautiful," Anne said. "Her hair was platinum and she had great big violet eyes, and whenever her tan faded even a little she took an airplane to *Hawaii!*"

"And she didn't have *any* hair on her legs," Joan said. "She told me she never had to shave them the way Betty does."

"Somebody set the table," I shouted rudely. "It's almost seven."

"Gosh, you're crabby!" Anne and Joan said together.

CHAPTER IX

OTHER FRIENDS AND ENEMIES

THERE is no doubt about it. Dog loving is closely related to the pounding-yourself-on-the-head-with-a-hammer-because-it-is-so-pleasant-when-you-stop school of masochism. But there are a great many of us dog lovers on Vashon Island. In this small beach community alone, since we have lived here, there have been a Dalmatian, a big black mixed, a collie, a boxer, a great Dane, a Kerry blue, a big yellow mixed, two Irish setters, two wire-haired terriers, a Malemute, a Boston bull, a dachshund, several of those fat, rheumy-eyed, long-haired, indeterminate creatures known as "the old dog," and several part-Tudor part-Trixie (a wanton who lives on the hill above us) puppies known as Trudors. Tudor, part Welsh terrier, part beagle, part rattlesnake and part mule but leaning toward beagle in looks, has fought them all. His bitterest enemies are Tiger, the boxer, and Trigger, a small rusty black, somewhat Scotty, who looks as if he might own a pawnshop. Tudor and Trigger are very evenly matched in size, age and bad temper, but when the going gets tough Trigger is apt to call in the Marines in the form of Timmy, a young vigorous Kerry blue member of Trigger's family. I guess it was after he lost most of his tail and part of one ear that Tudor decided to put into practice a few tricks he had learned from the raccoons he had been chasing for five years.

It was a summer morning of a very low tide, a sun

pleasantly muted by mist, the Sound dark and rippleless as a pool of yesterday's rain water and nasturtiums licking the edge of the silvery sea wall like flames. Anne and Joan and friends in bathing suits and oily as sardines were stretched out on striped beach towels on the sand. A small battery radio poured out King Cole singing "Embraceable You." The air was spicy with seaweed and sand steaming in the sun. All along the curve of the beach small children bobbed about in the flat water like corks, or crouched on their haunches on the sand, intent on some small project. I had come down to pick some nasturtiums for the table on the porch. I had picked perhaps half a dozen when Trigger's mistress wandered up to say hello and have a cigarette. Arranging ourselves comfortably on a huge, satiny, bone-colored log near the girls, we lit our cigarettes.

Down by the water Tudor was engaged in his favorite pastime of chasing sea gull shadows on the sand. As the sea gulls dipped and swooped he dipped and swooped, often turning a somersault in the air. Through eyes squinted against the sun we watched him amused. King Cole changed to "Sweet Lorraine." It was very peaceful. Then Trigger who had been quietly sitting on his mistress' feet, suddenly decided to go down and help Tudor. In spite of entreaties from all of us, he sauntered down to the edge of the wet sand where Tudor was playing and stood there a peaceful bystander.

"Don't say anything," I warned the girls. "Sometimes if you don't say anything, dogs won't fight."

"No rule that applies to normal dogs applies to Tudor," Anne said bitterly.

For a minute or two Tudor was unaware of Trigger's infuriating presence. Then, right in the middle of one of his backflips, he apparently saw him because he changed direction in the air and landed astraddle Trigger's shoulders. The girls began to shriek, "Do something! Stop them, Mommy. Get the hose. Get a club." Trigger's mistress and I, who had that summer already separated our doggies about eighty-six times, decided coolly that the time had come at last to let them fight it out. "Get it out of their systems," we told each other as we lit new cigarettes off the old ones.

For almost an hour we tried to interest ourselves in music, smoking, gathering shells and picking nasturtiums while our dogs lunged and snarled and swore at each other on the pretty sand by the blue blue water. It was uncomfortable, like trying to play bridge while an old aunt is choking to death on a fishbone in the same room. Especially as first Anne and Joan and friends, then our neighbors one by one ostentatiously herding their innocent little children, gathered up their paraphernalia and moved from the beach to the high safety of the sea wall, where they huddled watching.

The battle finally stopped, as it had started, suddenly all at once. Where there had been the dreadful, bone-chilling noises of a dog fight there were now only the peaceful soup-eating noises of the tide and *one* dog. We looked again. That was it, *one* dog. Tudor up to his stomach in salt water, was wearing a suspiciously triumphant expression. Trigger had disappeared. Trigger's mistress and I tossed away our cigarettes and ran down to the edge of the water. We found that Tudor was standing on Trigger, holding him under water. I yelled at Tudor. She waded out and retrieved Trigger and we both gave him artificial respiration, hampered somewhat by many sporting attempts on Tudor's part to kill him while he was semi-conscious. Trigger came out of the valley of the shadow very quickly, in fact snarling, and he and Tudor started another fight which I finally stopped with the bamboo lawn rake.

Tiger, the boxer, looks very large and powerful but he spent one evening sitting on my lap eating gumdrops, watching Mr. Peepers on television and proving that appearances are deceiving. At the time, Tudor was at my sister Alison's, supposedly guarding her against burglars while her husband was in Spokane, but actually killing her cats, sleeping on the boys' pillows and eating the duck food. Tudor brags of eating nothing but meat and canned dog food, but he will gulp down wild rice almondine with sour cream gravy or peanut butter and pickle sandwiches if it is meant for somebody else. Tudor was at my sister Alison's a week, which seemed like a second to me and like two years to Alison. During that time Tiger visited me every day. Sometimes just dropping in for a gumdrop or a drink of water. Sometimes stopping by to reassure me of his affection by putting his paws on my shoulders and licking my scalp. Often arriving uncomfortably early, say five-thirty in the morning, and staying all day.

We grew very fond of each other, Tiger and I. Then Tudor came home. I had called Tiger's owner and told her that Tudor was coming and she promised to keep Tiger at home, but something went wrong. I was sitting by the dining room window, writing, when I looked up and saw Tiger's dripping black muzzle pressed tight against the glass, his eyes pleading for a caress. I sprang to my feet and shrieked at Mother who was reading Angela Thirkell in the kitchen, "Mother-Tiger! Tudor! Do something!" Mother, who has great presence of mind but refuses to face the unalterable fact that Tudor doesn't, hasn't, won't mind, called in her gentle voice, "Come here, Tudor." Tudor came all right. He rushed between her legs almost knocking her down and hurled himself at the dining room door which is glass, shrieking, "Hand me my gun—gimme my switchblade—lemme out of here—lemme at him!" Tiger who was peacefully sniffing the camellias, at first either didn't hear Tudor or chose to ignore him. Then Tudor obviously called him some terrible thing, something even a television-loving boxer couldn't take, and Tiger, with a roar, came right through the glass. Mother who had come out of the kitchen but was still wearing her glasses and carrying *Before Lunch,* reached down calmly and picked up Tudor and carried him kicking and screaming into her bedroom at the other end of the house. I sent Tiger, who looked extremely apologetic, home and Don came up from the beach and began grimly measuring for a new window. A rather monotonous task, he said wearily. It was

about the eighth pane of glass he had put in that same location because Tudor always goes in or out of the house like
a policeman answering a cry for help through a locked door
under which gas is seeping.

In spite of the fact that he has never learned *anything,*
Tudor is really very smart and actually could understand us
if he wanted to. All dog lovers say this, I know, but we have
proof because Tudor learned Japanese. When we took a trip
to New York we were able to farm the girls out with relatives,
but we couldn't find anybody who would take Tudor and
whom we could trust to be nice to him, so we had to leave
him and Murra (our then cat) with Warner Yamamoto and
family, who assured us they "loved ahnimahl and will feed."

When we returned Murra had not changed. She was still
living on the mantelpiece and looking down on everybody
with complete disdain. Tudor didn't even look like the same
dog. He kept his head down close to the ground and didn't
speak English.

"Oh, Tudor, baby, we're home," I caroled to him as I
got out of the car.

With a sidelong unfathomable "wisdom of the East"
look, he sidled up to Mrs. Yamamoto. She spoke to him in
Japanese and he licked her hand.

"Come here, old boy," Don called heartily.

Tudor turned his head away and lowered his eyes which
seemed darker and more almond-shaped. Warner said something to him in Japanese and Tudor slithered over to him.

Later on when we went up for the mail, we discovered
that Tudor had also taken to hanging around with a cheap
crowd of mongrels who lived down by the dock.

For over a month he picked at his food and ignored us
when we spoke to him. Mother of course suggested that we
learn Japanese and speak to him in his native tongue but we
refused and, gradually, especially after a summer spent fighting American dogs, he returned to normal, and when we
called "Here, boy," at least turned his head and glanced at
us before running in the opposite direction.

If I am sick, Tudor takes up a vigil by my bed, whining, shivering, looking sad and occasionally, without warning, leaping up, pawing my bust and spilling my coffee. How loyal, how sweet! people say. But I know that these demonstrations are not made out of sympathy. He is afraid I might die and then who would take him to the beach.

Tudor has his own nice little smelly doggy bed, but he prefers to risk a daily beating with the hearthbroom and sleep on any bed, chair, couch, love seat or chaise longue not barricaded with spiky objects. He growls at babies. He snarls at all milkmen, laundrymen and neighbors. He can be depended on to leap against the back of your knees and try to knock you down when your are going down the path to the beach, especially in winter when it is slippery. When his water bowl is empty he takes it in his teeth and pounds it furiously on the kitchen floor.

His favorite resting places are in any doorway you intend to go through with a loaded tray, or pressed flat against a step in the middle of the stairway on the nights he is reasonably sure we will get a late telephone call. He has no gallantry and prefers to fight female puppies. He enjoys a swim or two in the icy Sound every day, even in winter. He is fifteen years which is 105 in dog years, but age has neither aged nor softened him. He is as lean and vigorous as Bernarr Mac-Fadden, as devious as Molotov and as determined as Dewey. Mother remarked throatily the other day, "Poor Tudor, he is getting so deaf." What she means is that he is stone deaf to any command or request by us, but can hear a plate being scraped in Sitka, Alaska.

Speaking of Alaska, about six years ago, somebody gave Anne a baby female Malemute flown down from Alaska. Mala was the most engaging puppy I have ever seen. Cuddly and loving and with many enchanting attitudes, one of which was sleeping with Anne with her head on the pillow. It was unfortunate that Mala was a moron. A complete moron. She never even learned her name. And when she was a great big two-year-old wolf, she was still coyly chewing up shoes and cashmere sweaters and pounds of butter. We have a swinging half door between the dining room and living room which Tudor has always been able to go through with facility. He merely lunges against it and on the third swing slips through. We tried for two years to teach Mala to push the door but she preferred to chew her way through. She was more successful chewing her way through the French doors, two sheep and a flock of Mallard ducks so we had to give her away.

Mrs. Miniver, our first cat, was a shy, affectionate, very fertile tortoise-shell, who was part Persian and part Angora. She used to walk the trail with me every morning and wait by the "big tree" for me at night. She had about forty-two kittens, off and on, four to a batch and was remarkably obliging about always having one yellow one for Mother who has a great weakness for yellow kittens.

Mrs. Miniver was a skillful ratter and caught at least one every day of her life, always displaying her catch at meal-times. She died of ratfish poisoning, as had many of her kittens.

Then a neighbor gave us Murra ("chimney sweep" in Swedish we were told), who lived on the mantel. She, also part Persian, part Angora, was a lovely dark brown with green-grape eyes. She had six or seven batches of gray kittens in Mother's closet, then one day we found her on the path, dead, from ratfish poisoning I suppose. The ratfish, I was told by old Mr. Blue, a caretaker for the beach, are caught and cast aside by the mud shark liver fishermen. When they are washed up on the beach by the tide, the cats eat them and die. Whether this is fact or fable I cannot say as I have never seen a ratfish but I have buried several beloved cats after a brief violent sickness.

I love cats. In spite of notions to the contrary, they are affectionate and loyal. The last time I came back from a trip, Marigold, our present cat, put her arms around my neck and rubbed her cheek against mine. Also, in spite of prevalent fallacies, cats do not have an easy time bearing kittens.

All of our cats have demanded that one of us stay with them during labor and Mrs. Miniver had such a hard time and cried so piteously that I always gave her some warm milk with brandy in it when she had the first pain.

Marigold, a beautiful orange kitty, was pregnant and had been badly treated by some children before we got her. She was in labor for three terrible days and finally had to be rushed to the veterinary, who told us that all of her kittens were dead, one was crosswise, and if she was to survive she must have an immediate operation. Her Caesarean section and hysterectomy were successful and now, though seven years old, she is very playful and a superb mouser.

Tudor has always chased our cats, but it was by mutual agreement and merely a gesture because dogs are supposed to chase cats. He would rush out the dining room door, yipping, and the cat would run up the cedar tree. Marigold would never tolerate this nonsense. From the first day we got her, thin, frightened and abused, she stood her ground with Tudor and slapped him hard on the nose when he ran at her.

Marigold enjoys walking on the beach, darting like a golden arrow from bleached log to bleached log, and loves picnic suppers and singing around the campfire. Her favorite spot is on the top of a huge old stump by the picnic table. Eyes blazing with mischief, tail switching anticipatorily, she crouches flat at the edge of the stump and grabs at the hair of any passer-by. When we sing she sits up straight and gazes mournfully across the water. When we throw scraps to the ducks she suddenly leaps off the sea wall into the middle of them and sends them squawking. Tudor often joins her at this game but invariably carries it too far and gobbles up all the duck food, once eating a paper cup.

Graybar, a mangy old Maltese cat left on the beach to go wild, came to us when he was desperately sick with some sort of dysentery. I doctored him with whisky, raw eggs, rice and boiled milk, but he grew steadily worse. I felt so sorry for him I couldn't bear it and one day in desperation mashed up five Nembutal capsules, mixed them with a raw egg and fed them to him. He looked at me trustingly and lapped it up. When he had finished he dragged himself over to the edge of the rockery by the rose bed and stretched out in the sunshine. I went into the kitchen and cried. Graybar lay by the rose bed all day. Once I went out and tearfully felt for a heartbeat. There seemed to be one. About sundown he disappeared. Anne and Joan and I cried and Don said sadly it was for the best. We all went to bed with heavy hearts—mine the heaviest because I was the murderer. The next morning Graybar showed up for breakfast, looking fine. The girls stroked him and cooed over him and he moved away from them disdainfully, flicking a little dandruff off his shoulders. I gave him hot oatmeal and cream and he drank about a pint. He has never had a sick day since.

Several years ago a raccoon decided to be our friend. We saw her first on the patio by the kitchen eating Tudor's food. The next night, naturally, Tudor didn't leave any food so Raccy came to the window and explained the situation. I mixed up a pan of Frisky meal, a bowl of left-over gravy, four old muffins and a rock hard piece of fruit cake. While I was fixing her supper Mrs. Raccy waited for me discreetly but appropriately behind the Unknown Warrior rhododendron. I set the pan in the rose bed in a spot clearly visible from both the kitchen and service room windows. As soon as I had gone indoors Mrs. Raccy waddled over to the rose bed and began eating. She chose the fruitcake first and finding it delightful held it in both her little hands and nibbled around it the way a child nibbles around the edge of a cookie. Watching her, Mother said that I should have also put out a pan of water as raccoons prefer to dip their food in water. I didn't put water out that night because I didn't want to frighten our new friend, but the next night when she announced her presence by sitting under a camellia and peering in the dining room window, I took out both supper (corn on the cob, mashed potatoes, chicken gravy and bones and a green salad) and a pan of water. She did appreciate the water, dipping each bite, but she showed us she didn't care for the green salad, by tossing it into the primroses.

The next spring when Mrs. Raccy returned she brought along either a close friend or a husband and two half-grown children. We were of course very glad to see them and I mixed up a big batch of dog meal (which we now buy in hundred-pound sacks), bacon grease, mashed potatoes, stale bread and stale cookies, dumped it into two large baking pans and set them up by the rhododendrons. Then I put a pan of water and a basket of left-over candy Easter eggs out on the patio by the dining room window. As soon as they had finished the entrée the Raccy family came around to the patio for dessert. Mr. and Mrs. Raccy, though dainty at the table and splendid about sharing, were very shy and ducked behind a camellia or rhododendron when we opened the door. The babies were quarrelsome and piggish about the candy but would eat out of our hands and showed strong leanings toward coming in the house and living with us. Sometimes the Raccys brought along neighbors but they were awfully nasty to them and wouldn't let them have a single Easter egg (we now buy these direct from the factory forty-pounds at a time) until they and their children were so full they were gagging. Mrs. Raccy is really more friendly than her husband and yesterday came down from the woods in the daytime and watched Mother prune the grapevine. I don't know whether she has a grapevine of her own at home and wanted pointers or whether she feels that women should occasionally seek the company of other women. No matter how friendly the raccoons become, no matter how often he sees them, Tudor, perhaps because of their black masks, insists they are robbers and goes shrieking after them every single night. So far they have treated him with amused, undeserved tolerance, unhurriedly climbing to the first branch of the cedar tree just out of his reach, but I really hope that some time, one of them, perhaps one of the quarrelsome babies, will give him a good scare. They are fierce fighters. We are now feeding six and all but two eat out of our hands.

Bucky, the deer, was our friend for over six years. Often in the very early morning, we could hear his footsteps like tack hammers on the front porch. Once I looked out of our bedroom window in that indistinct smudgy time when there is only a thread of silver across the darkness in the east, the lights of Seattle across the way are like tiny holes in a black kettle, but we can tell it is morning by the thin scratchy sound of birds' feet on the roof and swoopy shrill early-morning noises of the sea gulls. The air was soft and smelled like seaweed and marigolds. I was breathing deeply and wondering if there would be a good clam tide when I saw something moving by the wisteria tree. Something rather large. I watched and waited and pretty soon Bucky came up the steps from the lower terrace onto the patio. He walked around, nibbling daintily at the flowers. Finally surfeited with snapdragons and zinnias, he slowly, majestically climbed the steps through the upper rockery to the guesthouse.

One early morning he brought his doe and fawn down for a swim. Once we saw him running along the beach with vines in his antlers. We have seen him many times in the orchard, standing under a cherry tree as still as the mist around his knees. He disappeared the year they opened season for deer on the island. The sport who shot Bucky deserves the same badge of courage as the duck hunter who last fall rowed up in front of our sea wall and, when our flock of pet ducks hurried out to greet him, shot and killed all but four.

Joan and Anne brought Sheldon and Camille from the circus. Sheldon was a small green turtle and Camille a chameleon. Sheldon was no fun at all and spent his entire short life under the refrigerator. Camille lives in the blue garden where she darts around not changing color but apparently enjoying herself.

I do not like rats, but once one made me cry. It was when we first bought the house, before we built the new kitchen. There was a cupboard next to the stove which had at one time held a hot water tank. It had shelves in it and

I kept cereals and crackers there because the warmth from the stove kept them crisp.

One morning, Anne and Joan, who were still in that charming not-enough-publicized stage of childhood where all food, no matter how beautifully served, is given a thorough microscopic examination for foreign matter, announced in shrill horrified accusing voices that "the top of the PEP box *you* put on the table has been *gnawed* by *rats!*"

"Nonsense," I said from my corner by the stove where I was gulping hot coffee, staring at the wall, and wondering why I had chosen writing, of all things, as a means of satisfying my creative urge. What was wrong with those easy pursuits like dry-point etching or rhododendron hybridizing?

Anne said, "Look, Betty, tooth marks! Ugh, I don't want any breakfast!"

Joan said happily, "I think I see a little piece of fur sticking to the box."

With the eagerness and grace of a loaded burro I made my way to the breakfast table and looked at the box. The red Kellogg's on the left-hand corner showed a few but unmistakable signs of nibbling. I could see no large tooth marks or hunks of hair. I said, "Probably a little mouse. I'll set a trap. Now finish your breakfast. Nothing has been gnawing the toast or bacon."

Anne said, "Yes, but I think I see an ant in the jam."

"Where?" Joan said eagerly. "Show it to me."

I went back to my corner, poured out another cup of coffee, and changed my thinking to tidelands, striking oil, servants and breakfast in bed.

The next morning when I opened the door to the cupboard to get out the Cornflakes a large gray rat dived through a hole in the ceiling but left his tail hanging down like a bell cord. "I'll set a trap," I said to myself, but like most things I say to myself in the early morning it too passed away. I moved the cereals to the cupboard over the sink but I saw the tail every day because I put the soap powder in the rat cupboard. Then Don saw the tail and set a trap. A great big strong rat trap, cleverly handled with gloves and diabolically baited with young leathery cheese smeared with very smelly Camembert. The next morning while I was waiting for the coffee I eased open the door and peeked at the trap. It was empty and I was glad. Later that same morning I was huddled by the stove, writing, when I heard in the cupboard beside me a noise like a blast from a Luger followed by an anguished scream. I knew instantly what had happened and I felt like somebody who has beaten a tiny crippled old lady with her own crutches. Tears running down my cheeks I opened the cupboard door. . . .

Another time I saw tails but didn't feel any sorrow. That was also before we remodeled, and the dark hallway leading to the service room had exposed beams. It was one of my excess energy, uncreative days and I had already dusted the fireplace chimney, blacked the andirons and waxed the hearth and was wondering what vital task to attack next when I saw this nest snuggled in the joining place of two beams. I marched into the living room, grabbed the poker, a good long one, and from the safe retreat of the doorway gave the nest a big poke. Immediately right above my head like a moving fringe appeared twelve tails. I screamed and slammed the door. Don set the traps. That was during the time Murra lived on the mantel and, though she was deft and alert, not too many rats or mice ventured into her rather confined hunting preserve.

One summer some "plaidjackets" (family name for yellow jackets) set up housekeeping just beside the path going to the beach. Plaidjackets are not friendly little fellows and after we had all been stung on bare places we decided something had to be done. Don went purposefully up to Vashon and came proudly home with an expensive plaidjacket demolishing machine. "No matter how vicious or well entrenched, George said that this will get 'em," he told me confidently as he mixed up his poison. When the machine was loaded he strapped it on and strode down the path to the beach.

I heaved a huge sigh of relief because making the dash past the plaidjackets had already resulted in several skinned knees and twisted ankles, as well as the stings. Anne and Joan and my sister Alison's little boys, Darsie and Bard, were crowded by the railing of the front porch watching. Suddenly they began to shout, "Look out, Don, run!" and I could hear a noise like the whine of a distant saw. Then Don came pounding up the path, still strapped in his big machine, roaring, "Help, they're all over me!"

We all smacked and swatted and dejacketed him but he had more than a dozen stings.

It was my turn next. I waited for a day or so until Don's attack was just a memory in the plaidjacket home, then filled my fly sprayer with double strength DDT, sneaked down the path, put the nozzle of the sprayer clear into the hole and worked the plunger until the sprayer was empty. As I removed the nozzle several plaidjackets staggered out of the hole, shook themselves, then took off like jet planes, fortunately in the direction of the beach. A few more appeared at the entrance, then more, and then from back inside came the ominous whine, the sound of the distant saw. I ran all the way up to the house, angry plaidjackets breathing down the back of my neck, but I was only stung once because the ones that followed me attacked younger more succulent Joan and Bard.

Anne said she had noticed that all plaidjackets went into their house at night and didn't fly around. So that evening after dark, she and I crept down the path and again filled the plaidjacket home with DDT. We pumped two sprayersful into it. The next day the plaidjackets were still on their feet but definitely groggy.

Every night for a week we pumped their house full of DDT and finally one day we saw a for sale sign. "Whee! They're gone!" we shouted happily running to the beach.

"DDT will kill anything," I said smugly to Don, "and it is certainly a lot cheaper than that big useless machine you bought." I still don't know if the plaidjacket nest he showed me on the old stump by the picnic table is the same family or a new one. I do know they are just as unneighborly and twenty times as DDT-resistant.

CHAPTER X

MASTER OF NONE

IF YOU live on the salt water, I am informed by the old-timers, you can expect everything you own, even a great big stone fireplace, to break down eventually. This, they say, has something to do with the corrosive effect of salt air. My private opinion, solidified by experience, is that it has more to do with the corrosive effect of the eight million house-guests attracted by the salt air. Anyway, in addition to the icebox, beds, stove, etc., that were in the house when we bought it, we added, as fast as we could gather up the down payments, dishwashers, automatic washers, dryers, freezers, gas heaters, electric heaters on thermostats, chafing dishes, plant sprayers, septic tanks and more toilets with bowls eager for charm bracelets and little celluloid ducks, and with handles that must be juggled *ad infinitum* unless we want the toilets to run ditto. At inconvenient intervals each of these machines has stopped doing the thing it was hired to do and by means of smoke signals, grinding noises and pungent smells of burning rubber has indicated that it desired the evil eye of the local handyman.

The local handyman, always referred to as "Nipper" or "Gimpy" or "Mrs. Walters' Harry," will fix anything but, like a room that is tidy except for the underwear hanging out of the bureau drawers, the repair job is invariably left with tag ends. "The dishwasher's okay, now, Betty," Mrs. Walters'

Harry told me the time the dishwasher insisted on using only dirty cold water which it was apparently sucking up from the septic tank, instead of the nice clean hot water so handily piped into its abdomen. "But remember *no soap* and keep that big screwdriver of Don's handy to pry the lid up."

In my early island days I cuddled a cozy little notion that our country repairmen might not be as dextrous or have as big tool kits as their city brothers but they were a *lot* more willing and *much* cheaper. The willing part is true enough. Nipper, when you can find him (which he has not made easy by marrying an Estonian girl who speaks only one word of English, "hello," which she screams into the telephone before immediately hanging up), will attempt anything. Need your rowboat calked, your *Pittisporum tobira* transplanted, your Stradivarius tuned? Nipper will gladly take on the assignment, but *first,* and I mean before one broken fingernail or big rusty tool touches the job, he must send to Seattle for the most recent rate schedule for boat calkers, landscape gardeners or Stradivarius repairment. Your alternative is portal to portal pay from Seattle and maybe the lights are off and they are grinding the ramp of the dock down by hand.

Island repairmen also expect immediate payment. "Be sure and send the check tomorrow morning, Betty—I'm real short of cash and Elva's gittin' her new china clippers," New Motor Marvin told me after examining my steam iron the time it boiled and boiled but wouldn't let out any steam and so I set it out in the patio to blow up and Mother said, "Why don't you call Marvin? At least he can't say *that* needs a new motor." But he did, only he called it a "heat control unit and it will run you maybe twenty-twenty-five dollars."

Of course the pipes froze during the big snow and of course as soon as the weather warmed up we intended to put in new pipe. However, while the snow was still on the ground a delegation from the Spring Committee called on us. They were our neighbors on the beach, mostly summer people whom we had not met as yet, all male, the delegation, that is.

"The spring," they told us with great seriousness as they stamped the snow off their boots at the back door, "is on your property, but it is a community thing. We *all* have water rights. We *all* work together. We will *all* fix the frozen pipe. *Do not do anything yourself!*"

"What darling people," I said to Don after we had all had coffee and they had admired the way we had arranged the furniture and I had wished fervently I had washed the windows. "I just love community spirit. I adore people working together. I am so glad we live on an island."

Don said, "Did they say *when* we were *all* going to fix the pipe? I'm not exactly dedicated to carrying water?"

"I don't think they said when exactly," I said, "but I imagine it will be this afternoon. After all, nobody else has any water either."

But it wasn't that afternoon or the next or the next. Finally Don and Anne and Joan went back to the spring (I regret to say I protested this breach of community spirit and would take no part in the undertaking) wound rags and friction tape around the worst places in the pipe and that is the way it stayed until late spring when Don got hold of Zachary Millard Potts (colored) who wore tropical shorts and a sun helmet even on rainy days, sang calypso songs in French and signed his work, especially concrete variety: "Mended by Zachary M. Potts, 4/3/43." Zachary had no tools but he was very strong and could rip the threads off any diameter of pipe. Don bought the necessary pipe and wrenches and Zachary, between cups of coffee (he had a very nervous stomach which could not stand being empty even a minute) and cigarettes which he borrowed from me, removed the broken pipe, as I say usually removing the threads from the good piece, and put in new. Zachary was very artistic and instead of burying the pipe in the humdrum fashion of the former plumber, he allowed it to swoop in big natural curves, propping the lowest places with small forked willow twigs which rooted and eventually grew into little willow trees.

While he drank coffee with me, Zachary related incidents

from his full life. The only one I can recall offhand, is the story of a lady friend of his who tripped over a broken place in the sidewalk in Chicago and fractured her ankle. "She sue the city," Zachary told me, "but she don't get a penny. She can't understand why. 'The big mistake you made,' I tell her, 'is havin' your girl friend drive you to the hospital. What you should have did is lay on the sidewalk and wait for the avalanche.'"

When Zachary had finished and signed the pipe work, Don put him to work on the county trail. We were able to follow Zachary's remarkably slow progress on the trail by his singing which, though in a foreign tongue, had great volume and bounced off the hillside and rolled across the water with sonorous magnificence. When he had finished, Don and I walked the trail to check the results and found an ugly litter of paper bags, sandwich wrappers and Coke bottles, mingled with and following the course of the wilting nettles and slashed blackberry runners. Don told Zachary to clean up this mess but he was reluctant and without his usual zest.

"Waste of time," he told me when he knocked at the door for his seventeenth Coke. "Just trash along that trail anyways, what harm a few ole Coke bottles goin' to do? Mr. MacDonald's just wastin' money."

The next morning, Sunday, at five Don had a call from Zachary, who was in jail and needed bail. Don provided it that time and several others. Zachary explained that it was his weak stomach that always got him in trouble. "Two double sherrys and I'm a wild man," he explained sadly. When hot weather came and Don put Zachary to work on our new road, he quit. "My weak stomach won't stand that shovelin'," he told me. "I'll have to git me some sort of overseein' job. My last boss tell me I should be in charge of people. I'm a natural executor he tell me."

After Zachary came a pale artist named Egular Earhart who was studying oil painting by mail but for a dollar and twenty-five cents an hour offered to "put the place in shape." I had visions of weedless beds deep in peat moss, trimmed hedges, beautifully espaliered trees, slugless rockeries, wild morning-gloryless hillsides and everything very artistic. I told Don about Egular with a great deal of enthusiasm and he said evenly, "Is he very strong?"

I thought of Egular's shoulders like a bent coathanger under his threadbare tweed jacket, of his waxy face, his spindly arms, but I said, "He's not exactly husky but he's certainly willing."

"Well, try him out," Don said. "I guess he's better than nothing."

But he wasn't.

He came every morning at eight o'clock, checking in and collecting his tools courteously at the back door. Then he disappeared. I was writing, my typewriter on the small blue table by the kitchen window and I suppose I didn't pay as much attention as I should either to what Egular was doing or where.

I do remember going to the beach for bark occasionally (there was a strong feeling in our house at that time that writers didn't have to be warm) and wondering irritably as I fought my way through the syringa and blackberries on the path what exactly *was* Egular's idea of "putting the place in shape." Then one beautiful April Sunday, when the sky behind the black firs was the color of a milk of magnesia bottle, the peach tree was covered with pink tissue-paper rosettes, the wind had veered to the north which meant clear weather and the Sound was wrinkled green silk sprinkled with white ostrich plumes, Anne and Joan and Don and I decided to cook supper on the beach.

We were hunting for good marshmallow sticks when we found Egular's project—the project on which he had already spent eleven full twelve-dollar-days and on which I am sure he had intended to spend the entire summer. It was a lovely little design about three by four feet, made of beer bottles pounded into the hillside in the shade of an enormous wild blackberry vine. In between the beer bottle bottoms, Egular had transplanted some of my choicest alpines, some azaleas and two baby nettles. I do not know whether he intended eventually to pave the entire hillside with beer bottles or whether he intended to scatter these gems here and there in the garden, but Don said he didn't want to find out. Egular had to go.

Monday morning when he knocked at the back door I was ready with an evasive lie about Don's father, a landscape gardener from Scotland, coming to live with us and so, although we were just crazy about Egular and his work, we wouldn't need him any more, but perhaps I could get him some other jobs on the beach. . . .

Egular said, "Oh, that's all right, Mrs. MacDonald. I was going to quit anyway because I'm making pottery full time now."

Time is a great healer but I still remember the summer morning when Gimpy Hodgkins, hired to clean out the spring tank, told me he wouldn't be able to come until Saturday because he had "back door trouble."

The spring had a cement tank into which it flowed and from which the houses on the beach got their water supply. This tank was supposed to be cleaned once a year. "Don't you touch it," the Spring Committee had warned us. "Community project. We *all* get together and clean it." The tank was not mentioned again until one Sunday afternoon two summers later after a grueling weekend of fourteen adolescents, seven boys and seven girls, since Friday. It was about five-thirty in the afternoon and the houseparty had been up and eating (four more stacks of hotcakes and some more sausages, please Mrs. MacDonald) since dawn (more hamburgers—one without lettuce and lots of relish on mine but Mary Jean says she doesn't like onions) but were at long last on their way to the ferry and Don and I were wearily sitting down to a pitcher of martinis and some fried chicken, served on a cardtable on the front porch.

Don said, "I don't understand kids these days. When I was fourteen or fifteen if I had had a chance to spend a weekend at the beach I wouldn't have spent the whole time lolling around in the house giggling and listening to records. *I* would have been out in the boat fishing or hiking through the woods or digging clams."

I said weakly, "Oh, it's just that Anne and Joan seem to have so many good records. Have another martini. I'm on my third."

Then Tudor began to bark, which is a mild way of saying that he rushed between our legs, hurled himself off the porch and ran shrieking down the path to the beach. After an interval a neighbor appeared.

"Say, Don," he said ignoring the chicken cooling on our plates and our haggard faces, "we don't have any water. Haven't had any all day. Let's go up and take a look at the tank. Must be something wrong."

With an accusing look at me, Don got to his feet and followed Neighbor up the path to the spring. Tudor and Neighbor's dog came up from the beach and followed them. I gazed across the horizon and thought longingly of the Deep South where girls marry at fourteen. Don and Neighbor returned.

Neighbor said, "Tank needs cleaning. I'll get a bunch together and we'll all pitch in. Now, don't you touch it, Don. The spring's a community project. We *all* take care of it."

Don said, "Have a martini."

Just then Tudor and Neighbor's dog started a fight under the cardtable. I will say that the fight was undoubtedly started by Tudor who even now at fifteen still attacks great Danes and small females. I jumped up and Don and I both yelled at Tudor to "stop—stop it—stop it you naughty dog— stop it you little bastard!" As always Tudor ignored us and continued to hurl himself at Neighbor's dog's throat until the cardtable tipped over and our martinis and chicken were tossed over the railing and down the bank.

As I scrambled down after the silverware and pieces of plates, I heard Neighbor calling from the path, "Remember, Don, community project. We'll all get together."

So through another neighbor on the other side, not using the spring and not hampered by community spirit, we heard about Gimpy, and after his "back door trouble" had cleared up he came to work or rather came to the house and told me his dreams, read me some short stories he had written, looked up *my* dreams in *his* dream book, told me the exact number of germs in a cup of spring water and finally, I guess, cleaned out the tank. He also showed me how to sharpen old victrola needles, how to make papier-mâché out of newspapers, and the correct way to fry an egg. "Add a teaspoon of water to the bacon grease—no more no less—just one teaspoon. Keeps the white soft and smooth instead of all bubbly and starched like."

I loved Gimpy but like so many of the local artisans he was continually involved in some sort of factional dispute with the competition. "I seen him put sand in my motor but I couldn't prove nothin' especially with his dad bein' on the Chamber of Commerce." He finally left Vashon and went to Alaska.

For a while after we moved to the island the Puget Sound Power and Light Company had an electrician who knew what he was doing and did it. When the roaster lid got caught in a little spring in the oven element and filled the kitchen with lightning, when the pump was clogged with silt, when we had no water pressure and somebody was hammering inside the hot water tank, when I tried to unplug the vacuum cleaner and one prong came off and stuck in the wall socket—any of those little womanly emergencies—I called the Puget Sound Power and Light and they sent this nice man who located the trouble and also knew lots of interesting stories of buddies who grabbed live wires without their gloves.

Then for some reason the power company stopped this fine unselfish service and we were left with Orville Kronenburg who hated everybody in the whole world and whose wife wore her bedroom slippers downtown. Orville knew about electricity I guess, but he didn't consider looks important and, unless you stopped him, he would run wires across doorways and over pictures. Also he didn't measure when he cut holes for wall plugs and when he had finished putting the new wall plug in our bedroom, Don said bitterly, "It looks like a small raft in a large quarry." Orville also had a special kind of wall plug that even when just installed wiggled dangerously and made the lights flash on and off like beacons.

The time my Bendix shrieked and jumped up and down when I put anything bigger than a washrag in it, I called Orville and he came sullenly down and told me there was sand in our hot water tank. I told him to take the sand out and he did but after he had gone I tried out the Bendix and it didn't scream but it whirled like a transport propeller and threw a geyser of water out the soap hole. I called Orville and he said, "That's just the fledamora plankstaff. It will slow down after a while." It didn't, but I got used to it. Then after a time Orville went back to South Dakota and the Bendix began shrieking again and jumping up and down when I put anything bigger than a handkerchief in it so I called New-motor Marvin, and guess what the trouble was?

Anybody who has girl children over the age of ten knows the necessity of either having two bathrooms or learning to comb your hair and put on your lipstick by looking in the dog's pan.

Don and I decided to make the small bedroom next to our room into a combination dressing room and bath for us and to put a tub in the other bathroom and give it to the girls—which was certainly locking the barn after. . . .

This was still during the war and basins and bathtubs were impossible to get, to say nothing of carpenters and plumbers. We had a friend around the Point who was a good amateur carpenter and who offered to do that part of the work for us in the evening and on the weekends. Through the ferry-commuters' grapevine we heard that there was a plumber living at the other end of the island who also sold plumbing supplies and could get us the fixtures and install them. Don immediately contacted this phenomenon, a Mr. Curtis, and one evening he came to the house and we showed him the bathrooms and he drank brandy, and the deal was made including a large septic tank which Mr. Curtis was going to install in the south patio with a sump down on the beach. We were also at that time putting in a road which was at the deep-cut, knee-deep-mud stage but which, Mr. Curtis assured us, after some brandy, would make bringing in the pipe and fixtures a cinch. Just a cinch!

The carpentering of the bathrooms went along very rapidly. We bought hand-wrought black strap hinges and knotty pine and in no time at all our friend turned them into closets and drawers and shelves.

The plumbing seemed to be at a standstill. Don called Mr. Curtis and called Mr. Curtis and called Mr. Curtis, and Mr. Curtis said his back hurt, he couldn't work in the rain, he was using his secret powerful influence to get the fixtures, was the road paved yet (it was barely bulldozed), he would let us know.

Weeks later, about eight o'clock one evening, Mr. Curtis and his wife appeared. Mr. Curtis wore a light polo coat and a brown Fedora. His wife had on jeans and a mackinaw. This was not too unusual a combination in a place where husbands go to the city while wives dig clams and get wood, but in the case of the Curtises it had a special significance, we learned. We offered them a drink which he readily accepted in the cause of his back and she refused, rather wistfully I thought. Don threw another log on the fire and we prepared to settle down and discuss the current ferry strike. To our amazement Mr. Curtis downed his drink in one gulp, leapt to his feet and said, "Sorry, Don, but we must get to work." Firmly he took his wife's arm, led her into the service room and handed her a pick. She chipped where he pointed.

They worked pretty steadily after that. She did all the heavy work, chipping cement, digging the hole for the septic tank, laying the sewer pipe, and so on, not done by Don and his carpenter friend who also dragged all the pipe and the fixtures down the road and set them in place. Mr. Curtis, who never once removed his polo coat or Fedora, in addition to directing the job, did a little screwing on of different things. He performed this rite delicately with his tapering fingers.

We had quite a celebration when the job was finished. Two bathrooms, wheeee! Then the girls reported that if they wanted to take a bath in their new tub they had to fill it with the shower because the faucets wouldn't turn on. Don said, "Nonsense!" and went masterfully upstairs with his pipe wrenches. He came out in a minute soaking wet and told me to call that "fellow Curtis."

There was no answer at the Curtises' house. I called every day for a week but there was never anyone home.

Then one very rainy morning Don and I were getting dressed to go to town. I finished first and was downstairs drinking a cup of coffee when I heard an agonized howl from upstairs. I ran up and found Don on his knees by the washbasin, his forefinger in a hole in the floor shouting, "The shutoff—find the shutoff!"

"What's the matter?" I asked.

Don said, "I was shaving and suddenly my shoes were full of water and the pipe came apart and dropped down below the floor and water was spurting up. I finally found the pipe and put my finger in it but for God's sake hurry and shut the water off."

"Where is the shutoff?" I asked reasonably.

"How in hell should I know," Don shouted. "Curtis put it in."

Then, Joanie who was home from school with a sore throat and/or history test, said, "I think it is outside my window. I'll go and see."

In a few minutes she announced that it was the shutoff and she had turned the water off. Don took his finger out of the dike and stormed down to call Curtis. Mrs. Curtis answered the phone and apparently told Don that Mr. Curtis was lying down. Don yelled, "Get him up. Get him to the phone." Apparently she told Don it was Mr. Curtis' back because Don yelled, "His back'll hurt a lot worse after I get hold of him." So Mrs. Curtis finally said she'd have him come right up.

Don and I explained to Mother, who was visiting us but had as yet not experienced all of the pleasures of island living, about Mr. Curtis, his weak back, need for brandy, loose connections, and so on. I actually believed that Mother thought we were exaggerating, but she promised to see to everything. That night when we got home Mother said, "Well, Mr. Curtis came. He limped in, introduced himself and asked me if I had any brandy. I said no so he said he'd have to go to Vashon and get some as his back was hurting. He came back after a while with a strong breath and two pints. I took him upstairs, pointed out the trouble in both bathrooms and went downstairs. In about three minutes he came down and told me everything was fixed. I said, 'How about that pipe in Betty and Don's bathroom?' He said, 'All fixed. But say, Mrs. Bard, tell them not to *brush* against it.' "

Mother asked him if he had fixed the shower in the girls' bathroom and he said yes and so Mother asked him to test it. He said sure so he and Mother went into the girls' bathroom and he pointed at the bathtub and said, "See, everything's okay here now."

Mother said, "Turn on the faucets, I want to see if they work."

"Well, sure," said Mr. Curtis, sitting down on the edge of the tub in his polo coat and Fedora. "But it's not necessary. I put in bell top crossers and street elbows." (I think those are the terms, but of course it might have been California trap crosses or flow flanges.)

Mother said, "Turn on the faucets."

"Well, okay," said Mr. Curtis reaching over and turning on both the hot and cold water full force, "but it's not necessary." Just then the shower, on fine spray, went sssssssssssss all over Mr. Curtis' polo coat and Fedora.

Mother said Mr. Curtis looked very hurt. "I can't understand it," he said. "Everything is tight as a drum. Maybe it's the sissom joints." He took a drink of brandy out of the bottle he had in his right coat pocket.

Mother said, "I'm going to stay right here in this bathroom while you fix those faucets."

Mr. Curtis said, "My coat's all wet, I might catch cold and I've got a bad back."

Mother said, "It must be the valve that releases the shower."

"Say, you got something, Mother," Mr. Curtis said, taking another drink of brandy for his bad back.

Mother said, "Fix it," and he did finally so that anybody equipped with a wrench could have a shower *or* a tub as they wished.

Then came the trouble with the septic tank. We were made aware of the fact that there was trouble in rather a harsh fashion. It was on a weekend with eight houseguests, two of them under two. Saturday afternoon we (that is all of us who weren't chained to the sink) were lounging around in the living room watching the fire and listening to (it was nap time) a Brahms symphony, Toscanini conducting. The record player was turned to full volume so every instrument came through very clearly. Especially one that made a strange gurgling sound, like an oboe filled with spit.

After a while I noticed that the gurgling sound was accompanied by a distinct splatting noise. Then both noises were supplemented by the remarkably penetrating sound of a toilet running over.

I yelled for Don who came unhurriedly upstairs, lifted the copper ball in the back of the toilet and stopped the water. Then everybody was upstairs and somebody confessed to flushing a didy down the toilet.

Several people said, "Call a plumber."

Don said, "Don't call Curtis. Look in the phone book."

I looked in the Vashon phone book, but the yellow section under P produced only Paint Dealers, Painting Contractors, Photographers, Physicians, Plasterers, Plastics, Printers and Pumps.

I called a neighbor. She gave me the number of her plumber. I called him but his wife said he was at church and wouldn't work on weekends anyway. I asked her if she knew the name of any plumber who would work on weekends. She said, "Yes, call Mrs. Grisert at 3478 and ask her if Henry has came home from war."

I did and he hadn't, but Mrs. Grisert gave me the number of her plumber. I called him. His number didn't answer. I asked the operator if she knew where he was. She said yes, he was in Mexico, but she gave me the number of *her* plumber. I called him. He said he would come Monday if he could squeeze me in. I told him that this was *Saturday* and water was running down the front stairs but he said he couldn't come until Monday, adding cheerfully, "Don't use the toilet until I get there."

Mr. Olsen came at seven-thirty Monday morning and by six-thirty Monday night he had chipped away all Mr. Curtis' wife's cement and exposed the sewer pipe clear to the septic tank. Tuesday he lifted the blocks in the patio and exposed the septic tank. He removed the blocking didy—then recovered the septic tank and pipe to the accompaniment of constant admiring demands that Don and I "yust look at dem tees, yust look at dem yoints, yust look at dem nipples—I never seen so many," but that was the last we ever saw of him. Moved away I guess.

Now when we want plumbing we call the television man who relays the information to a friend of his who is reputed to do odd jobs including plumbing, but I wouldn't vouch for this as I have left him at least a hundred calls which he hasn't answered and anyway Don gave me my own plumber's snake for a valentine.

Next we had the sprinkler system installed. Up to the time we got ours (unconsciously apt expression), my conception of a sprinkler system was a lady in a lavender voile dress lying on a chaise longue on the cover of The Small Home

Owner's Weekly. The lady's left hand was wrapped around a glass of lemonade and/or gin—her right around a small brass handle protruding shyly from the floor beside her. Surrounding the lady's chaise longue in every direction was a Kelly green mohair lawn, roughly about thirty acres of it. At about three-foot intervals all over the lawn, sprinkler heads were tossing crystal showers of water into the sunshine.

We got Bubby Hadlock of North Beach to install our sprinkler system. I showed him the picture of the lady but he said, as we had hardly any lawn and lived on a hill besides, our problem had to be handled differently. It certainly did. Bubby put copper pipe and sprinklers all over the place but arranged for each one to be operated independently *if* you are able to find them. Also the little handles are very close to the ground, well really *in* the ground, so you cannot take hold of them, and they must be hammered on and off. Also so located that when the lady in the lavender dress has crawled up the hillside, scrambled under the lilac, pushed aside the azaleas and found the —— —— valve, she is in for a surprise because good old Bubby placed all the sprinkler heads just above the valves and when they are turned on they soak first the operator, then the wisteria tree, the arborvitae, etc.

It is really not fair to lump Warner Yamamoto in with the island handymen because he was not really an islander nor handy. We got hold of him through the United States Relocation Center, a sort of clearing house for the Japanese who had been interned. This was just before we left for our trip to New York. Don and I felt very sorry for the returning Japanese who could not find places to stay and so we offered our house for the six months we would be gone. We offered the house and a dollar an hour for any work Warner did while we were gone.

As I remember time was very short, as Warner did not show up until half an hour before we were to leave, but I did manage to give him a few instructions such as: "You might divide this enormous clump of Siberian iris and clear off that hillside." Of course I meant clear off the weeds.

We were in New Mexico when we got a rather frantic letter from Mother saying, "Are you planning to cement the bank in front of the house? Warner has cleared off every living thing and is smoothing the dirt with a trowel." The next report was received in Dallas, Texas. "No need to cement the bank," Mother wrote. "Warner has divided the iris and is setting it out, spear by spear in neat rows over the entire bank. The place is beginning to look like a rice paddy."

Our first card from Warner came in Los Angeles. It said,

Am thanking God for opportunity to stay in this beautiful place. Earthquake did not do too much damage.

Your friend,
WARNER YAMAMOTO

Wildly we called home. What earthquake, they asked? We haven't had any. Don said it must have been the wash from an aircraft carrier pounding the beach.

The next card was received in Tampa, Florida. It said,

Am thanking God for opportunity to be in this beautiful country. Still raining. Big slides not too near house yet.

Your friend,
WARNER YAMAMOTO

We called home. Mother said, "An old snag fell across the road. It brought down a little dirt but Cleve has cleared everything away. The place really looks like a rice paddy now. Warner has now taken everything out of all the rockeries, including those heathers from Scotland, and thrown them away. He has almost finished filling the crevices with iris spears."

But Warner Yamamoto did have a green thumb and now we have more Siberian iris than Wayside Gardens. He also had a very pretty wife who spoke little English, had obviously never held a broom in her mothlike hands, but wished to help me with the housework, so Warner informed me, after we had come home and cleaned the house and they had settled elsewhere on the island.

As the female counterpart of the handyman is much more difficult to come by—island people being very proud and housework being considered menial, which it certainly is—take it from a menial who knows—I naturally snapped up Fumiko with no questions asked but several answered such as —How much pay an hour? Not do windows? Eight o'clock morning okay? Scrubbing floors too hard, yes? Not expect in rain? When important company come, Fumiko dahnse? She do both crassikar and moderne—take twenty minute, okay?

The first morning Fumiko staggered in with an armload of Japanese records and old photographs. For several hours we sat on the couch and looked at faded pictures of indistinct people who all looked exactly alike. Occasionally Fumiko would say, "Mama," and point at one tiny figure in an enormous group of tiny figures in front of a temple. "Mama beautiful," I would say politely, pronouncing each syllable loudly and clearly and pointing at what I thought was Mama. Fumiko would burst into giggles. "That Papa." "Well," I'd say, standing up, "I guess we had better get started." "More picture," Fumiko would say, quickly turning the page. "See, brozzer."

When we finally finished that batch of photographs she took out the records and her fans. To "Oh Beautiful Hiroshima in Cherry Blossom Time" (I think) she performed a long long series of small steps and angular postures. Then it was lunchtime. While she watched, I set a place at the kitchen table, heated some soup, made a tuna fish sandwich and opened a can of peaches. While she was eating, I sneaked out the back door and went down to the beach. Japanese people are notably polite and I thought that Fumiko thought that as long as I was in the house she must entertain me. About two o'clock I looked up from the beach and saw all the living room rugs hanging over the railing of the porch. "Ah, that's more like it," I said to Tudor.

At five-thirty when I came up from the beach the rugs were still on the railing, the living room chairs were all lined up in rows as if we were expecting Billy Graham, the floor had not been swept, the lunch dishes were on the table, and from our bathroom upstairs I could hear a voice humming "Oh Beautiful Hiroshima in Cherry Blossom Time."

At six-thirty, Warner came for Fumiko. She was still upstairs—the rugs were still on the railing. He called to her in Japanese and she came tripping down and began gathering up her photographs and records. Warner said to me, "Le's see—eight o'clock to six-thirty—that ten dollah fifty cent plus one dollah cah fah."

After they had gone I went upstairs—none of the beds had been touched, crumpled towels still littered the bathrooms, the mirrors were splattered with toothpaste, but the brass fixtures on our bathtub had been polished until they looked like gold.

That night I sat down at my typewriter and typed out a long list of things I expected Fumiko to do. The next morning I gave it to Warner and told him to read it to Fumiko in Japanese.

He did and all the time he was reading she giggled hysterically. I did not think that "Take ashes out of living room fireplace—Bring in the rugs—Wash and wax kitchen floor," and so on, was very funny but perhaps it gained something in translation.

Fumiko worked for me for five months or rather I worked and she performed. I finally did teach her to make beds, wash dishes, mop floors and wash windows after a fashion, but I couldn't make her bring in the rugs. I finally resigned myself to the fact that I was up against sort of an oriental superstition.

Marlene wore striped mechanics coveralls and used water and ammonia on everything. Don complained because the couches and rugs were always damp and the girls said the house smelled like the bus-terminal toilet but I couldn't let Marlene go because there wasn't anybody else and, anyway, her two sons were in the service and her husband was in a mental hospital. As she put it, "Boris's real sick in the head." She finally left to work at Boeing and as soon as the house had dried out a little I got Margaret, who was very pretty but had a low I.Q.

Margaret demanded long handles on all tools and used a gallon of wax a week. One day I found her waxing around a slice of bread on the drainboard. What was worse she was using the floor applicator with the long handle. "Margaret," I said sternly, "I've told you again and again that when you wax around a slice of bread you should use a *cloth.*"

Each Monday, Wednesday and Friday as Margaret ate her lunch, she told me about her boy friends. She had hundreds. One day she said, "Mrs. MacDonald, you wanta know why I got so many boy friends?"

I said, "I imagine it is because you're so pretty." (It certainly couldn't have been her brain.)

"Uh-uh," she said, taking a reflective bite of oatmeal cookie. "It's because I *like* 'em to git fresh with me."

I told her that with an attitude like that she was wasting her time on Vashon Island. She should go to Hollywood.

She laughed but she quit soon after that without notice or any reason, just failed to appear ever again. I heard that she had left the island. I am still checking the movie magazines' new faces departments for a picture of Margaret captioned probably, "Cecile Lamont—fascinating new French import." Cecile says, "I have leetle Eenglish but many many boy friends." (Hollywood version of "I *like* 'em to git fresh with me.")

CHAPTER XI

BRINGING IN THE SHEAVES

ACCORDING to tidbits I have picked up from my reading over the past twenty-five years, it seems to be an accepted fact that the *happy* woman is the woman who has some interest other than bearing children and the subsequent washing and ironing and cooking and sweeping. These backbreaking tasks, thrust upon her with her wedding ring, are her lot and she is expected to perform them with willingness, dispatch and quiet efficiency, but, we are told, the discussion of them is not interesting to the husband—that lucky pup who goes downtown every day to meet new people and eat in restaurants.

If you want to keep your husband's love, so say the instructions, you should *always* look pretty, be *fun,* keep your house *immaculate,* get up and cook your husband's breakfast, *and* have outside interests. There is one thing to be said for this state of affairs—it offers a challenge—a challenge about as easy as getting along with Russia.

When we moved to Vashon Island my outside interest was working for that contractor.

It was an outside interest, though, and I could fill up the evenings telling my husband and children how tired I was, how incompetent everybody else in our organization was and how much cabbage was selling for in Alaska. Then in February my sister Mary decided that I should become a writer and introduced me to an editor who told me to bring him a five-thousand-word outline of *my* book. Never having dreamed of writing a book I was not as quick with the outline as I might have been. In fact, I had to stay home from work to write it and some pal in the office told the boss what I was doing and I was instantly fired and thus became rather unwittingly an author. The job of being a lady writer not substantiated by any regular salary has always been regarded by my family with the same tolerant amusement they accord my efforts toward making my own Christmas cards. "All I ask," I tell them, "is one quiet spot where I can write." (This is a lie, of course, and they know it. What I really want is a million dollars so I won't ever have to write another word.)

When I am writing I itch and hate my family, especially during that painful period known as "getting into the book," when I am trying to decide whether I shall be Marcella Proust or Thomasina Wolfe and know I shall end up being Betty MacDonald and sobbing over nasty reviews. Thank goodness, I am not alone in this, because I read *The Cost of a Best Seller* by Frances Parkinson Keyes and another book about writing by Kenneth Roberts and they had their feelings hurt—in Europe too. Apparently the only writer who is never sorry for himself is Ernest Hemingway and according to a recent article by his wife, he is not only well adjusted but usually stripped to the waist. I have tried writing in the kitchen, the dining room, the living room, our bedroom, the guesthouse, the porch, the patio—it is always the same. I am first last and always a wife and mother and must stop whatever I am doing to—"try and remember where you left the big screwdriver"—"I am up in Vashon and I lost the list— what was it you wanted?"—"read the directions and see if Weevil Bait can be used for slugs"—"give me the recipe for chicken in olive oil and wine"—"I'm bringing the children over for the weekend." . . .

Late in the spring of our second year on the island, a week or so before school was to let out, I moved my typewriter out to the umbrella table and Don and I decided that if I was ever to have a minute's uninterrupted quiet Anne and Joan should also have an outside interest and earn at least part of their school clothes. The girls, who had already planned a summer of sleeping late, swimming, talking about boys and not helping, did not greet this decision with hand-clapping. In fact for days and days we ate our meat and potatoes to the broken rhythm of—all the children on Vashon earn money by picking berries—I always worked when I was a boy—I always worked when I was a girl—we do too like you —you can go swimming when you get home, anyway berry picking is not steady work—we do *not* want your money for whisky—it is *not* against the law for children to pick berries —of course we don't expect you to walk ten miles, the farmers call for the pickers—because nobody wants to adopt two great big girls, that's why. . . .

The berry picking was not much of a success. Late rains had almost ruined the strawberry crop, not enough rain had withered the raspberries, the currants had blight, the mean old man who had the cherry orchard made tiny crippled children climb clear to the top of huge trees just for three wormy cherries, and have you ever seen the thorns on goose-berry bushes?—well, picking nettles would be more fun.

Every morning I injected the girls with maxims—the idle man does not know what it is to enjoy rest—all work, even cotton spinning, is noble—fixed them hearty lunches and shoved them out the door. When they came dragging home in the late afternoon I looked hopefully for signs of self-reliance and found only boiling resentment and berry stains which almost looked as if they might have been smeared on purposely and wouldn't come out even with Chlorox.

In July Mary telephoned and offered Anne a job as mes-senger for her husband's laboratories. Anne was delighted. At last she was returning to her rightful place in the *city,* and she was going to earn lots and lots of money and perhaps, this was a secret hope, Don and I might become so dependent on her earnings we wouldn't *let* her go back to school.

Joanie, who to date had earned exactly $3.87, heaved a sigh of relief because certainly we wouldn't expect her to pick berries alone, and got into the rowboat where she intended to spend the rest of the summer.

Then Anne received her first week's pay and came staggering home under a dazzling load of skirt material, new white socks, panties with ruffles, a new blouse, paprika lipstick and nail polish and blue eyeshadow. Joan said, "Old First-Born always gets everything. She *is* your favorite. She always has been."

Anne said, "Favorite! That's very amusing. All you do is lie around on the beach getting brown while I run all over downtown in the boiling sun carrying terribly valuable reports. When I'm not running, I'm washing test tubes and how would you like to eat your lunch in a place that smells like boiling urine?"

"Do they really boil urine?" Joan asked.

"Of course *we* do," Anne said importantly. "And *we* kill rabbits by injecting air in their veins. It's for the pregnancy tests."

"Yeah, but look at all the money you make."

"I earn every cent of it," Anne said. "Those laboratory technicians work me like a slave. I don't even get to sit down, all day long."

"I wouldn't care if I sat down or not if I had all that money," Joan said. "I sure wish I had a job like yours."

"Perhaps next year," Anne said grandly. "When you're older. Now you're considered a child and nobody will hire you except the berry farmers and that's just because they're such big cheaters and don't want to pay anything."

I said, "I feel sorry for the berry farmers. From what you have told me all you and your little friends did was drink Cokes and throw berries at each other."

"That was only when we were too tired to pick any more," Joan said. "You should just be out in that boiling sun, crawling around in the dirt trying to find those wizened-up little strawberries."

With her next paycheck Anne bought a new bathing suit and some huaraches. Joan examined them enviously but continued to spend her days in the rowboat, spearing sole and chasing crabs with her friend Bobby.

With her next paycheck Anne bought two men's sweaters—one pale blue and one yellow. As she laid out her purchases she said to Joan, "Labor Day is only two weeks away you know."

Joan said, "Oh, you just think you're smarter than anybody in the whole world." But Monday morning after she had washed the breakfast dishes, she made a telephone call. Then with elaborate casualness she approached the umbrella table where I was miserably huddled being creative. She said, "Mommy dear, would you do me the biggest favor in the whole world?"

"Of course," I said heedlessly thinking in terms of another request for macaroni and cheese, or perhaps some new huaraches.

"Well," said Joanie, "I just called Karen and she says that maybe I can get a job picking peaches at Hawkins' orchards. They pay sixty-five cents an hour but if you stay all season you get eighty-five cents. Karen says it's not hard and last year she earned eighty-two dollars. Will you call the Hawkinses for me, Mommy?"

"Of course," I said getting up. "Do you want to start tomorrow?"

"Yes," Joan said, "and tell them they can pick me up on the road by the Falcon's Nest."

So I gave the Hawkins number to the operator and after a while a female voice that had been tempered in a forge yelled, "Yeah?" and I said timidly, "Are you hiring peach pickers?" and the voice said, "Any experience?"

"Oh, my yes," I said.

"Where you live?" the voice asked.

"At Vashon Heights," I said. "Right near the Falcon's Nest."

160

"Way down there?" the voice said. "Golly, I don' know. How many of you?"

"Four," I said, making a mental note that this was not a lie as there were four in our family.

"Okay, then," said the voice. "We couldn't come way down there for less. Be on the road at seven-thirty tomorrow morning."

I hung up the phone. Joan said, "What'd they say? Will they take us?"

"Us is right," I said grimly. "They won't come down here for less than four. Can you get anybody else? What about those little girls that live down by the store?"

"You mean the Hansens?" Joan said. "I'll call them but I think they are visiting their grandmother. *They* have fun in the summer. *Their* mother says picking berries is for Indians."

I said, "In wartime everybody works. In England countesses are milking cows and shoveling manure."

"Why don't they let their servants do it?" Joan asked.

"Because the servants are working in war plants and all the men are at war," I said. "Now call the Hansens."

But the Hansens were at their grandmother's not working. "See," Joan said hanging up the phone and sighing heavily.

"Try somebody else," I said briskly.

"Who?" she asked.

"Your school friends," I said.

"I don't know any of their telephone numbers," Joan said.

"Look them up," I said.

Finally, after a great deal of urging, she called the few of her schoolmates whose names she could remember and learned that they were all either already working at Hawkins' or in some other peach orchard.

"Oh, ho," I said spitefully. "I thought you and Anne were the only children in the whole wide world who had to work in the summer."

Joan said, "Well, I can't work because you said Hawkins won't come down here for only one." I knew then what was coming as I had known from the minute Mrs. Hawkins said hello.

Joan said, "Why don't you come, Mommy? You're not doing *anything* and that would be two."

That night when Anne came home she announced that she had quit her job because Aunty Mary thought she should have some vacation and, anyway, she had all her school clothes but her shoes and a new coat and Aunty Mary didn't think that even Don and I were mean enough to expect little children to earn their own coats. She also said, "It's certainly going to be too bad for you when school starts, Joan, unless you can persuade your friend who gets her clothes off the city dump to take you along on her next trip."

Joan said, "You don't have to worry about me, Miss Barbara Hutton; Mommy and I are going to pick peaches."

"That's not fair," Anne said. "Betty, you didn't help me with my job."

"It's just for one day," I said. "The Hawkinses wouldn't come down for only one picker. Tomorrow Joan will arrange with some of her school friends to take my place."

Don said, "I thought the girls were to learn self-reliance and independence. Why can't Joan make her own arrangements?"

"Nobody could make arrangements with that voice," I said. "It even scared me. Anyway it is only for one day."

"Be sure and fix plenty of sandwiches," Joan told me the next morning when we were getting ready. "Picking makes you awfully hungry. What have you got for dessert?"

"What's the matter with peaches?" I said. "We'll be in a whole orchard of them."

"Mr. Hawkins doesn't let you eat the peaches when you're picking," Joan said.

It was a hazy morning, with a long white plume where the Seattle shore should be, but the sky behind the big firs was already a clear glassy blue and showed it was going to be a hot day. I put on shorts but when I came out to the kitchen Joan said, "Mrs. Hawkins won't let the ladies wear shorts, Mommy. She says they're indecent."

"Who does this Mrs. Hawkins think she is?" I said crossly. "Everybody wears shorts in summer, even old ladies like me."

"Wear them if you want to," Joan said, "but she won't let you pick. Karen said she sent Ethel and Mary Everts home because they were wearing cut-off jeans and they're only fifteen and sixteen."

So I changed into jeans and a white sweatshirt and wooden shoes, which we wear on the beach. Joan wore jeans and a red sweatshirt and huaraches.

As we crunched along the beach at seven-fifteen, Joanie said, "Lucky old Anne, still asleep."

I said, "She's been getting up early for weeks and weeks while you've been sleeping."

"But she didn't have to be at work until ten o'clock," Joan said. "Look, deer tracks. I bet Bucky has been down taking a swim. Next year I'm going to get a job in town."

The Hawkins truck stopped for us promptly at seven-thirty but before he would let us in Mr. Hawkins yelled, "Where are the others?"

"Home, sick," I said.

"Whatsa matter with them?" he asked suspiciously.

"Flu," I said. "Sort of intestinal flu with nausea and dizziness."

"Will they be okay tomorrow?" he asked.

"Sure," I said, "that flu never lasts long."

"Okay," he said. "Climb in."

The tailgate of the truck was as high as my chest but I managed, with the help of the ten or eleven children, to scramble in, just as Mr. Hawkins with a roar and a lurch started off. There wasn't straw or gunny sacks or anything for us to sit on and Mr. Hawkins immediately turned off the paved highway and drove like double greased lightning over what appeared to be partially cleared land. By the time we got to their ranch, Joan said she felt like a milk shake.

After he had unloaded us, Mr. Hawkins said, "Can't start pickin' until the mist gits off the trees. You can set around and wait. But the pay don't start until you start pickin'."

The pickers put their lunches and jackets in a heap, then lined up on the porch of the packing shed to watch the mist on the trees and look woebegone. Joan, her friend Karen, a pixy-ish little girl with black pigtails and freckles, and I wandered down into the orchard and ate slightly green peaches while Karen gave us the lowdown on picking.

"Pick them with the palm of your hand, like this," she showed us. "If you use your fingers you get bruise marks and they count against you. We all have numbers so they know who picked what boxes. Mrs. Swensen is the forelady and she's the meanest old crab you ever saw: 'No talking in the orchard, girls.' 'Faster, girls! Work faster, girls!' 'You're leaving finger marks, Karen!' 'Number seventeen report to the packing shed, I've tattled on you!' "

"Which one is she?" I asked.

"She wears a big green straw hat," Karen said, "but she's still in the house, drinking coffee and tattling to Mrs. Hawkins. When you get tired, and you sure do in the afternoon, climb up to the top of your ladder and sit and eat peaches. You can see the old crab before she sees you and pretend to be picking like sixty. Yesterday she sneaked up to where I was picking, but I saw her coming and when she was right beside the ladder I dropped a great big rotten peach on her head. 'Oh, excuse me, Mrs. Swensen,' I said, then busted out laughing. She was awful mad but she couldn't do anything because I picked the most boxes yesterday. We picked till nine last night and didn't get home until after eleven."

"After eleven!" I said. "How awful!"

"Yeah, it is," Karen said, "but Mr. Hawkins won't drive the pickers home until they are all through in the packing shed."

"What about dinner?" Joan asked. "We only brought lunch."

"Oh, they give you sandwiches and Cokes," Karen said. "Two halves of a sandwich and one Coke. I could have eaten twenty. I ate about a hundred peaches but they aren't very filling."

It was ten o'clock before Mr. Hawkins gave us our tickets and told us to start. I was number twenty-seven—Joanie was twenty-six. Karen had already showed us where the best trees were, so we went down to the other end of the orchard about a mile from the packing shed. The land between and under the trees had been plowed and disked thoroughly and recently, and walking in it was like walking over sand dunes. Joan's huaraches filled with dirt immediately so she took them off and went barefoot, like Karen. My wooden shoes also filled with dirt and I kept stopping and dumping them.

Karen said, "It would be better if you could take your shoes off too, Mrs. MacDonald, but Mrs. Swensen won't let the older ladies go barefoot. She says it makes them look tough."

I was pretty slow filling my first two or three boxes because I couldn't tell which peaches were ripe enough to pick and was very conscientious about not putting finger marks on them. Joan and Karen filled five boxes to my one, ate peaches by the dozen, threw the rotten ones at each other, skittered up and down their ladders like squirrels and by noon were so far ahead of me I couldn't even hear their giggles.

The trees were so loaded with fruit, almost every branch had to be supported with a stake. The peaches were very large, a deep golden yellow with flagrantly painted cheeks. Their color was a lovely contrast to the bottle-blue sky, the pointed drooping silky green leaves. As I stood on my ladder and with the heel of my hand gently twisted off a plump golden peach and tucked it in the box beside other plump golden peaches, I decided that this was the life. Beauty, independence and a feeling of harvest. This would be my chosen work. I could see our car loaded with camping equipment, Anne and Joan and Don and me crowded happily inside, singing as we spun along the highways heading for the hop fields, or the orange groves or the apple orchards. What a life! To say nothing of seven or eight dollars apiece per day—let's see—eight times four is thirty-two dollars a day! Heavens! It *was* the life. I reached way above my head and picked a small ripe red peach, bit into its sun-warmed juicyness and then nearly fell off the ladder as a nasal voice zinged up at me, "You have two finger marks, Number twenty-seven, and you are not cleaning the trees properly."

Quickly tucking the small bitten peach into my box, bite-side down, and choking down what was in my mouth, I said, "You mean I am leaving ripe ones, Mrs. Swensen?"

"I certainly do," she said. "Come here."

I climbed down. Peering at my wooden shoes through her steel-rimmed spectacles, she said, "What on earth do you have on your feet?"

"Wooden shoes," I said. "We wear them on the beach."

"Well, they may be all right for the beach but they are certainly inappropriate for picking peaches," she said. "Look here, this peach is ripe," deftly she twisted it off. "And so is this one, and this and this. Where is your flat, Mrs. MacDonald?"

"Up on the ladder," I said. "I'll get it."

When I brought it down she immediately reached in and grabbed the small peach I had been eating. "That one is too small," she said, then seeing the bitten pieces she added, "Eating the fruit is not encouraged, Mrs. MacDonald. After all, this fruit belongs to the Hawkinses. It represents money to them. Helping ourselves to their fruit is like helping ourselves to their money."

She handed me the bitten peach and I accepted it humbly with hanging head. "Now," she said briskly, "you are very slow. Let me see how you are picking."

I reached over my head and got hold of a peach that looked ripe but was as hard as a stone and apparently cemented to the tree. I twisted and twisted and yanked and twisted and it stayed on the tree.

Mrs. Swensen said, "Here, let me show you." She reached up and snapped the peach off and laid it in the box.

I felt like telling her that if somebody would loosen them up for me I wouldn't have any trouble either, but instead I tried another and it did come off finally, after I had wrung it like a dishrag.

Mrs. Swensen had on great big mustard-colored culottes, a long-sleeved Kelly green silk blouse, brown Red Cross oxfords with medium heels and the big green straw garden hat. I said, "Isn't this a lovely day?"

She said, "It has been a very disappointing day for the Hawkinses. Those early mists make picking so late."

I said, "On the beach where we live the mist was almost gone at seven o'clock."

"That's impossible," she said. "I could hardly see to drive at seven."

"It was, though," I said. "We are on the southeast side. Perhaps the wind blew it away."

"It seems very unlikely that it would be foggy at Hawkins' and clear at your place. That's a green peach you just picked."

"I'm sorry," I said. "What shall I do with it—throw it away?"

"Of course not," she said. "It will pack, but be more careful in the future. You must work faster too. You're way behind the others. Perhaps if you had on sensible shoes like these you could go up and down the ladders faster."

"I could go barefoot," I said eagerly.

"Mrs. Hawkins doesn't approve of the women going barefoot," she said. "It makes them look tough."

I saw that the sun was directly overhead. "What time is it?" I asked.

"I don't wear a watch," she said. "I can tell the day is over when my work is finished."

Just then there was a loud banging, like somebody pounding on a wash boiler with a hammer.

"There's the lunch gong," she said, still picking.

I kept picking, too, because I was afraid to stop. After ten minutes or so I heard Joan and Karen calling to me, "Betty, come on! Where are you?"

"Down here," I answered. "Aren't you going to eat lunch?" I asked Mrs. Swensen.

"I'm not hungry," she said, drawing her lips into a small lavender rosette. "I've been having a little upset. Anyway I want to finish this tree."

"I'll help you," I said weakly.

Then Joan and Karen came running down between the trees, carrying the lunch bags. "Come on, Mommy," Joan said. "We only get a half hour and half of it's gone already."

"Well, I guess I'd better eat my lunch now," I said to Mrs. Swensen.

"As you wish," she said, not looking up.

Long before we were out of earshot, Karen said, "How come you were stuck with the old Crab Patch?"

"She was teaching me," I said, adding sadly: "She said I'm slow and don't pick right."

"Oh, she tells that to everybody," Karen said. "She thinks she's the only person in the whole world that can pick those darn peaches. If they'd let her, she'd pick the whole crop all by herself."

It was very hot and dusty between the rows of trees, but under each tree was a circle of cool dark green dappled shade. I suggested going under a tree to eat our lunch but Karen said no, because of the yellow jackets swarming over the peaches on the ground. We finally ate on the porch of the packing shed along with the other pickers. The sun had swung around and was shining directly on the heap of jackets and lunch and our sandwiches and milk were warm. After we had gulped down our food I said I wanted a drink of water. Karen said we had to drink out of the faucet in the yard. The water was warm and tasted like it had been standing in a tin can.

As I stood up and wiped off my lips, Joanie said, "Gosh you look hot, Mommy! Your face is as red as a beet."

"I am hot," I said, "I wish I'd worn a thin blouse."

"Karen and I are going to take off our sweatshirts," Joan said. "We've got halter tops on underneath. I wish I'd worn my short jeans."

"Let's cut 'em off," Karen said. "Here, I've got a pocket knife." She jabbed the blade of the knife through the material of her jeans at the inside seam, gave a yank and ripped off one leg. Then she cut off the other. Joan asked her to cut off hers. When they went back to work a few minutes later they had shed their sweatshirts and in their bare feet, halters and very short jeans, appeared as cool and carefree as pearl divers. I clumped hotly along behind them through the orchard.

About two o'clock my wooden shoes felt like they were made of iron and my throat was so dry it crackled. The tractor, hauling a sled that picked up the peaches and left empty boxes, went roaring by leaving a cloud of chokey tan dust. I climbed down from my tree and went in search of water. Ten or twelve trees away I found Karen and Joan. I asked Karen if there was any water nearer than the packing house. She said, "Ask the Crab Patch, she's supposed to have it hauled down to the orchard." I finally found Mrs. Swensen whispering to one of her lady friends behind the packing shed.

"Could we please have some water in the orchard?" I asked her.

She said, "Didn't you get a drink at noon?"

I said, "Of course I did, but it's awfully hot and the dust from the tractor is terrible."

She said, "Well, I'll take it up with Mrs. Hawkins." She looked very disapproving of the whole idea.

I went defiantly over to the faucet in the yard, took a long lukewarm drink, washed out and filled Joan's and my milk bottles and started back to work. Once I looked back and saw Mrs. Swensen pointing me out to Mrs. Hawkins. Joan and Karen were grateful for the water but instead of drinking it, poured it on their heads.

"Makes you cooler," Karen said and I wished I had wet my hair when I was up at the faucet.

About four o'clock the tractor hauled down a ten-gallon can of water and a tin dipper to a place about in the middle of the pickers. The word went through the orchard with a whoosh. "Water!" the pickers called from tree to tree and we all hurried up to the sled. Mrs. Swensen was disbursing it as if it were vintage champagne.

"Don't waste it," she kept warning us. "Don't crowd— don't loiter—don't be piggish—don't push—be careful!" When my turn came I deliberately poured two dippersful over my head, then drank one.

Mrs. Swensen watched me with horror, then said, "I think we should all be very grateful to the Hawkinses for this nice water, Mrs. MacDonald. Mr. Hawkins filled the can and hauled it himself. I don't think we should waste it. Mr. Hawkins is a very busy man."

My hair was apparently thick with dust because the rivulets that ran down my face and neck were muddy. Joan and Karen giggled and said comfortingly, "Golly, you should see yourself, you look awful!" I didn't care. I wanted to look awful. I was tired and hot and my legs ached and I had bleeding blisters on both heels and I hated peach picking more than anything in the whole world.

About five o'clock Mrs. Swensen announced that we would pick until dark, which was not until about ten as we were on double daylight saving at that time. I told her that I would have to call home and she said, "Well, I don't know. Mrs. Hawkins doesn't like the pickers to use the phone."

"I don't care what Mrs. Hawkins likes," I shouted. "My husband won't know where I am and unless you want the sheriff coming down here I'd better telephone."

"Well, all right," she said. "But I think arrangements should be made before you come to work."

"How, by ouija board?" I said. "When I telephoned yesterday nobody told me that we were going to work until dark. I naturally assumed that we would quit at five or five-thirty. Where is the telephone?"

"I'll show you," she said.

"And tattle on you to Mrs. Hawkins," Karen said to Joan audibly.

"You watch yourself, young lady," said Mrs. Swensen turning around to Karen.

"Yes, ma'am," said Karen, hurrying up her ladder.

The telephone was in the packing shed where about twenty women were sorting and packing peaches and screaming pleasantries to each other. It sounded like a hen house invaded by a weasel. I couldn't even hear by own voice when I gave the number to the operator. I thought I heard Anne say that she and Don were going to my sister Alison's for dinner but I wasn't sure. Anyway, I was quite certain she understood that Joan and I would be late.

Mrs. Hawkins, a small sturdy brown woman with bright blue eyes, stopped her packing and came over to me. "How you getting along?" she asked.

"Fine," I said, "but I'm awfully hot. I wish I could wear shorts."

"Why don't you?" she asked.

"I thought the women weren't allowed to," I said.

"Nonsense," she said. "Wear your bathing suit if you want. We don't care. Just so you don't mark the peaches."

I looked at Mrs. Swensen and she had her lips drawn into the lavender rosette.

We stopped for supper at six. Mrs. Swensen brought the sandwiches and Cokes to us. The sandwiches were egg and peanut butter and there were only two halves apiece. I could have eaten twenty and judging by Joan's forlorn expression, she could have eaten sixty. Mrs. Swensen didn't eat any. She said she was still upset and she didn't like peanut butter anyway.

"Can I have yours, then?" Joan and Karen asked together.

"I suppose so," said Mrs. Swensen ungraciously.

The long shadows of evening, with the soft bird sounds and a breeze from the Sound, gave us all a second wind. I was barefoot and even the earth between the trees, which had been as hot as a griddle during the afternoon, felt cool and cushiony to my tired feet. As we straggled finally up to the packing house I worried about Joanie. She was only thirteen, and seemed so small and slight to be doing such hard work. I asked her how she felt and she said, "Keen! I earned seven dollars and eighty cents at the very least and if they pay me eighty-five cents an hour like they are supposed to if you work the whole season but Karen says they never do because Mrs. Swensen chooses the ones that get eight-five cents, I earned ten dollars and twenty cents. Isn't that keen, Mommy? You earned that much too," she added generously.

I didn't answer and she tucked her arm in mine and said, "It won't be so hard tomorrow, Mommy. Karen says the first day is always hard."

I had absolutely no intention of seeing what the second day was going to be like but didn't want to bring it up at this time.

I sat down rather dispiritedly on the edge of the packing house porch and watched other packers, even two very old ladies, bustle gaily, untiredly around gathering up shawls and jackets and lunch buckets. I decided that if I did have to work the next day I would bring a big thermos of coffee—I also realized I hadn't had a single cigarette all day. I took one out and lit it and immediately Mrs. Swensen materialized in the darkness beside me and said, "Mrs. Hawkins doesn't allow smoking on the premises."

"Okay, then I'll let *her* tell me to stop smoking," I said.

Mrs. Swensen flounced away. Joan and Karen giggled

but Joan said, "Please don't smoke, Mommy. None of the ladies here do and it makes you look funny."

"You mean tough," I said, "like wearing shorts or going barefoot?"

"Oh, Mommy," Joan said. "You know what I mean."

"I do, sweetheart," I said, "but I'm so tired I don't care. I need a cigarette right now and I'd like a martini."

"Shush," Joan said. "Don't talk like that. Somebody might hear you."

"I could sure go for a can of cold beer," a pleasantly loud voice said behind me.

"Make it two," another answered.

"What about them?" I asked Joan.

"Yes, but they're not mothers," Joan said.

Wearily I stamped out my cigarette and accepted half of Joan's lukewarm Coke in its place. Mr. Hawkins didn't finish cleaning up and locking the packing shed until after eleven. It was eleven-thirty when he slowed up the truck just a little and Joan and I tumbled out at the top of the Sanders' road. My blisters were so painful I couldn't wear my shoes, so I carried them and walked in my sock feet. The road had recently been graded and covered with crushed rock, which was like walking over broken glass. It was also very dark as the road followed a wooded ravine sheltered from the moonlight by the steep hills, and we couldn't see the larger rocks until we either stepped on them or banged them with our toes. We were stumbling along complaining about how tired we were when we saw the lights of Don's car at the top of the hill back of us.

Joan said, "Mommy, don't let's tell Anne how awful it was. Let's tell her it was fun and all we did was sit under the trees and eat peaches for eighty-five cents an hour."

It seemed a reasonable request, so when Don slowed up and we climbed in, I tried to leap a little and appear sprightly.

"How was it?" Anne asked immediately.

"The most fun I ever had," Joan said. "The peaches

are enormous and delicious and you can eat all you want and all Karen and I did was sit under the trees and eat peaches and giggle and I earned ten dollars and twenty cents."

"Ten dollars and twenty cents!" Anne said. "My gosh, I only got fifteen dollars for a whole week on my job."

"Well, come on and pick peaches," Joan said. "They need more pickers."

"Do they really?" Anne asked.

"Yes, they do," I said. "You know I had to promise Mrs. Hawkins we'd have four or she wouldn't have come down for us."

"Well, I'm going tomorrow," Anne said. "Ten dollars and twenty cents! I could get new saddle shoes *and* loafers."

The great advantage of having Anne along was that she became friends with the Hawkinses' daughter and learned that we could have as much water as we wanted and as many sandwiches as we could eat for supper. The tiny portions had been Mrs. Swensen's idea. Also Anne stayed loyally behind with me and let Karen and Joan scamper ahead and be champions. I wore shorts and tennis shoes and a thin blouse the next day and was much less tired. Mrs. Swensen sniffed when she saw me and hovered around my trees like a yellow jacket but didn't say anything.

We didn't work late every night and after a while I wasn't so terribly tired when I got home. We were all paid off at eighty-five cents, a pleasant surprise. We went to town the Saturday before Labor Day and had a rich, well-earned spree. The girls spent all their money for clothes and records and charms for their bracelets, but I got a new typewriter ribbon, some new pots and pans, and a large white Lotus camellia bush.

Don was very proud of all of us and Joan said that next year maybe he'd like to pick.

Anne said, "Oh, no, Mrs. Swensen doesn't like men pickers. She says men smoke and use dirty language."

"Description fits me like a glove," Don said. "Guess I'll have to dig clams."

CHAPTER XII

TRIPLE THAT RECIPE

IT WAS a baby shower for a neighbor and we were all invited. Don, who does not approve of women's clubs or women's luncheons or women's bridge parties, or sororities or even two women talking together on the phone, elected to stay home alone with Tudor and Mrs. Miniver. When Anne and Joan and I came downstairs in our ironed dresses and perfume, carrying our presents and our good shoes, he was sitting by the radio, looking sad.

"How do we look?" I asked him.

"I thought you told me you didn't like women's clubs," he said, his voice dripping disappointment.

"This isn't a women's club," I said. "It's a baby shower for Elspeth Carlyle. All the other husbands are coming."

"Do the men bring baby presents?" Joan asked.

"Of course not," I said. "They just stay in the den and drink and play poker, the lucky dogs."

"Come on, Don," Anne said. "You'll have a good time and it's scary walking the trail in the dark."

"If you want me to, I'll walk you down," Don said. "But I won't go in. A baby shower!" He spoke with great resentment. "Who ever thought that up?"

"I think it's very nice," I said. "And I think it was very considerate of Mrs. Adams to ask the husbands and Anne and Joan."

"Say, it's almost eight o'clock," Anne said. "We'd better get started."

"Are you coming?" I asked Don.

"No," he said. "But I will walk the trail with you."

"You don't have to," I said. "We've each got a flashlight. Just keep up the fire." I gestured with contempt at the four pieces of bark about the size and thickness of slices of meat-loaf, the burning of which would leave the copper boiler we use as a wood box, entirely empty. "You don't expect that to last all evening, do you?"

"You tend to your women's clubs and I'll tend to my wood," Don said, turning the bad news on the radio up louder. "What time will you be home?"

"About eleven, I expect," I said.

"Do you think you'd like a sandwich?" he asked.

"Oh, no," Anne said. "This is a party. We'll probably have tons to eat."

Hopefully Joan asked, "Do they have weenies and buns at baby showers?"

"Oh, heavens, no," Anne who had never to my certain knowledge been to one, answered confidently. "They have things like chicken salad and hot rolls and ice cream and cake, don't they, Mommy?"

"I hope so," I said, adding to Don, "But if you're planning on any kind of an extra-good sandwich, like peanut butter on dry bread, save me one."

When the guest of honor had picked up the last package, admired the stork paper and the rattle tied to the bow, squealed, for the twenty-third time that evening, "What a darling card!" and as she undid the wrappings, "Just what I needed!", handed the box to the woman on her left who said, "Oh, how darling! Just what you needed!", passed the box to the woman on her left ditto, until the box had gone all the way around the room, the hostess appeared and said, "And now, ladies, if you will follow me."

We all got quickly to our feet, no mean accomplishment for those of us in the stranglehold of African camp chairs, lounging in which always brings back vivid unpleasant memories of waiting for the obstetrician, and, like all women following their hostess into the dining room, afraid to appear either too eager or too reluctant, we began backing and filling and lurching ahead very much like freight cars trying to follow an engine onto a siding.

The refreshments, laid out on the dining room table buffet style around the pink candles, stork centerpiece and little pink and blue candy baskets in the shape of folded didies, consisted of a large lumpy salad in lettuce cups, homemade banana bread, black olives and lukewarm very weak coffee. After we had helped ourselves, moving left to right around the table and ending up with the sugar and cream, and I had made Joan put back six olives and told Anne for the eighth time she could not have coffee, we carried our plates and cups and saucers back to the living room. I hurried just enough to avoid getting stuck in one of the African camp chairs again, but not enough to spill the coffee.

After I had arranged myself on the floor beside the coffee table with the girls beside me, I looked and looked at my salad trying to guess what it was. When it could not be avoided any longer I took a bite and it *was* tuna fish and marshmallows and walnuts and pimento (just for the pretty color, our hostess explained later when she was giving us the recipe) and chunks of pure white lettuce and boiled dressing. I almost gagged, both Anne and Joan nudged me and giggled, but most of the other ladies shrieked, "Delicious!" "Heavenly!" and "So different!" (that I could go along with) and so the beaming hostess gave us the recipe and we all wrote it down, using the same pencils and pads we had used to guess rivers beginning with B—cities with A—authors with B and historical events with Y, and Anne had won the crocheted coasters.

It was at another baby shower that I first encountered a ring mold of mushroom soup, hard-boiled eggs, canned shrimps (that special brand that taste like Lysol) and lime

Jello, the center heaped with chopped sweet pickles, the whole topped with a mustardy, sweet salad dressing.

An evening party during elections produced casual refreshments of large cold slightly sweet hamburger buns spread with relish, sweet salad dressing, dried beef and cheese, then whisked under the broiler just long enough to make the cheese gummy and the relish warm.

At another shower (wedding, I believe) we were served *tuna fish* chow mein with rancid noodles. A garden club meeting, creamed tuna fish and peanuts over canned asparagus. A hospital group dredged up a salad of elbow macaroni, pineapple chunks, Spanish peanuts, chopped cabbage, chopped marshmallows, ripe olives and salad dressing.

I could go on and on *ad nauseam* and not even scratch the surface of the desserts which veer toward you "just take a devil's food cake, make a filling of whipped cream, peanut brittle, chocolate chips and custard . . . and freeze." I don't know what is happening to the women of America but it ought to be stopped.

Another thing, why do terrible cooks always have their houses so hot, their coffee so cold?

The other day as I ironed I listened idly to a radio program for housewives. I was immediately irritated by the commentator, or whatever she calls herself, because she said "prolly" for "probably." I was further irritated when, with a great deal of self-confidence and speaking slowly so that the listeners could get it all down, she gave a perfectly ghastly recipe for one of my favorite foods, pot roast. As nearly as I can remember she said, "This being spring you are prolly at the end of your ropes as far as meal planning is concerned and would prolly just love to know about an easy delicious meal to surprise your family. Well, here it is. Individual pot roasts. All you do is take a pot roast and cut it up into pieces, so that each member of the family has one, put them in individual casseroles, cover with plenty of water, add a couple of carrots and a turnip and bake until done. What a surprise for the family! Everybody with his own little pot roast!" From her recipe I would say, "Everybody with his own little chunk of boiled army blanket."

Another female household-hinter gave a recipe for a big hearty main dish of elbow macaroni, mint jelly, lima beans, mayonnaise and cheese baked until "hot and yummy." Unless my taste buds are paralyzed, this dish could be baked until hell freezes over and it might get hot but never "yummy."

These women are also strong for what they term "tossed" salad and into which they tell their gullible listeners to "toss everything you have in the refrigerator."

It is pretty obvious to me that they, as well as most of the cooks in the women's magazines, operate on my grandmother's old theory of "Don't make it so awful good—men, the pigs, will eat anything."

The only really good cook I have encountered via the women's magazines is Ann Batchelder of the *Ladies' Home Journal.* She has managed to retain a taste for simple food with good flavor and she obviously likes to eat, two infallible rules for a good cook.

Men's magazines have much better recipes than women's magazines, but are apt to go to the other extreme and demand "six tiny bitter oranges from the island of Crete, one-fourth litre of St. Emilion, Château Ausone, pounded into two pounds of fresh truffles."

Everyone in our family likes to cook. My sister Mary, if she can be controlled on her occasional flights into "turnips stuffed with grated orange and old brandy," is a marvelous cook. Anne and Joan are divine cooks. I am sometimes a very good cook but my weakness is "if a little is good a whole lot is better" and my leftovers are often carried from the table in tubs. My mother seldom varies from her goal of good food, simply prepared, well seasoned and beautifully served.

Most of the time when I am cooking I feel that I have been more than usually fortunate in my choice of a mate, because Don is a true gourmet and a delight to cook for. He has only one tiny flaw in this department—he would like Beef Stroganoff for every meal. I like Beef Stroganoff but it is quite a bore to make with its "strips of beef the size of a lead pencil," should be served as soon as it is made and does not combine well with guests who prolong the cocktail hour until eleven P.M.

Every time I make Beef Stroganoff I think of the first time we entertained my managing editor. It was one of those unexpectedly raw spring days we specialize in up here. A day when your flesh seems all huddled around your neck and you feel as if the wind were blowing directly on your bare bones.

We met George at the two-thirty ferry and, though he was wearing a thin raincoat and looked blue, he didn't protest when Don suggested a drive around the island. I sat in the back, and he sat hunched in the front and nobody said much as Don drove seventy-five miles an hour past cemeteries, the Vashon dump, the big patch of burned-off land on Maury Island, mud flats, abandoned farms, farms which should have been abandoned because the well was obviously dry, the old brick yard. It was pretty depressing, made more so by the fact that I was shy, George was shy, Don was shy and the heater was broken.

At four o'clock we came home. Don said, "Betty is going to make Beef Stroganoff for dinner."

George said, "That's fine."

I said, "I love Hollywood. In fact my secret vice is reading movie magazines."

George said, "Oh, no!"

Then I remembered that he had been editor of the *Saturday Review,* and I was just going to change the subject to a book by André Gide, when Don handed us each a martini and said, "Betty certainly does like movie magazines. Last week she spent two dollars and seventy-one cents on them—the week before three dollars and eighty-seven cents—the week before three dollars and forty-five cents—the week before . . ."

The upshot of the whole thing was that I had the Beef Stroganoff done and on the table at four forty-five and we were all yawning by seven five.

I invited Maggie Cousins, the Managing Editor of *Good Housekeeping,* to dinner during my first early innocent days of being a writer—before we remodeled the kitchen. Anne and Joan and I planned the menu of baked ham, stuffed peppers, scalloped potatoes, hot rolls, green salad and wild blackberry pie. Everything to be baked, but the salad, and we had only one small oven. As a result the ham was raw, the potatoes curdled, the green peppers burned, the rolls hard and the pie runny but Maggie was darling.

One thing about Good Old Don, his drinks are always frequent and strong, and even without a signal of distress from me, he can be counted on to have those not already under, crawling to the table or at least softened past the point where they might be pettish about scorched string beans.

Don likes to cook too, but like most males in the kitchen even the making of a fried-egg sandwich produces the attitude of a Vienna-trained surgeon repairing the trachea of a new-born baby. "Hand me that pan! Where is the butter? Now some coarse ground pepper, careful not too much. Is the bread buttered? Heat the plates! Have you made the coffee? Hand me the spatula, no, the big one. Move faster, things are getting cold." He demands much of his staff as he busies himself turning the clean kitchen into something that looks as if it had been attacked by a gang of dope-crazed teen-aged vandals.

One of Don's culinary specialties is Monte Cristo sandwiches, a concoction of ham, Swiss cheese, turkey between two slices of white bread, the whole dipped in egg and fried in butter. He will make them any time for anybody but prefers serving them to favorite friends around three A.M. Came our second New Year's Eve on Vashon and we had invited some of our dearest friends to celebrate. The morning of New Year's Eve dawned and I realized that I had what was unmistakably the flu. I was hot and my chest hurt and I didn't even want to read. Don brought me a cup of coffee and two aspirin tablets and then later another cup of coffee and two more aspirin. Each time he asked me wistfully if I didn't feel well enough "to get up now?" I drank the coffee, took the aspirin, got up and washed my face and then got right back in bed again. I felt awful. Like bulbar polio with double pneumonia and a touch of cholera.

At lunchtime Anne brought me a bowl of heavenly vegetable soup she had made especially and asked me hopefully if I didn't feel all right? "Like getting up now?" I ate the soup, took two more aspirin, got up and washed my face then fell back in bed. Later on, Joanie built a fire in the bedroom fireplace and Anne brought me a pot of tea.

"Now do you feel like getting up?" they asked anxiously.

"I feel rotten," I said. "Terrible. I guess you'll have to be the hostesses for the party tonight."

Don came in with some coal for the fire (we were beginning to learn something about fuel by that time) and said, "Oh, you'll be all right by tonight. Just stay quiet this afternoon and you'll feel fine by tonight."

But I didn't. I felt worse if anything and finally reminded the family, who were still urging me to my feet and post at the helm, that after all I had had t.b. and it was time they realized that I was not as big and strong as I apparently looked. I added faintly that my sight was dimming and I ached all over. Anne called Mother, who came out on the next ferry and all I can say is that I know that there have been great strides made in psychiatry and I realize that analysis is a fine thing, but just let somebody try to cut my umbilical cord. Mother merely walks into the house and there is peace. Peace, comfort and smoke.

"I feel horrible," I told her tearfully, "and I'm feverish and all Don and the girls do is try and prod me to my feet, like a sick horse. They're worried about that damn party."

"I don't know why anyone should worry about the party," Mother said, lighting what was undoubtedly her ninetieth cigarette for that day. "The house looks lovely, there is plenty of food and liquor and wood, and unless the people are bores they should have a good time. It's not your fault you're sick and the party will be good experience for the girls. I'm going to move you into my room away from the noise. I've got two hot water bottles in the bed. Mary sent you out these sleeping pills and here's an Angela Thirkell you haven't read."

About two A.M. I was awakened from a deep sleep by Don switching on the light and slapping a plate down on my chest. "Look what I brought you," he said proudly. "Eat it quick, while it's hot."

I knew it was a Monte Cristo sandwich, a big, greasy, hot Monte Cristo sandwich and next to a spinal puncture, it was the very last thing in the world I wanted. I still felt horrible and in addition was half drugged. Weakly but kindly, I said, "I'm really not a bit hungry, dear."

"Of course, you are," Don said heartily, turning on two more hundred-watt lights. "The trouble with you is that you haven't eaten all day. Anyway, this is the very first sandwich I have made tonight and I want you to taste it."

I said, "Why don't you taste it while I wake up?"

"Okay," Don said cheerfully picking up the sandwich and taking a huge bite. Immediately with his mouth open wide he began to howl, " 'Oothpicks, 'atch out for 'oothpicks." He began pulling halves of toothpicks out of the roof of his mouth like quills from a porcupine.

While he was occupied, Anne and Joan came in with a cup of coffee for me. Anne said, "I told you not to break those toothpicks in two and hide them in the sandwiches, Don."

Joan said, "You had better get back to your cooking, Don, the whole house is filled with smoke."

As soon as Don had gone, they both began to laugh hysterically. "What's so funny?" I asked sleepily.

Joan said, "Well, I came out in the kitchen and Don was breaking eggs into a bowl. Squashing them in his hands and letting the egg run through his fingers the way he says chefs do. I noticed a couple of feathers and an awful lot of pepper in the bowl but I didn't say anything until he finished cracking the eggs and began grinding in more pepper. Then I said, 'Aren't you putting an awful lot of pepper in that batter?' He said, 'I haven't put *any* in yet.' I said, 'You did too. I saw it. Look.' I showed him the billions of black specks and he said, 'That isn't pepper.' I asked him what it was then and he said, 'Probably just a little old chicken manure.' Then I looked at the eggs and they were the ones he always gets from that crazy Mrs. Elchin and of course they were covered with feathers and chicken manure. I told Don he'd better throw the eggs out and start over and he said, 'Vitamin B-12 is very healthful. Anyway nobody will know the difference' and kept right on grinding the pepper."

Anne said, "And I told him everybody would puncture the roofs of their mouths on those broken toothpicks but he wouldn't pay any attention. He's using about a pound of butter for each sandwich and he has grease splattered clear up on those high windows."

"How is the party going?" I asked.

"Oh, it's all right," Anne said. "Everybody is talking loud and laughing, Harriet Crawford's drunk, but she was when she came, Mary Arden is acting like a goo-goo over Bob Crawford and Mrs. Roanoke is giving Joan and me hard eyes because we aren't in bed."

Joan said, "Don's been adorable. He only let the fire go out twice."

"What's Margar doing?" I asked.

"Smoking and talking to people," Joan said. "She offered to help Don with the sandwiches but he said he wanted to do the *whole thing himself.*"

"Do you think we should tell Margar about the chicken manure?" Anne asked.

"Let Don tell her," I said, laughing. "After all he's the chef."

"Wow, it's almost two-thirty," Joan said, looking at my clock. "Gee, I love to stay up late."

"Don't you think you'd better go to bed?" I asked anxiously.

"You said we could stay up as late as we wanted on New Year's Eve," Anne said, yawning.

"I know," I said, "but aren't you tired?"

"Kind of," Anne said. "But we don't want to go to bed until we watch the people eat those awful sandwiches. Do you feel better, Mommy?"

"Lots better," I said.

"Well, then we'd better flush this sandwich down the toilet before you get sick again," she said, beginning to giggle. They were both laughing hysterically as they left.

One of the nicest things Don ever did for the girls was to find the "Turkey Squasher" in a small obscure cutlery shop. One fall day when he picked me up at the dentist's, he said with the ecstatic look of a man who has just come upon a ten-pound chunk of ambergris, "I've got something to show you. Something wonderful!"

We drove downtown and after he had parked the car, he took my arm and led me into the cutlery shop. The foxy little man who owned it said, "Ah, ha, you brought her," and disappeared behind a dark green portière at the back of the shop. In a few minutes he came staggering out with a plank about the size of a door, attached to one side of which was a large shiny machine. Setting it down carefully on the counter, he said, "Now, what do you think of that?"

"What is it?" I asked unenthusiastically.

"What is it?" the man repeated scornfully. "What is it? Why it's a carving board. All you do is put the bird here, lower the prongs, set the vise, adjust this screw, loosen this spring nut and the bird is secure, ready to carve."

Don's face bore the enraptured glaze of the true gadget lover. "Isn't it a dandy?" he said. "Just what we needed?"

Taking my clean handkerchief out of my purse, I removed a heavy coating of dust from the machine part, then said evenly to the foxy little man, "Not too much in demand, are they?"

"Very scarce item," he countered quickly. "All hand-made."

"Looks awfully complicated for just carving a turkey," I said.

"Complicated!" Don and the cutlery man said together. "It's not complicated, it's simple."

"How much is it?" I asked suspiciously.

"Only twenty-five dollars," the cutleryman said smoothly, the implication being that twenty-five dollars was a mere coin in the fountain.

"Twenty-five dollars!" I shrieked. "It would be cheaper to send our turkeys to France and have them carved."

"It *is* expensive," Don said seriously, as he stroked the carving board, "but it is very well made and will last a life-time."

"It would last a lifetime if it was made out of crêpe paper," I said scornfully, "because nobody would ever use it. Anyway we can't afford it."

"I know it," Don said sadly. "I just wanted you to see it."

When, with a triumphant smile I said goodbye to the little cutleryman and thanked him for his trouble, I had a feeling he looked smug.

I didn't give another thought to the carving board until Christmas morning when I came downstairs and saw under the tree, at my place, a box as big as a coffin that could only, and of course did, contain a Turkey Squasher.

Owing to about forty unexpected guests and at least twenty expected ones, the Christmas turkey even though the approximate size and weight of an ostrich, was forgotten and cooked to death. It took Anne and Joan and me, all armed with spatulas, to maneuver it onto the Turkey Squasher's board in one piece. After we had propped it up here and there and garnished it with parsley, we summoned Don to carry it to the table. He came eagerly, grasped the handles and started proudly for the dining room. His en-trance was spoiled somewhat by the fact that the Turkey

Squasher would not go through the door frontward and he had to sidle through. Fortunately we had arranged for the turkey to be carved on a serving table by the window. When he had lowered it to its carving position Don called *everyone* to come and see the wonderful new appliance. When all had assembled, he ground a little handle until the machine and prongs were as high as they would go and well above the turkey's breast bone. Then he adjusted a flange, took a reading for weather, checked the oil, twirled a knob or two and nothing happened.

"Where are the directions?" he asked me.

"What directions?" I asked. "You mean instructions on carving?"

"I mean the directions that came with this turkey board," Don said, adding plaintively. "If you were interested you would know."

"I am interested," I said. "In fact I'm starving but you threw away the box the board came in. You probably burned them."

Cleve said, "Say, Mac, there are two wing nuts on this side you haven't loosened and it looks to me like your carburetor's dirty."

Dede's husband said, "Rev her up, Mac, she's still on the ground."

Don said, "Anne and Joan, did you see the directions?"

Joan said, "What do they look like?"

Anne said, "Just keep turning things. It'll work, Don."

Don smiled at her gratefully and pressed a little lever. Instantly the whole machine came down on top of the turkey, squashing it flat. Juice and goblets of stuffing sprayed generously over the onlookers and the window. A big hunk of dark meat skidded off the table right into Tudor's waiting mouth, which surprised him so he could hardly swallow. Anne and Joan began to laugh. Finally everybody, even Don, joined in. For the rest of the Christmas holidays the sight of the turkey carcass, finally in the soup kettle, occasioned great mirth. We still use the Turkey Squasher but only as a carving board, sans the machine.

I remember that when Anne and Joan were quite small one of their favorite expressions was "You want to know somebody I hate?" Well, you want to know somebody I hate? I hate Katherine Reynolds who has no help and invites you to dinner and when you get there she looks beautiful and her house looks beautiful and her husband looks happy and not once does she leave her guests during the cocktail period yet at eight o'clock she summons you to the dining room and there is dinner complete even to hollandaise sauce on the asparagus and Yorkshire pudding around the roast beef and last but worst, if you force her to let you help carry out the plates, you find the sink empty and the kitchen looking as if it had just been painted. There has to be a secret—either she throws her dirty pots and pans down cellar, she has the food sent in from the Olympic Hotel, or she is a hypnotist. My sister Mary is the most well-organized woman I know and entertains constantly, in spite of three adolescents and a doctor husband which is like saying she entertains constantly in spite of advanced arteriosclerosis, but she always has someone in the kitchen. Here on Vashon there ain't no such animal. What I mean to say is that you don't have somebody "in the kitchen." You have another member of the family who shares your table, your problems, and your pleasures and is usually just as unenthusiastic as the family about housework, or you have nobody. In the long haul, I have found it less harassing to make do with a hoer-outer brought in once, twice or thrice a week.

So I am still left with the problem of getting the gravy made without abandoning my part in the colloquy on the real purpose of the United Nations.

"I do everything in the early morning," Mary says blandly. That is all very well as far as peeling the potatoes, washing the romaine and making the cheese dip is concerned. It would also be fine for hot weather dishes, such as jellied chicken, or cold boiled salmon, if we had any hot weather.

The home economist's answer to the problem is the one-dish meal, and she hands out recipes for some ghastly hazelnut, sardine, chocolate chip, lima bean, avocado casserole.

My answer is a large kitchen with a fireplace and comfortable chairs. My next house isn't going to have a living room, or drawing room or parlor at all. Just an enormous kitchen with two dishwashers, two fireplaces, one for me and one for the guests, several couches, one for me, a big bar, four ovens, twelve burners, perhaps television and a record player, and scattered here and there among the couches and chairs, little vending machines filled with peanuts, popcorn and potato chips.

CHAPTER XIII

WHY DON'T YOU
JUST RELAX, BETTY?

W HEN I contemplate my own household and our way of life with fountain pens washed in the Bendix, candy bought for the raccoons, the small fireplace tongs burning up in the cedar tree, my greenhouse devoted to little sailboats, big plastic alligators and suntan oil, twenty-four sheets to the laundry on Mondays, and $183.50 long distance phone bills, I think longingly of a neighbor who always has her cuticle pushed back and buys her ground roundsteak one pound at a time.

"Well, one reason I'm glad we have this house," Anne said, "is because now I can invite all my friends to visit me."

Joan said, "Who am I going to invite? I don't have any friends."

Don said, "I think before anybody invites anybody we should talk things over."

Anne said, "Of course I'm not sure any of my friends would care to come *way* out here?"

Joan said, "Who'll I invite? I don't have any friends."

I said, "Anne and Joan, you can invite your friends, Don can invite his friends, I can invite my friends and if *we* feel like singing 'The Star-Spangled Banner' at three in the morning *we* can."

Don said, "I think we should talk things over. I think I should be consulted."

Anne said, "Of course I'm not sure any of my friends . . ."

But as it turned out everybody had friends and relatives and they were all glad to visit, especially in good weather and nobody ever talked things over until the guests had gone and then often in loud voices, and I learned right away that the big difference between island entertaining and any other kind is that on an island guests stay all night or for two weeks or a couple of years. Even the few rare good sports who try to go home usually miss the last ferry or the ferry company hears you are having people to dinner and knocks down the dolphins or stops running the ferries just for the hell of it.

The point being, if you are not an "I always defrost on Wednesday" kind of housekeeper, but still enjoy having people in for dinner, you can stuff that four gallons of half-finished and a little scorched currant jelly under the sink; tuck the large stack of *Popular Mechanics, The Farm,* and *Country Gentlemans,* which Don insists on keeping on the kitchen window sill so that he can get at them easily, in with the ironing; toss the beach coats, the dog dishes and my manuscripts in the back hall with the vacuum cleaner; light the candles; put some good music on the record player; mix up a pitcher of very dry martinis and you are ready.

But when people stay all night too, such slap-dash methods will not pass muster and there are the items of the so-revealing morning sunlight, the medicine cabinets, and the jam cupboards in the back hall where we also keep old magazines, the Christmas candles, the coloring books and the weed killer.

Of course, there is the thing about staying up until two or three or four A.M. If we have congenial people and they are having a good time, it is easy to stay up most of the night, especially when it is a houseparty and some of the guests are slightly hysterical at being out of their traps, away from clawing little sticky hands for a change. I like to stay up late too and I like to have a good time, but four o'clock in the morning is not a time to make decisions. Shall I clean up before I go to bed and perhaps not get to bed until dawn or let it go and probably be just as tired in the morning and the house will still look like a saloon.

In the meantime, all the guests have popped off as has Don, who keeps calling hoarsely, "Betty, come to bed. Why don't you come to bed, Betty?" Another thing, I love children and almost always have some tiny friend with me. Some tiny friend who goes to bed at seven and gets in my bed at six. Oh well, sleep is just a habit, the psychologists say.

There are all kinds of guests. Fun, no-fun, hard, bores, nasty, crazy, alcoholic, religious-fanatic, old pals who have gotten fat and dull, old pals who have gotten rich and dull, old pals who haven't succeeded and are on the defensive, relatives, babies, foreign friends who know no English dumped on you by Mary, adolescents who play the record player from 7 A.M. to 3 A.M. and paint their toenails while I wash the dishes, bright young friends of Anne and Joan's who are fun, bright young friends of Anne and Joan's who are no fun and don't help, foreign men who light my cigarettes lingeringly and tell me "Youth is so gauche, so raw," then try to lure Anne or Joan out on the porch, and FBI agents who should open a school.

One summer we rented our town house, which we had bought to lessen the domestic shame while the girls were in their last years of school, to five FBI agents with whom we naturally became friends and whom we naturally invited to spend their weekends on Vashon and one of whom Joan later married. Now *that* was a summer I enjoyed.

They helped, in fact, did all the work, portioning it out in a most businesslike way and not accepting any excuses. They were good cooks, they were bright, they sang, they never got drunk, they liked children, they made the beds (there is a housewifely differentiation here between "made" and "spread up warm over the newspapers") and they loved the country. As far as I am concerned J. Edgar Hoover can billet his whole staff on me any old time, for as long as he wants.

My idea of heaven would be an enormous house, preferably one with twenty-four bedrooms and twenty-four bathrooms, thousands of guests, mostly FBI agents and foreign men, a great many excellent unobtrusive servants, and no work to do. As my alternative is a house with four bedrooms, a guesthouse, three davenports, a lawn swing, three chaise longues and the floor, thousands of guests, many of them under four years old, and no servants, I often go six months without getting to the beach. Don says that my problem is that I don't relax. He usually says this to me early in the morning after I have been up until three o'clock anyway and then gotten up again with somebody small who has thrown up in the upper bunk.

I prefer to believe that I am not abnormally tense—that all over the world there are wives who, under similar circumstances, are not relaxing. How could I relax, for instance, when Anne invited her friend "Okay Honey" to spend the summer and that was the year we were building a big kitchen with a fireplace and I was making do in the service room with orange crates for cupboards and no drainboards on the sink? Okay Honey was very small, with enormous blue eyes, long golden brown hair, almost black lipstick, wine-colored fingernails an inch long, and an I.Q. which I estimated to be about twenty. I guess the reason Anne and Joan liked her so much was that she was not pressing with her opinions and she knew so many boys. I say I guess, because, though she was here for over a month, I never heard her say one thing but "Okay, honey."

Don kept growling, "Who invited her? Why am I never consulted about anything any more?" as Anne and Joan and Okay Honey spent hours covering themselves with sun-tan oil and lying motionless on the chaise longues on the porch, painting their toe- and fingernails, listening to records, pinning up their hair and eating. I used to wonder if Anne and

Joan mightn't have bought Okay Honey in a drugstore. She certainly looked as if she could have come wrapped in cellophane and she was unfamiliar with even the simplest forms of housekeeping, such as putting two pieces of bread in the toaster and pushing down the big hard lever.

Anne and Joan were willing, even eager, to cook for her, serve her, wash and iron her clothes, row her in the boat, light her cigarettes, drive her to the movies, make her bed, but if I asked them to empty the ashtrays or pass the cookies, they roared like wounded bison and said, "Work, work, work, that's all we ever do around here! I thought this was *summer vacation!*"

They were also wearing their hair long and limp, their fingernails painted deep maroon, their lips almost black. It was very trying and seemed to be alarmingly permanent. Then one day somebody named Buzz telephoned from Seattle and Okay Honey went to the phone and said, "Okay, honey" and took the next ferry home.

"Buzz is her steady, home on leave from the Navy," Anne and Joan told me, after they had packed her things and driven her to the ferry.

"*Steady!*" I laughed loudly. "And just who were all those millions of other Charlies and Phils and Tommies and Donnies—friends of her mother?"

"Do you always have to be so critical of our friends?" Anne said wearily as she settled herself at the kitchen table with a box of Kleenex, a bottle of polish remover and a new bottle of Deep Plum nail polish.

Of course I'll *never* forget the summer I took care of my sister Alison's three- and five-year-old boys because she was expecting a new baby, and Joanie invited her steady to stay with us because she was so sorry for him because she didn't love him; I invited a dear friend who was an alcoholic but didn't feel that she was quite ready for psychiatry; a couple whom I had met somewhere in the Southwest and carelessly asked to "come and see us any time—we have plenty of room" took me at my word and dropped in for the month of August; my Norwegian cleaning woman's husband had a heart attack; and Anne, who was leading her own life in town being a model, kept bringing home for the weekends and recuperation another model who looked like a Madonna but whose husband was everlastingly blacking her eyes and knocking her against "our new twenty-seven inch T.V. set" because she was so attractive to other men.

The weather was fair and by that I mean gray and cold, but I forced everyone to eat supper on the beach every night —paper plates, no dishes. Things might have worked out after a fashion if my alcoholic friend had not been deeply suspicious of the woman from Arizona, who had one of the first chic short haircuts, and if the woman from Arizona had just once gotten up before three in the afternoon. Her husband was disgustingly hearty and arose and went swimming in the icy Sound at five-thirty A.M. and was lathering around in the kitchen ready for a *big* breakfast at six.

When the woman from Arizona did finally appear, she demanded that I sit with her while she ate her breakfast, which I was glad to do because it was sitting. However, we would no more than get settled at the table and she, with a few raspberry seeds between her teeth, would be outlining in detail the biography of Ivan Fegenscu she was readying herself to write, when my alcoholic friend, by this time on her eighteenth bourbon on rocks, would weave out and hiss in my ear, "Wash out lil' lady, tha's the ole build-up"; or Don would telephone from the dock in Seattle (sometimes he can't wait to bring the bad news all the way home) that we were $598 overdrawn and he had forgotten the meat; or one of Alison's little boys would come sloshing up from the beach to tell me that he had fallen out of the rowboat in his last clean clothes; or in a low throbbing voice Joan would plead with me to do something about her steady who was contemplating suicide in the porch swing; or my sister Mary would call up and tell me that she was on her way out with Mrs. Ellis and her three children or "Arenthau Salavochic and his adorable wife, actually a count and countess but working for the Ellises just to learn American ways and they don't speak a word of English but you will love them and they want to meet you more than anything in the world and I am bringing a salmon and what else do you need?" As I write this the thought occurs that it is a very strange thing that the ferry has never broken down bringing people —only when it is supposed to be taking them away.

Then of course there was the Saturday afternoon when Don and the girls and I came staggering along the beach with our loads of groceries and a male voice yelled "Yoohoo!" at us from the *roof* of our house and it was Don's old buddy, the very same old buddy who, refusing to believe that "ole Don" had finally taken the step, spent our weekend honeymoon in Don's apartment *with* us.

Although he did not come down off the roof, we drew closer to home and finally could see clearly that Old Buddy's face was suspiciously flushed and that he was crawling around loosening the shakes in none too steady a fashion. I sent Don out to "talk" to him while the girls and I put the groceries away. Mary and some Navy people were expected on the next ferry and I still had a great deal of rapid stuffing and tidying and flower arranging to do and I didn't intend to be hampered by Old Buddy.

I set Anne to making clam and cream cheese dip and Joan to filling little dishes with nuts and sunflower seeds and olives. When I had finished my tidying I opened the back door and called to Don to start the fire. Don didn't answer, but Buddy peered at me over the edge of the roof on the steep water side and said, "Heigh-ho!" I slammed back into the house and into Don who was making two drinks.

"You've got to get him out of here," I said, wiping the soda water out of my eyes.

"Why?" Don asked mildly. "He's up on the roof out of the way."

"I don't think you're funny," I said. "Mary and those

Navy people are coming on the next ferry and anyway think of the girls."

"Yes, think of us," the girls said.

"Why don't you all relax?" Don said. "Everything will work out. Let's all be sweet."

He went out the door carrying the two drinks.

Leaving Anne and Joan with the hors d'oeuvres I dashed upstairs, washed my face, put on my tight black slacks and a white sweater and was splashing on perfume when from my open bedroom window I heard Mary and the Navy people crunching along in the sand, and then from overhead I heard Buddy calling out to them "Heigh-ho!"

Anne, who had come in to inspect my makeup and borrow a handful of perfume, said, "Oh, Mommy, honestly, I think he's perfectly disgusting. Can't Don get rid of him?"

I said, "He's Don's oldest friend, Andy, we'll just have to be understanding."

It really wasn't too hard as Mary and her friends were fun and Old Buddy stayed on the roof all evening only asking for occasional favors in the way of drinks and the binoculars so he could examine the crevasses on the moon.

One of the Navy officers (there were three) had brought a guitar and after dinner we went out on the porch in the moonlight and he played sad songs and sang to us. It must have been after three when I was stumbling around emptying ashtrays and brushing potato chips off the mantel while Don hissed at me from the upper hall, "Why don't you come to bed?" that I remembered about Buddy and realized that we had not heard from him for some time.

"What are you going to do about Old Buddy?" I whispered hoarsely. "He's still out on the roof."

"Nothing," Don said. "His responsibility. Now come to bed."

"I'll be along in a minute," I said, sweeping the hearth.

As I put the glasses in the dishwasher and put away the liquor and the enormous amount of equipment Don uses for fried-egg sandwiches, I thought again about Buddy out there on the roof in the cold night air. What if he rolled off and broke his neck? What if the raccoons, who favor our roof as a playfield, clawed him?

Humming happily, I went up to bed.

The next thing I knew there was sunlight dappling the rug, Don was handing me a silver fizz and up from the patio floated the cheerful thrumming of a guitar.

"What happened to Old Buddy?" I asked Don as I patted the silver fizz off my lips with the sheet. "I was so worried about him last night I couldn't sleep."

Giving the cord that pulled back the draperies a yank, Don said, "Take a look."

Draining my gin fizz, I got warily out of bed, walked to the window and looked out. Below me, spread-eagled in the lawn swing, a white goatskin rug clutched around his throat, was Old Buddy. One of the Navy officers was kneeling beside him strumming his guitar, the other was propping up his head, feeding him a gin fizz.

Anne and Joan and Mary came in with coffee. Anne said, "You'd better hurry and drink this, Mommy, that Lieutenant Commander and I have breakfast almost ready. We are making buttermilk hotcakes and sausages."

Joan said, "What's that one's name with the guitar, Aunty Mary?"

"Johnny," Mary said.

"Well, Johnny and I are going out sole spearing right after breakfast."

Lighting a cigarette, Mary said, "It's heavenly out here, Betty. So relaxing."

CHAPTER XIV

ADVICE, ANYBODY?

I DISLIKE telephoning and have never been able to approach the telephone with the easy nonchalance of most people. My sister Mary, for instance, who embarks upon any telephone conversation with the zest of a person carrying new ice skates happening on a huge frozen lake and can glide effortlessly from the stupidity of publishers to cooking pheasant in sour cream to the dangers of cortone to the peccadillos of her recent maid, for two hours without even changing hands. One of my sister Dede's favorite stories is about Mary and the telephone. It seems that Dede's little boy, the second one, had an attack of asthma and so Dede, as we all do, called Mary for sympathy and unofficial medical advice. Mary took the call in her bedroom where she holds many of her medical and psychiatric clinics. Before Dede had half finished the symptoms Mary had made her diagnosis and prescribed the treatment. She said, "There is only one way to handle asthma. You must:

1. Remove all wool from the room.
2. Remove all dust from the room.
3. Wash down all the walls and woodwork.
4. Put an allergy cover on the mattress.
5. Put an allergy cover on the pillow.
6. Remove all toys which might contain allergic materials.

7. See that the child has plenty of rest.
8. Bring the child down to the laboratory for interdermals.
9. What little stinker put shrimps in my wastebasket?

Lifting up the telephone receiver gives me immediate constipation of the brain and long distance calls also affect my vocal cords so that who ever I'm talking to thinks he has been mistakenly connected with the porch rocker. Even so, every single time I am on the telephone Don materializes at my side and gives me long accusing looks indicating that *my* frivolity is delaying *his* call to the coroner. As soon as I spot Don I try to finish up any conversation but he seldom wants to use the phone, just wants me to know that he disapproves of women telephoning to other women. This is rather common among husbands, I am told, especially Elizabeth Gage Wheaton's husband, Everett, who one day grabbed their telephone by the throat, yanked it out by the roots and threw it through a window that was not open.

I do not remember just how I first got entangled with Elizabeth Gage Wheaton and Everett and Little Donny and Little Gail and Little P.J. ("Percival Jarod after Everett's father because Everett insisted but it is such an ugly name we only use the initials") and Baby (Little Elizabeth Gage). I think it was through my sister Mary and the telephone. Anyway Elizabeth Gage was terribly nervous and run-down and cried a great deal and her children all wet their beds and their panties and her husband had a great big boat even though Elizabeth Gage didn't even have a washing machine and Mary thought that if I could find them a place on our beach they would all sort of dry out and cheer up. Mary thought also I could help Elizabeth Gage fix herself up and show her how to clean a house and discipline her children. She was terribly intelligent but not very well organized.

Fortunately, I could not find them a place on our beach because there weren't any for rent, but I did find, at the other end of the island, an attractive beach house with two sets of double bunks, another bed in the living room, knotty pine walls, a big fireplace and a Bendix. By that time I had met Elizabeth Gage who had big damp blue eyes, hair like sphagnum moss, and didn't wear a brassière.

I was quite excited about the house—it was attractive— the beach was sandy, the rent was only seventy-five a month and there was that washing machine. I called Mary so that she could tell Elizabeth Gage and I wouldn't have to tele- phone, but Mary had gone fishing in Canada so I had finally to call Elizabeth Gage myself. Elizabeth Gage's telephone voice was low and sad like a receptionist in a funeral parlor and when she said, "Hello there, honey," I almost began to cry myself she sounded so beaten and woebegone. I told her about the marvelous house I had found and she said well, she'd look at it but she was thinkin' more of a little farm. I said that I didn't know of any farms for rent, in fact I didn't know of anything else for rent. She said, "It was darlin' of you to look, honey, but I'm not sure Everett will approve. He has been so mean lately suckin' up liquor like a hog and sleepin' in the guestroom and all, but we'll come over to- morrow. Isn't there a ferry about ten?"

Elizabeth Gage was a graduate of Smith College and her father was a prominent attorney somewhere in Texas and she was really beautiful, but when she and Little Donny and Little Gail and Little P.J. and Baby got out of the Buick station wagon the next morning I felt like a California fruit grower in *The Grapes of Wrath*. Nobody's hair was combed, all faces were dirty in a grubby long-standing way, supple- mented by chocolate, doughnut crumbs, and suckers, and all but Elizabeth Gage, Sr., had on wet panties.

Elizabeth Gage was wearing a pair of faded jeans with enormous legs and a broken zipper, a dirty white T-shirt of Everett's, no brassière and red satin mules. The children had on wet dirty coveralls with at least one strap pinned with big rusty safety pins, dirty T-shirts and scuffed brown shoes with broken knotty laces. Like Elizabeth Gage, the children had good features and lovely blue eyes and could have been attractive if they had been clean or dry. Their thin, limp, light hair hung in bangs below their eyebrows and their scalps were crusty with oil and dirt.

When she was with her children Elizabeth Gage seemed in a kind of coma—a coma produced by the millions of little attendant interruptions and confusions with which children, especially completely untrained ones, delight in surrounding themselves. She also seemed tired to the point of collapse and on the brink of tears. I suggested a cup of coffee and she accepted gratefully, sinking down into one of the kitchen chairs like a sack of meal. While we drank our coffee at the kitchen table, the children raced through and in and out of the house like a pack of hounds after a fox. Doors slammed, windows rattled, vases quivered, Tudor barked, Baby, who was only two, fell down and bellowed. Elizabeth Gage didn't even glance at them. She put four lumps of sugar and plenty of cream in her coffee, stirred it sadly and said, "I know I'm too fat and should be reducin' but I'm so darn tired all the time I just have to take sugar and cream to keep up my energy."

"Maybe you need iron," I said, flinching a little as the children streaked past, joggled my elbow and spilled my coffee on the clean tablecloth.

"Oh, no," Elizabeth Gage said, lighting a cigarette. "I just had a physical and the doctor said I'm in perfect health. He said it's all mental 'cause I'm so worried about Everett. I just told him everything—I told him how Everett drank and didn't come home to dinner and slept in the guest-room. . . ." The children galloped past again and sent one of the braided rugs skidding into the fireplace. "The doctor was real sweet. He said I needed a vacation. I told Everett and he said why don't we go to San Francisco and I said I couldn't because Little P.J. hasn't finished his allergy shots, he has terrible asthma you know, and Everett said, 'Well my God, I didn't expect to take the kids. I thought you and I were going to have a vacation' and I just told him that even if he didn't like his own children, I did, and they would go wherever I went and if he didn't want them along then perhaps he didn't want me either. Oh, we had an awful row. I cried for two weeks straight."

The children had paused in their marathon to ask Elizabeth Gage for something to eat. While awaiting her reply they pushed the heavy oak captain's chairs back and forth on the brick floors with a raw scraping sound that was very disturbing. Ignoring the children's requests for food and the scraping noise, Elizabeth Gage went on, "On Thursday night I just called Mama in Texas and I was cryin' so hard she could hardly understand me and Little P.J. pinched Baby's fingers in the desk drawer and she was bawlin' and honestly Mama was scared to death and wanted me to come right home but I told her that I couldn't go anywhere until Little P.J. finished his allergy shots and she said she would fly up and I told her not to bother as I didn't know where I would be but I did tell her how wonderful Mary has been to me and she was tryin' to get me a house on the beach and she said to let her know and Donny, honey, did you make that big puddle on Betty's clean floor—shame on you a big boy of six! Where was I . . . oh, yes and so I told her that you were lookin' for a beach house for us and she said to let her know where and she would fly up and was there anything that she and Daddy could get for me and I said no nothin' because last Christmas they sent me a sable scarf and I've never had it on because you certainly can't wear sables with jeans and that's all I ever wear—No, sister, don't play with the barometer . . . where was I . . ."

My cleaning woman was there that day and I tried tactfully to suggest leaving the children with her but Elizabeth Gage said, "Love me, love my dog and anyway Baby won't stay with anybody but me." Then I suggested giving the children something to eat but she said, "Oh no, they've been just stuffin' on the boat. Candy, pop, ice cream and Little P.J. insisted on eatin' a chocolate bar and he knows he's allergic to it and will probably have asthma all night long."

Fortunately the real estate man was busy with some

people who wanted to buy a farm and asked me if I would take the key and show my friend the house. As we drove away I saw him come to the doorway and peer after us. I resolved to remember to tell him that Mr. Wheaton was a prominent attorney with a big boat. The minute we got to the house the children climbed in the bunks and bounced on the davenport in their wet panties while Elizabeth Gage looked vaguely around and told me about another mean thing Everett did and how she cried for four weeks when he bought the boat and of course would never go out in it because the children might fall overboard—after all they were so little with Donny the oldest only six and Baby just a baby. . . .

I asked her how she liked the house, making a big fuss over the Bendix, and she said, "Well I really wanted a little farm—you know so the children could have a pony and it does seem rather cramped—I'll see. . . ."

I told her she'd have to make up her mind right then, as there were lots of people looking for places to rent on Vashon, and she finally said, "I did have my heart set on a little old farm but I guess this will have to do. . . ."

From that day forward Elizabeth Gage called me every single day and talked for at least an hour telling me how mean Everett was and how tired she was and how she had really counted on a little farm and if I heard of anything to let her know. . . .

Two weeks later Little P.J. finished his allergy shots and Elizabeth Gage and the children moved in and I invited them to dinner that night and almost fainted when I saw mean ole Everett who looked just like a harassed edition of Gregory Peck. Elizabeth Gage had on the same jeans, another dirty T-shirt and nurse's white oxfords. The children were as wet and dirty and boisterous but when they began to race through the house Everett shouted, "GO DOWN TO THE BEACH, ALL OF YOU!" and they went quite quickly and Elizabeth Gage moved over beside me at the sink and said in a low conspiratorial voice, "See how mean he is.

That's what liquor does to him." As Don had not even finished making the martinis I reasoned that maybe Everett had been drinking before they came. But when Don handed him one a minute or so later, he said, "I've been waiting all day for this."

I had intended to have the children eat in the kitchen or at the umbrella table while we ate in the dining room, but Elizabeth Gage got tears in her eyes and said that not eating with their parents made children feel left out and her children were never going to feel left out and so we ate dinner to the constant scraping of the chairs, interruptions in the form of "Don't cry, darling, Betty didn't know that none of us like peas." "Just push that to one side, Gail, honey, Mommy'll fix you a peanut butter sandwich later on." "Don't hit sister, P.J." "Oh, look, Baby spilled her milk on the nice clean tablecloth, naughty baby." "Children, don't throw your food on the floor—the doggy doesn't want your potatoes, Donny. . . ."

Everett looked defeated and embarrassed and Don gave the details of his plan for a children's wing which he intends to build some day—plans involving steel bars, cement floors, noiseproof walls—all very unsubtle. After dinner, which seemed interminable, I suggested that Elizabeth Gage might like to put the children down for naps. She said, "Oh, no, they don't like to nap in strange houses. They will just run around. Food does seem to give children a great deal of energy, doesn't it?"

Don and Everett retired to the porch to drink brandy and every time one of the children put a toenail on the porch, Everett shouted, "GO DOWN TO THE BEACH!" even after it was dark.

At one A.M. all the children except the baby, who had fallen asleep on the living room floor, were in the kitchen scraping the chairs and whining, Elizabeth Gage was sitting at the kitchen table drinking bourbon and water and telling me how mean Everett was and how she couldn't wash her hair oftener than once every two months because her scalp was so sensitive. Don and Everett had moved indoors in front of the fire. Everett was still drinking brandy and he was quite drunk. When they finally left, about ten minutes of two, Elizabeth Gage paused dramatically at the kitchen door with Baby in her arms and Little P.J. clinging to her knees and said, "Pray for us, honey. Everett's too drunk to drive, but he will anyway."

The next morning about eleven she telephoned to tell me how sorry she was that they had stayed so late, but I was such a darlin' and so understandin' she just wasn't aware of the time when I was around and the drive home was just horrible but they made it and she was so exhaused from it all she had just waked up but Everett was still asleep. I asked her how the children were and she said they had torn the house to pieces and nobody would take the blame, but one of them had broken Daddy's telescope and he was just goin' to be wild.

She called every day the next week talking about an hour each time, to tell me how small the house was, how cramped the kitchen, how they had really wanted a farm, how she wouldn't let the children go near the beach because of the poison jellyfish (there aren't any) and the undertow (the house was on a small very quiet harbor) and how she was thinkin' of having the Bendix taken out she was so terrified one of the children might get ground up in it. Each time she telephoned Don materialized beside me and looked pained and after I had finally disengaged myself from her, I would tell him how sorry I felt for her but how infuriating she was and he said, "My God, let's chop it off. She's like a barnacle."

Friday she called and asked if Don and I wouldn't like to go on their boat with them. I hurriedly advised her of the telephone number of a very capable mature baby-sitter but she said, "Oh, I think I'll just take the children, they love the water so much." I said, "I wouldn't risk it, if I were you. They are *so* active and they might fall overboard." She said,

"I'm going to buy them all life jackets." So I said I'd talk to Don and call her back.

Don said he liked Everett immensely, but he couldn't stand another session with those brats and did I know that the last time they were at the house one of them had broken the record player and somebody had been playing with the barometer and one of them put the hearthbroom in the fire and there was Fig Newton ground into the wing chair and wet panty marks on both davenports. I kept putting off calling Elizabeth Gage and finally, about ten that night, Everett called and said that he had engaged the baby-sitter and they would come by for us the next morning and would Anne and Joan like to come along too? I told him that Anne and Joan were going away for the weekend, but Don and I would be ready.

Saturday turned out to be a perfect boating day with a clear faraway pale blue sky, a stiff breeze from the north and water well wrinkled but not too choppy. Don and I had new dark blue top siders and I had a new long high-necked striped shirt supposedly worn by Basque fishermen, but which Don surveyed critically and finally said made me look exactly like a hornet. However, I felt nautical and Vogue-ish and, anyway, one nice thing about Elizabeth Gage even if I wore my old bathrobe with one sleeve torn out and rubbers I knew I would be better dressed than she would be.

At about ten o'clock, as Don was fixing his emergency sailing kit of Scotch and Scotch and Scotch, there was a honking out in front and I looked out the window and a boat just a tiny bit smaller than the *Queen Mary* with sails was easing up. "Good God," I said to Don, "do you suppose this is Everett's boat?"

"Could very well be," Don said without emotion. "Everett said something about taking college boys along as crew."

"Well, no wonder Elizabeth Gage has no washing machine," I said heatedly. "I'm surprised they have *food*. That boat must have cost at least fifty thousand dollars and imagine the upkeep."

"Speaking of food," said Don, "are we supposed to be bringing any?"

"No," I said. "I offered but Elizabeth Gage said she had everything."

One of the crew rowed in for us in the dinghy and Everett immediately said that I looked terribly chic and where did I get the shirt. He looked wistfully at Elizabeth Gage who had on red pedal pushers with enormous legs, an over-all jacket, the kind plumbers wear, and high-heeled straw sandals. She was different though, without the children. Not at all sad, very witty and a superb cook. As is always the case on a boat, hunger was a constant thing but Elizabeth Gage produced marvelous food at intervals until one o'clock in the morning when we finally dropped anchor in the bay by our house, and there were several other couples besides the Wheatons and Don and me aboard and the galley left much to be desired. When Elizabeth Gage wasn't handing around loaves of hot fresh French bread hollowed out and packed with fried chicken, she was baking strawberry shortcake or brioches or stirring tiny hot meatballs to be speared with toothpicks. I was amazed and even Don heaped lavish compliments on her. She only said in her sad little voice, "It's nothin'—I like to cook, it's easy for me."

That night when we were brushing our teeth, I said to Don, "There must be more to that marriage than meets the eye. Elizabeth Gage was charming today, and she is certainly an inspired cook. She couldn't be as inefficient as she seems."

Don said, "Connie Pegler is certainly attractive."

Connie Pegler had jet-black curly hair, deep blue eyes, dimples, weighed less than a hundred pounds and bought her clothes in the children's department. She had given me these statistics just as I was asking for a third piece of chicken and accepting a second ear of corn. Elizabeth Gage had said, "Now you hush up, Connie, just because you're no bigger than a gnat you have no call to make the rest of us feel like hippopotami."

Like many little women, Connie Pegler liked to curl up on big things like davenports or other people's husbands' laps.

Her own husband was nice in a pale factual way. He wore glasses, had plump pink arms sprinkled with tan freckles and little stiff red hairs, and he knew more about plankton than the Bureau of Fisheries. It was while he was telling me about plankton in southern waters that I noticed Connie and Don heading for the prow with a blanket. The moon had just come up and we were in Admiralty Inlet just off Marrowstone Island. Everything was silvery and very romantic. I looked hopefully for Everett but he was occupied, I was happy to see, with Elizabeth Gage. They were lying back on a coil of rope looking at the stars. Her head was on his shoulder and he was giving her drags of his cigarette. I had found it very frustrating to sit in a pool of moonlight and listen to Paul Pegler drone on about protozoa and entomostracans. Also it had gotten quite chilly.

I said, "For anybody as adorable as Connie Pegler keeps telling everybody she is, she certainly nabbed herself a dull husband."

Don said, "You should know, you spent enough time with him."

I said, "What else could I do with you sneaking off in dark corners with Connie and a blanket."

Don said, "Oh, for heaven's sake. Connie had forgotten to bring a jacket. She was cold."

"I'll bet," I said.

The next morning when Elizabeth Gage called me up she said, "Say, lil ole Connie was sure makin' time with Don, wasn't she?"

"I despise little women," I said bitterly. "Especially ones with naturally curly hair and eyelashes seven inches long."

"I thought you'd feel that way," Elizabeth Gage said,

"and really, honey, there's no point because she's just crazy about that weevil she's married to. Always has been and he's so dull he even bores P.J. It's sure hard to realize though that Connie has four children. She is a whiz, her house is always slick as a whistle, she always looks pretty and she is one of those mean little things that keeps their figures no matter how many children they have. She is always after me to reduce, but I just can't. I'm too tired all the time."

"How was the baby-sitter?" I asked.

"Oh, that poor woman," Elizabeth Gage said mournfully. "When we got home all the kids were up runnin' around and bawlin' and she was almost out of her mind. I'll never leave them again, I told Everett."

"Maybe that's the trouble, maybe you don't leave them enough," I said.

"Be that as it may," Elizabeth Gage said levelly, "that woman certainly doesn't know the first thing about handling children. I don't know who recommended her to you, but she's no good at all."

"I'm awfully sorry," I said. "Lots of people on the beach have used her and they think she is fine. Anyway, you and Everett seemed to be having a wonderful time last night."

"Oh, we were," Elizabeth Gage said without enthusiasm. "He is always as sweet as peaches in front of people, but when we got in the house he hit the ceiling. He said we have the worst-behaved brats in the world and I cried and the children cried and it was real embarrassin' for the sitter."

Poor Elizabeth Gage, she was really so sweet but she was letting her children ruin her marriage. I said, "Why don't you all come to supper. We'll have it on the beach."

"Oh, that would be fun," she said, "but Everett's got to take the boat back to the yacht club. He wanted me to come along but I can't leave the poor little children with a sitter again. I sure wish I could think of somebody. It would mean so much to Everett. Of course I don't know a soul on the island but you. Oh, well, I'll just have to tell Everett."

"Leave them with me," I said, wondering as the words left my mouth what I would tell Don and wasn't I just trading places with Elizabeth Gage and ruining *my* marriage with *her* children.

"Oh, honey, you really mean it?" she said. "You aren't just foolin'?"

"Of course I'm not," I said bravely, looking around to see if Don was within hearing distance.

"Oh, Betty, you're wonderful!" she said. "The sweetest person in the whole world and the children will be so thrilled, they adore you."

At this point Don materialized beside me and so I said quickly, "Don wants the phone, I'll see you in a little while."

"Who were you talking to?" Don asked. "Elizabeth Gage?"

"Yes," I said.

"Do they want us to go out in the boat again?" he asked eagerly.

"Well, no," I said. "Everett has to take the boat in to the yacht club and Elizabeth Gage was just telling me how much she'd like to go along."

"Why doesn't she?" Don asked.

"She's going to," I said and went upstairs to put rubber sheets on all the beds. Mercifully Elizabeth Gage was in a great hurry when she delivered the children and drove away before I herded them into the kitchen and Don yelled, "Good God, what's this?"

I said, "We're going to have a good time, aren't we, children?" Baby began to scream. I picked her up and she screamed louder. "Do you know what's the matter with her?" I yelled at Little Donny.

"Uh, uh," he said, his forefinger in his nose up to the second joint.

Little Gail said, "Yesterday Baby cried from early in the morning until way late last night when Mommy came home."

Little P.J. said, "I'm hungry."

I said, "I'll make some sandwiches and we'll all go down to the beach." I put Baby down and she stretched out on the floor and began pounding her heels in time to her screaming. Leaning over I yelled, "Want a cookie, Baby?" No answer. "Want some candy, Baby?"

Little Donny said, "She's sleepy. Mommy said so when she brought her over."

I picked up Baby, carried her kicking and shrieking upstairs and into our bathroom, ran a full tub of water, peeled off her gray, wet clothes and dumped her in. She stopped screaming and began to play. The other children who had crowded in with us said, "We want a bath too." I told them to start undressing but they said they didn't know how. I told Little Donny who was six and Little Gail who was five that they were big enough to be undressing themselves and now was a good time to learn. When I had them all in the tub I poured in a whole box of bubble bath, tossed in some little plastic boats I keep for just such emergency and went downstairs for the shampoo, some dishtowels, a huge piece of oiled silk I kept sprinkled clothes in and some scissors.

I washed all the hair to the accompaniment of blood-curdling howls and great flailing of arms and legs, scrubbed them all thoroughly, rinsed everybody off in the shower, then took them out one by one. After I had dried them, I sprinkled them plentifully with bath powder, swathed them in dishtowel diapers covered with oilsilk and one of Don's pajama tops pinned over. Then I combed their hair, cut the girls' bangs, brought them down to the kitchen, gave them peanut butter sandwiches, milk and ice cream and put them all down for naps. After I had scoured out the bathtub I put all of their clothes in the Bendix. I felt very noble, like a Red Cross worker in a flood area.

When Don came in for lunch, he asked suspiciously, "What have you done with them?"

"Bathed them and put them down for naps," I said virtuously.

"Why do you get yourself into these traps?" Don said.

"Because I'm unselfish," I said. "I try to do nice things for other people. I don't just sit around thinking about myself all the time."

"You're not unselfish," Don said. "You're just a sucker. I'll bet you ten to one Elizabeth Gage has had somebody taking care of those brats of hers ever since she had them. Anyway why does she need help so much? Everett makes lots of money and he told me that Elizabeth Gage could have a nurse and a maid if she wanted."

"A likely story," I said. "She didn't even have a washing machine but I notice that Everett has a fifty thousand dollar yacht."

Don said, "I think Elizabeth Gage is one of those women who likes to be pitiful. She gives me a pain."

Just then Connie and Paul Pegler came in. Connie was wearing the tiniest pair of white shorts I'd ever seen and a hand-knit, burnt-orange, turtle-necked sweater. She looked beautiful. Don fixed drinks and headed for the living room. I quickly suggested that we all go out on the porch because the children were asleep in the bedrooms off the balcony.

"What children?" Connie asked.

"Oh, I'm taking care of Little Donny and Little Gail and Little P.J. and Baby," I said airily.

"So that Elizabeth Gage can have dinner with Everett and try to make the mean ole thing happy?" Connie said, laughing.

"That's the picture," Don said.

Connie curled up on the white chaise longue, the largest and most becoming spot on the porch, and said, "Listen, Betty. I've known Elizabeth Gage and Everett Wheaton for years and years. I have also taken care of Little Donny and Little Gail and Little P.J. and Baby so that poor little Elizabeth Gage could have dinner with mean ole Everett and try to make him happy. Would you like to know what the next step is?—you get the children for two days, then for two weeks and then for the summer. You hose them down, cut their hair and try to housebreak them. The minute Elizabeth Gage gets them home she undoes all your good work—nobody is goin' to tell her how to bring up her children. Then you get Elizabeth Gage and the children because Everett is drinkin' and he can't stand the children and he is so mean and once he even told Elizabeth Gage she was sloppy and he was sick of livin' in a hog wallow. They will stay with you for a week or two—in the meantime of course your own husband moves out because Elizabeth Gage immediately makes any household into a rabbit warren. If you are really a sucker you try to clean up Elizabeth Gage—put her on a diet perhaps, even cut her hair and give her a Toni. Then one fine day Everett appears—drunk because he has been so lonely —Elizabeth Gage runs into his arms—he says what have you done to yourself—she says that mean old Betty cut my hair and made me diet—he says where are the children—she says that mean old Betty has them all takin' naps all the time (this is all whispered, of course, with Everett giving you dirty looks over her shoulder). So they scoop up the children and leave and all the way home Elizabeth Gage entertains Everett with all the mean things she has said about him, only she puts them in your mouth and the next time you see Everett he either doesn't speak or barely chips off one small icy hello. Of course you and Elizabeth Gage know the same people and you're bound to run into each other and she can be cute and funny and before you know it another summer has rolled around and she has another baby—the others are still wetting their panties and their beds—Everett is still drinkin' and bein' mean and, if you're a softie like me, you're off to the races again."

I knew that Connie was probably telling the truth but it was hard to give up my Red Cross work so suddenly—to part with my picture of Elizabeth Gage, thin and tastefully dressed with her hair combed and wearing a brassière, standing in the doorway of an immaculate house, surrounded by clean dry children, waiting for Everett, who would have gained a little weight and lost most of the deep furrows in his cheeks. After the reconciliation, of course, they would all come down to my house to thank me, with tears streaming down their faces, for saving their marriage.

Then Anne and Joan came home and after they had been introduced Joan said, "You look awful, Betty, what's the matter? What have you been doing?" I noticed then that I was awfully rumpled and damp and remembered also that I had not put the children's clothes in the dryer. I jumped up and ran out to the service room, the girls following. As I took the things out of the Bendix, Anne said, "What are those grubby little things?"

"Elizabeth Gage's children's clothes," I said. "I gave them a bath. They are upstairs taking naps."

"Not in our rooms," the girls shrieked.

"I'm afraid so," I said. "But I put rubber sheets on the beds."

"Oh, Mommy," Anne said. "Those children are just gruesome."

"No they aren't," I said stoutly. "They are just pitiful and neglected. Now let's go out on the porch."

The children awakened from their naps about three. Baby opened her eyes and her mouth at the same time and shrieked and shrieked and shrieked. She didn't even stop for breath but like a singer pulled in new air via her diaphragm while holding one high shrill note. Then Connie appeared in the bathroom and yelled at the top of her voice, "BABY, STOP THAT NOISE!" To my astonishment she did. Leaning against the basin, Connie said, "I had that for two weeks once, only it was Little P.J. Paul finally stopped him. He yelled louder than P.J. It's the only way."

After Paul and Connie had gone Anne and Joan helped me with the children. We had them all fed and in bed again at six-thirty—then went out on the patio and I had a martini while the girls broiled steaks. It was very peaceful. After the second martini I felt sorry for Elizabeth Gage all over again. I said, "Andy, couldn't you fix Elizabeth Gage's hair?"

"Sure I could," Anne said, "but she'd have to wash it first. Imagine washing your hair only once every two months. Ugh."

Don said, "Let's talk about something else."

Joan said, "You know, Betty, you're just asking for trouble when you try to change Elizabeth Gage or her children. She must like the way she is or she wouldn't be like that."

Anne said, "Oh, that's not fair, Joanie. She has four babies and she's always tired."

Joan said, "Connie Pegler has four babies too, she told me. Wow, she's pretty."

Don said, "Can't we talk about something else?"

When Elizabeth Gage and Everett came for the children, about 1:45 A.M., they were both pretty high. Elizabeth Gage was flushed and disheveled and really looked awfully pretty even if she hadn't combed her hair, had two runs in her stockings and a great many spots on her suit. We had a nightcap with them then Elizabeth Gage and I went upstairs to retrieve the children. On the way up Elizabeth Gage said, "Where are Anne and Joan?"

"Oh, they're sleeping in the guesthouse," I said. "They love it up there." This was not exactly true as Anne and Joan had finally been driven to the guesthouse like sheep to the slaughter, reluctant and bleating.

The minute Baby opened her eyes and saw Elizabeth Gage she began to scream. Elizabeth Gage picked her up and murmured into her neck, "Poor little Baby. Did Mommy leave her with mean ole Betty? Did she miss her Mommy?" As Elizabeth Gage murmured and cooed Baby stopped screaming long enough to give me a triumphant look over her mother's shoulder. Then we gathered up the other children who were all wet and sad and cross. Elizabeth Gage made them sadder by telling them how pitiful they were— how mean Mommy was to go off and leave them—how mean Daddy was to make Mommy go off and leave them. She asked me if she could borrow the pajama tops and a blanket to take them home in and I said yes and so she herded them downstairs and through the house and up the backstairs and then Everett who was having another nightcap with Don wouldn't come right away. Elizabeth Gage cried, all the children cried and I finally pushed Everett out the door.

The next morning Elizabeth Gage called me up and told me that she was sorry that I had felt it necessary to give her children a bath. She tried to keep them clean but it was so hard, and she hadn't wanted the girls' bangs cut as she was trying to grow them out so they could wear pretty little ribbons and Little Donny had said that they had been in bed most of the time and she was certainly sorry her children had been so much trouble but after all I had *asked* to take care of them—it certainly had not been *her* idea. . . .

I found myself apologizing and explaining earnestly that the only reason I had given Baby a bath was because that was the only way I could stop her crying and the other children had asked to get in the tub, and so on, and so on. Elizabeth Gage listened politely then crisply said goodbye. I never saw the blanket or the pajama tops again.

Anne and Joan were very dramatic about their rooms and Anne threw all the bedclothes, excluding the mattress only because she couldn't lift it, out onto the patio and told me to have them "disinfected." Joan said her room "smelled."

I learned from Connie that a Mrs. Anderson and her husband moved in to the cabin next to the Wheatons and for the rest of that summer she got Little Donny and Little Gail and Little P.J. and Baby and finally of course Elizabeth Gage because Everett was drinkin' because "that cabin Betty made us take is so cramped we all feel like animals."

When I saw Elizabeth Gage on the ferry the other day it was the first time in five years. She seemed very glad to see me and, as we drank our coffee and she ate two doughnuts ("I should be reducin' but I'm so nervous and tired"), she told me that she and Everett have bought an old run-down farm on the west side of the island. They don't have lights or running water but the children have a pony, and there is a nice dock for Everett's newer, much bigger boat. They have six children now—Little Mary Louise and Little Alexandra Dean (Baby) and Elizabeth is very pregnant with a seventh. She hopes it will be Little Everett, Jr. All the children had runny noses and most of them had wet panties and hair hanging in their eyes. Elizabeth Gage's hair still looked like sphagnum moss and she had on maternity jeans, a dirty T-shirt with no brassière, what was almost certainly a corduroy bathrobe and black ballet slippers. She said that Everett is drinkin' again and meaner than ever. She says she bought all the children life jackets and they always go out on the boat with them. She said bein' so pregnant she hadn't had time to stop at the store or she would ask me to lunch, but all they had in the house were graham crackers and honey. What could I do but ask her to lunch and when lunch seemed to be running into dinner I couldn't push her out, could I? She called Everett and told him to stop off here and he is as handsome as ever but thinner, more nervous and drinks ten times as much.

When they left at one or two A.M., Elizabeth Gage said, "We don't have lights or runnin' water and I still don't have a washing machine but we do have a telephone. I'll call you in the morning, honey. It will be just like old times."

CHAPTER XV

ADOLESCENCE, OR PLEASE KEEP IMOGENE UNTIL SHE IS THIRTY

THE tricky thing to remember about adolescents is that they seem so miserable doing what they are doing that you, their loving and bewildered parents, assume that they would be happier doing something else. They wouldn't. Adolescents are going to be miserable no matter what they are doing but they would rather be miserable doing the things *they* choose. This is all so easy for me now that Anne and Joan are twenty-four and twenty-five, charming, intelligent, beautiful, companionable, adult and married. Don and I adore them and can't see enough of them, even if Don did design a Christmas card showing him on the roof shooting at the stork.

But during that long pull between fourteen and twenty (they were both married at twenty) it came over us with a flash, well really more like a punch in the stomach accompanied by the splash of tears, that the English are truly more civilized than we are and they know what they are doing when they send Imogene away to school—and by "away" I mean from Rangoon to England or vice versa—at age seven and bring her home reluctantly when she is thirty.

The summer Anne and Joan turned fourteen and fifteen and both bolted themselves in the bathroom for hours at a stretch and wore lipstick to bed, Don and I sent away for the catalogue of a fine school in Canada. It had the splendid English approach, we could tell, because the catalogue said, "No need for them to come home for any of the holidays—we will keep them all summer." Anne and Joan found the catalogue and cried, not because we didn't want them home in the summer but because the school demanded that all pupils have their hair chopped off even with the ear lobes and wear black oxfords with Cuban heels.

Frankly I do not know any easy answer to adolescence. About the only thing to do is to try to hang on to your sanity and pray much as you would if you were lost in a blizzard without a compass or were adrift in a leaky canoe and could hear the roar of the falls just ahead.

While you are hanging on I will reach down into the black pit of my experience and give you a few things to think about, in case they aren't already glaringly apparent:

1. Adolescents do not hate their parents. They merely feel absolute contempt, occasionally coated with condescending pity for them, their tiny brains, ridiculous ideas, unfair rules and obvious senility. They all refer to their father as "oh him" and their mother as "she": "*She* won't let me go, naturally. *She's* scared to death I might have a little fun for a change." "Who was that on the phone? *Oh him!* What did he want, his overcoat again?"

2. All adolescents are masters of the double- even triple-cross. This does not mean that they will grow up to be either Communists or politicians—it is merely an indication that in adolescence, loyalty is no long-term emotion, and best friends can turn brown quicker than gardenias.

3. All adolescents "go steady." Daughters with boys who appear to be oily, weak-chinned and untrustworthy. Sons with girls who appear hard-eyed, brazen and, if not downright immoral, certainly not wholesome sister types. No par-

ent gets anywhere combatting these great romances. How can anyone as stupid as "oh him" evaluate a big wheel like Billy? (A big wheel who lies on the couch more than the dog and has a vocabulary of thirty words.)

"It just so happens that Billy is left half on the football team and president of SqueeGees, *the* high school fraternity."

What can "she" possibly know about a wonderful girl like Charlene (with her skin-tight skirts, fuchsia lipstick apparently put on with a putty knife, and scintillating conversation of "Gollee, Anne, Johnny may have the mind of a boy but he sure has the *body* of a *man!*"). *She* is just jealous because Charlene was voted sweetheart of the SqueeGee *four times*" (no wonder).

The thing that is so difficult for fathers to remember is that very few, if any, of the brilliant lawyers, bankers, doctors, architects or statesmen, a facsimile of which they desire for a son-in-law, ever took out girls when they were in high school. They were too shy and too busy studying to be brilliant lawyers, etc. Big Wheels in high school are, always have been, and undoubtedly always will be the smooth, shifty-eyed, self-confident non-studiers.

The thing that comes as such a blow to the mothers is the fact that little Conroy is not attracted to Ermingarde Allen, who "has such pretty manners and will be very nice-looking when her skin clears up and after all her mother was my classmate at Bryn Mawr." Conroy, who is shy and unsure, refers to Ermingarde, who is shy and unsure, as "that pimply creep," and spends all his time trying to get a date with Carmen Smith who is reputed to let the boys take off her sweater in a parked car. If it is any comfort, isn't it really better for Conroy to satisfy his curiosity about Carmen Smith at sixteen rather than, say, forty?

4. All adolescents telephone. This is part of the cohesive quality that makes them all eat in the same beanery, walk in bunches, knot up in hallways, keep in constant touch. United we stand—divided we might learn something. (You will not solve anything by having two telephones, "Wow, *two* tele-

phones!" Anne and Joan's friends said, and kept them both busy.)

5. All adolescents intend to have the family car all of the time. To accomplish this they resort to the gentle nag or water-on-stone method, the smooth lie, or the cold tearful silence. They will always win if you try to reason or appeal. They have the least resistance to the cheerful impersonal "no."

6. Adolescents are not careful of their own possessions, but they are absolutely reckless with anything belonging to their parents. Don's gray flannel slacks, Don's shoes, my small radio, my toast-colored cashmere sweater, Don's bathing trunks (about four pairs), my jeans, our sweatshirts, our beach towels, hit the adolescent trail and were never seen again.

7. All adolescent girls would prefer to live in a bathroom.

8. All adolescent boys would prefer to live in a car.

Examining in retrospect that first long wet difficult winter when daylight was only on weekends and keeping warm was the motivating force, I am overcome by how wonderful Anne and Joan were. How co-operative and uncomplaining and hard working and dear. Of course, viewing things in retrospect does blunt corners and point up bright places, but they were such little girls to be getting wood, cooking dinner, making beds and smiling, and I repeat again they were such little girls and they did smile. I wondered if they were happy living on an island and leaving for school in the dark. After all, they were used to my large family and our hordes of friends, I told Don.

He said cheerfully, "Look at the Brontës, Saki, Ruskin, Lincoln. All great people who thrived on isolation."

I said, "When I was a little girl I always came home to a house smelling of gingerbread and filled with people."

Don said, "I always came home to a house smelling of funerals and filled with Methodists. I think Anne and Joan are lucky."

I said, "Perhaps we should have waited until they were older before moving to the country."

He said, "Living in the city doesn't solve everything. Think of all the city children who are alone because their parents are in Palm Springs or down at the Athletic Club getting pie-eyed or in New York attending the National Convention of the Juvenile Delinquency Prevention Society. Anyway there weren't any houses for rent in the city. Remember?"

One stormy night Don met on the ferry and brought home to dinner a widower who lived by himself on the other side of the island. Anne, home from school with one of her fleeting unlocalized ailments, had stuffed and baked a salmon and made an apple pie. The man couldn't get over it. "That little girl, that wonderful little girl!" he said over and over again as he passed his plate for more salmon and watched Anne swishing competently around making boiled coffee and cutting the cheese.

Joanie said, "I'm wonderful too, aren't I, Mommy? I rowed out and bought the salmon from the fishing boat and I carried up a root so big Don can't get it in the fireplace."

"You don't know how fortunate you are," the old widower told Don and me, with tears in his eyes. "I've never seen anything like it." Anne and Joan glowed like little fireflies and in his honor after dinner, when they were doing the dishes, kept their fighting down to quiet slaps, hissed insults and one broken saucer.

Sunday morning the girls always climbed in our bed, Don lit the fire in the fireplace and we took turns going down and getting coffee, orange juice and the Sunday papers. After we had read the papers, accompanied by a great deal of shoving and spilling and jerking of the covers Anne and I got up and cooked a big Sunday breakfast. Kippered herring and scrambled eggs or clam fritters and bacon or shad roe or eggs scrambled with Olympia oysters no larger than a thumbnail. While Anne and I cooked, Joan and Don got wood and built the fires. We never bothered with Sunday dinner, preferring soup and sandwiches whenever we got hungry.

Sunday afternoons we took walks, gathered bark, wrote and acted out plays, popped corn, made fudge, sang into the recording machine, read aloud, helped with homework, took trips in the rowboat with the outboard motor, cleared land, fed the deer and played with the kittens. In spite of my occasional misgivings, we were a very happy, enthusiastic family and I was delighted that Anne and Joan had accepted Don so easily as my husband and their friend.

Then Satan, in the form of adolescence, entered the Garden of Eden and turned it overnight into a jungle. A jungle filled with half-grown, always hungry, noisy, emotional, quarrelsome, rude, boisterous, snarling animals.

The first manifestation was the hair. Anne had bright copper-colored curly hair which she wore shining clean and hanging shoulder length. Joan had pale blond curly hair which she wore shining clean, if I caught her, and hanging shoulder length. One early evening Anne began rolling her pretty hair into small wet snails, about six hairs to a snail, secured tightly with bobby pins crisscrossed like swords.

I said, "What are you doing to your hair?"

Sighing heavily she said, through a mouth filled with bobby pins, "Oh, you wouldn't understand."

"Why shouldn't I?" I said.

"Because you don't know anything about style and anyway you want me to look ugly."

"Your hair looks lovely just the way it is," I said unwisely.

"I knew you'd take that attitude," Anne said, beginning to cry. "I knew you'd get furious if I tried to fix my hair the way *everybody* is wearing it."

Joan said, "That's right, Mommy, *everybody* puts their hair up in pin curls. They all think we look like hags."

"And bags."

"And scrags."

"I'm not furious," I said, getting a little furious. "But I don't see much point in curling curly hair."

"You don't see any point in *anything!*" Anne sobbed. "You don't know anything about anything! You even like to live on this Godforsaken island."

Joan said, "Say, Laurie told me that Helen told him that Bobby likes you."

"When?" Anne said, sucking the tears back into her eye sockets and brightening up.

"Yesterday," Joan said. "I forgot to tell you."

"You stinker," hissed Anne. "And now I promised Jimmy I'd go to the Friday dance with him. I could kill you."

"Go ahead," Joan said calmly, "but if I'm dead I won't be able to tell you what else Laurie said."

"What?" Anne said.

"Say 'cross my heart I'm not going to kill you,'" Joan said.

"Don't be silly," Anne said.

Joan said, "All right then, promise you'll help me with my theme."

"I promise."

"Well," Joan said, "Laurie said that Helen said that Bobby is going to ask you to the Seaview Boys School football dance. What are you going to wear?"

"Something ugly and childish and old," Anne said bitterly. "And all the other girls are rich and will smoke and have on strapless formals."

"Karen Hendricks isn't rich," Joan said, "and she goes steady with the president of the sophomore class."

"Yes, but she doesn't live on a corny old island," Anne said.

"If I had red hair and a bust I wouldn't care where I lived," Joan said wistfully. "Say, the subject of my theme has to be Why I Want to Go to College."

"Ugh, what a repulsive title," Anne said.

"You promised you'd help me."

"I know," Anne said, "but it will have to be all lies."

"I'll get my notebook," Joan said.

"Wait," Anne said. "I have to finish pinning up my hair. I'll do yours too, if you want," she added generously.

"Oh, boy," Joan said rapturously.

From then on Anne and Joan and all their little female friends spent at least one third of their lives rolling their hair into the small snail curls. Over the snails they tied bandannas of different kinds—one year dishtowels, one year men's bandannas, one year woolen scarves, one year enormous silk squares. The strange thing was that except for special occasions such as the Friday night dances, SqueeGee formals and Junior Proms, we never ever saw these curls unfurled. Their hair was pinned up when they left for school, it was pinned up again the minute they got home.

Saturday before last, my sister Mary's middle daughter, Sally, who is sixteen, came to see me, bringing three of her school friends. I flinched when I saw their hair, wound into little snails, each snail secured with the crisscrossed bobby pins. I decided to ask Sally, who is not my daughter and therefore doesn't feel called upon to give me the "diamond drill eye" or to turn all my simple questions into personal affronts, why adolescents keep their hair pinned up all the time. Stepping softly, I said, "Sally, would you answer a question for me?" Instantly she and her three friends exchanged looks and moved closer together.

She said suspiciously, "What do you want to know?"

I said, "Why do you keep your lovely blond hair pinned up all the time? In the past two years I've only seen it combed out twice."

She said, "Well, it comes out of curl."

"When?" I asked.

"At school," she said. "I comb it out as soon as I get to school in the morning."

"And you put it up again the minute you get home?"

"Of course," Sally said. "Somebody might come over."

"What if somebody doesn't?"

"Then it's all ready for dinner."

"Do you comb it out before dinner?"

"Daddy won't let us come to the table in pin curls. He's so darn crabby I think he must be going through the menopause."

"Then you put it up right after dinner."

"Of course."

"Why?"

"Somebody might come over."

"Then you put it up again before you go to bed?"

"Of course."

"So it will be ready for school in the morning?"

"Uh, uh."

"Wouldn't it be easier to have a permanent?"

"Oh, no, permanents are corny."

I said, "What about riding back and forth on the ferry with those little wet snails all over your head?"

She said, "Oh, we combed our hair while we were waiting in line."

"How did it get curled again?" I asked. "The ferry ride only takes twelve minutes."

"We rolled it up while we were waiting for the ferry to dock."

"Are you going to take it down again before you get back on the ferry?"

"Of course, you don't expect us to ride on the ferry with our hair in pin curls do you?" Accompanying scornful laughter.

Of course everybody knows that adolescents, in spite of a repulsively overconfident manner, are basically unsure. We read it in books. It is pointed out to us in lectures. There are even articles about it in the newspapers. But you have to live with an adolescent to realize that in this half-ripe, newly hatched, wet-feathered stage they are not aware they are unsure. They consider themselves wise, tolerant, responsible adults. Adults so mature they have a phobia against anything childish. Thus the pleasant Sunday mornings in our bed came to a sudden end. Instead Anne and Joan rushed down and got the papers, fought over them shrilly for a while, then came into our room, sat on the bed, drank the coffee which we had gotten ourselves, and complained. "Gosh, you look hideous in that nightgown, Betty," was one form of greeting, followed quickly by, "Raining again!" heavy sigh. "It seems like it has been raining for years and years." Another heavy sigh. "Do you think Tyrone Power's going to marry Lana Turner, Mommy?" They were both wearing Don's pajamas, their hair was of course in pin curls, their faces smeared with calamine lotion, their fingernails were long, ruby-colored and chipped, their eyes sad.

I said, "Let's get dressed, have breakfast, build a big fire in the fireplace and play charades."

"Charades? You mean that baby game where you act out words?" Anne said.

"It isn't a baby game," I said. "You remember we played it last summer."

"I don't want to play," Joan said. "It's too much like school work."

"I wish I had a pink Angora sweater," Anne said. "Marilyn has two. A pale blue one and a pale pink one."

"Two?" Joan said. "Are you sure? They're twenty-five dollars, you know."

"Marilyn's rich," Anne said. "She gets thirty-five dollars a month just to spend on clothes."

Don said, "I can't understand why we let the Russians into Berlin."

Anne said, "Marilyn's going to spend Christmas in Palm Springs."

I said, "Palm Springs is the last place I would want to spend Christmas. Who wants hot weather and palm trees for Christmas?"

"I do," Anne said wistfully. "I'm so sick of rain I could die."

"Me too," Joan said. "Marilyn's going to get her own car when she's sixteen."

Don said, "Of course Russia had the world bluffed and our policy of appeasement, uncertainty and double-talk isn't fooling anybody but ourselves."

I said, "Possessions don't bring happiness. Happiness is something you must find in your own self."

"Well, it would be a lot easier to find if I had a car of my own," Anne said.

Joan said, "If we had a car of our very own we could drive to California next summer."

"You could not," I said.

"Why?" they said together.

"Because I don't believe in young girls' driving around the country by themselves. It's not safe."

"Well, next summer we'd be fifteen and sixteen."

"That's not old enough to take a trip by yourselves."

"It certainly seems funny to me that we are always old enough to do what *you* want but never old enough to do anything *we* want."

Don said, "Listen to this, 'Peace is largely beyond the control of purpose. It comes as a gift. The deliberate aim at peace passes into its bastard substitute, anesthesia.' "

I said, "Why don't you girls get dressed?"

Don said, "You never listen to anything I say."

I said, "I do too. But it's hard to concentrate on Russia when the girls are leaving for California in their own car."

Anne said, "Don't you think Joan and I are old enough to drive to California, Don?"

"What about South America?" Don said. "It's farther away."

"Who'll go down and get me a cigarette?" I asked.

"You go," Anne said.

"You go," Joan said.

Don said, "Here, smoke one of mine."

Anne said, "Gosh, I hate Sunday. Nothing to do but damned old homework."

"Don't swear," I said.

"Why not?" Anne said. "You do."

"You swear all the time," Joan echoed.

"Let's get dressed," I said, getting out of bed.

To be sure they weren't missing out on any new vital beauty aid, Anne and Joan studied *Glamour, Mademoiselle, Charm, Vogue, Harper's Bazaar,* as well as all the movie magazines. They knew instantly if Burnt Sugar was the latest color in lipstick and they pled and bled until they got it. When they got it they wore it out in about two hours because they put on a new complete makeup when they got home from school (this one was for getting wood), another for eating dinner and of course another before doing the dishes because "somebody might come over." On occasion they would experiment with different blemish removers.

One night when they both came in to kiss us goodnight coated entirely with some pure white stuff that smelled like creosote and made them look like plaster casts, I said mildly, "Are you sure that is good for your skin?"

Anne, her voice throbbing with bitterness, said, "If it's deadly poison it's better than having to go to school with a face that is always just one big running sore."

"Where are all these running sores?" I asked.

Bending down so that the lamp shone on her face, she said, "Look."

I looked, but all I could see was one small red lump on her chin. I said as much and she stamped up to bed.

Joan said, "Look at my face. My pores are so enormous I look like a cribbage board."

I examined her face as well as I could through the white paste and said, "Your skin looks fine to me."

"Naturally you'd say that," Joan said. "Because you don't care. You cook rich foods all the time because you want us to break out and look ugly."

Don said, "What have you got on your hair?"

"Straightener," Joan said. "It's not stylish to have curly hair. Nobody has it any more. It's corny."

"White stuff on your face, straightener on your hair, what are you trying to do, pass over?" Don asked.

I thought it was very funny and laughed. Joan flounced upstairs.

Leg shaving began the summer Anne was thirteen and before either of the girls had so much as one picker on their skinny legs. But leg shaving was considered sophisticated and so they scraped their legs almost as often as Don did his chin, and always with his razor.

After a while I got pretty foxy, and when I saw Anne and Joan come limping out of our bathroom, their legs sporting bloody ribbons of toilet paper like tails of kites, I would dash upstairs, wash out Don's razor and put in a new blade.

Then there were the clothes. So vitally important. Everything long and loose and pitiful. Boys' coats. Men's sweaters. Don's shirts. Boys' jeans and T-shirts. Wooden shoes, loafers, dirty saddle shoes. Exactly the right kind of white socks turned down an exact number of inches. The first high heels and the furious outburst in the shoestore— "You're glad my feet are so big because you know it hurts my feelings!"

No matter what garment I bought Anne and Joan the grass was always greener in somebody else's closet. They and their schoolmates exchanged clothes constantly. Anne and Joan would leave for school in one outfit, come home in another. It was hard for me to understand this because all the skirts, blouses, sweaters and coats were exactly alike and all made the girls look like figures in faded photographs of long-ago picnics.

Next in importance to clothes were eating and dieting. For weeks everything would be so-so. The girls would come home from school with their accompanying wake of Jeanies, Lindas, Ruthies, Sandys, Bonnies, Chuckies, Normies, Bills and Jims, go directly to the kitchen and the icebox door would begin to thump rhythmically like the tail of a friendly dog, as they devoured everything not marked with a skull and crossbones or frozen. During those intervals any old thing I cooked, stew, spaghetti or deep-fried pot holders, was greeted with "Is that *all* you made? We're starving."

Then one morning I would decide to get up early and cook something very nice for my growing girls and their long chain of Ruthies, Jeanies and so on, who apparently didn't care if they slept six in a bed or in the fireplace just so it was every night at our house. "I'll make French toast," I said fondly to Tudor as I flitted happily around getting out the real maple syrup and crowding another place on the table each time another gruesome little figure in a torn petticoat, bobby pins and calamine lotion appeared and asked me where the iron was.

When I had a stack of golden French toast about two feet high, ordinarily a mere hors d'oeuvre, I called loudly that breakfast was ready and sat down in my corner with a cup of coffee and a cigarette. After an interval the girls began straggling in, dripping with my perfume and, of course, wearing each other's clothes.

"Hurry and drink your orange juice," I said proudly. "I've made French toast."

"I hope you didn't cook any for me," Anne said loftily, sitting down at the table and unscrewing the top on a bottle of nail polish. "I'm dieting and all I want is one hard-boiled egg."

"Why do you always fix orange juice?" Joan said. "Tomato juice only has fifty calories."

The various Ruthies and Jeanies said to my offers of French toast, "None for me, thanks, Mrs. MacDonald. I'm just going to have black coffee"—or warm water and lemon juice, or a hard-boiled egg.

After they had gone I grimly dumped the lovely golden brown French toast into the raccoons' pan and decided that this was the last time I would ever get up and cook breakfast for my disagreeable little daughters and their ungrateful little friends.

After school the locusts arrived on schedule, but only the boys ate. The girls sipped tea and smoked. Then came dinner and no matter what I cooked, rare roast beef, brook trout, ground roundsteak broiled, it was never on their diet. Also I could count on either Anne or Joan or both of them saying, "So much! Why do you always cook in such enormous quantities?"

I don't know what diet they were on, but it was apparently the same one Mary's daughters and friends are using today, a special high school diet that calls for one plate of fudge, three Cokes and a pound of cheese eaten in private and one small celery stalk and half a grapefruit nibbled at the dinner table. Mother used to infuriate Anne and Joan by quoting:

> There was a young lady named Maud
> Famed both at home and abroad,
> She never was able to eat at the table
> But in the back pantry, my God!

Of course you can't examine adolescence without getting on the subject of sex, the discussion of which occupied a prominent place in our dinner table conversation during those years. Don and I tried to be very frank with Anne and Joan and encouraged them to be very frank with us. We answered their questions with medical terms, as many as we knew, and, we hoped, the correct casualness. The result was that no matter who came to dinner, the conversation was dappled with rather clinical discussions of sex in which Anne and Joan and their friends seemed to be extremely interested. Adolescents enjoy, in fact will go to most any length to get, the center of attention. In our quiet little home this was accomplished rather easily. We sat down to dinner, Don began to carve, I took a bite of salad and Ruthie said, "Did you know that Ellen broke up with Bob?" There was an excited chorus of No! When! Why! Where! Then Anne remarked in a very conversational tone, "It was bound to come, after all they have been having sexual intercourse every five minutes for years."

Dropping my lettuce into my lap, I said, "Anne Mac-Donald, what a dreadful thing to say!"

Reaching for another biscuit, Joan said, "Don't get so worked up, Betty. It's common knowledge."

Putting down my salad fork I would launch my standard, worn-to-the-fraying-point lecture on reputations, their preciousness, their gossamer fragility and so on, and so on. The girls waited impatiently but politely for me to finish, then Anne said, speaking patiently, slowly, the way you discourse with mental defectives, "But, Betty, we're not hurting Ellen's reputation."

Ruthie broke in eagerly, "That's right, Mrs. MacDonald. Yesterday she told the whole botany class about Bob and her."

Sighing heavily Don said, "Can't we change the subject?"

Sitting up straight, I began an interesting discourse on the new book I was reading.

I learned after a while, a long while, that if I displayed shock or any other interesting reaction during these discussions they went on and on and on. So I became able finally to toss it off—to say casually, "Please pass the gravy," right in the middle of the gory details of the story about Murdene Plunkett, who didn't wear panties to the spring formal. . . .

I encouraged Anne and Joan to read from the time they first learned how. Our library is large and varied, and beyond casual suggestions I made no attempt to monitor their selections. One rainy school morning Anne asked me for a piece of wrapping paper. I asked her why she wanted it, merely to determine the kind and size, and she said she wanted to wrap up a book so it wouldn't get wet. I offered to wrap the book for her and she handed me *Lady Chatterley's Lover*. I said, trying very hard to speak casually, "Why are you taking this book to school, Andy?"

"Because I'm going to give a book report on it," she said just as casually as she adjusted her bandanna.

"Have you read it?" I asked.

"Part of it," she said. "It's awfully dull, but D. H. Lawrence is supposed to be a good writer, isn't he?"

I tactfully substituted *The Turn of the Screw* by Henry James, as a little more suitable for high school English, just as dull and a lot easier to carry in the rain.

Of course the girls eventually came across and read *Ulysses* quite openly on the couch in the living room, but they didn't attempt to do a book report on it. They adored *Gone with the Wind,* but they thought *Kitty Foyle* was corny. They loved *A Farewell to Arms* but couldn't decide about *The Grapes of Wrath* because of "that absolutely *disgusting* ending." They loved *Tortilla Flat,* but were not enthusiastic about *Invitation to the Waltz* or *Alice Adams,* two of my favorites. Their favorites were Dickens, Thackeray, the Brontës (Anne read *Wuthering Heights* five times one winter) E. B. White and Thurber. They read *The New Yorker, The Saturday Evening Post, The Ladies' Home Journal, Good Housekeeping, Time, Life,* as many movie magazines as they could get hold of, and all the magazines exploiting charm, glamour, beauty and so on.

They loved all movies except the ones depicting Hollywood's conception of college life. They were wildly enthusiastic about any stage play or musical, but only Anne and I enjoyed the symphony or concerts.

Anne and Joan and their friends talked a great deal about sophistication, tight strapless black evening dresses and long cigarette holders, but when boys appeared they screamed like gulls, laughed like hyenas and pushed one another and the boys rudely. One day I came into the living room and found Anne lifting a chair with two great big boys in it. I was horrified and that night I gave the girls lectures #10874-598734 on Being a Lady—Nice Manners—Charm—Womanliness. They listened with half-closed cobra eyes until I had finished, then yawned and stretched rudely, shoved and pushed each other up the stairs, and locked themselves in our bathroom. The thing that troubled me the most was that none of Anne and Joan's friends was as rude as they were.

All the Ruthies and Jeanies, etc., said please and thank you, stood up when I came in the room and wrote their bread-and-butter letters. I wondered what magic their mothers used and when, as they were at our house most of the time.

Then one day Don and I were at a cocktail party and a strange man came up to us and said, "So you're the parents of Anne and Joan. They go skiing with us quite often, you know, and Mrs. Alexander and I think they are the *most charming girls* we have ever met. They are also very witty and very bright but, right at this point, it is their *manners* that impress us the most. You see, Carol," (I realized all of a sudden that this was one of the mysterious parents of Carol, quiet, exquisitely mannered Carol, who had been with us off and on, mostly on, for over a year) "ever since she entered adolescence has apparently been taking a behavior course from Al Capone." Of course we told him about Carol and how beautifully she behaved at our house and he went on and on about Anne and Joan, and then he said, "I can't keep this to myself," and rushed off and got Mrs. Alexander, and we went over the whole thing again. We all left the party looking years and years younger.

Anne and Joan had always been to my prejudiced maternal eyes, normally truthful children. Joan told me when she broke the windshield of the Alcotts' car. Anne told me when she spilled nail polish on my new bedspread. Joan told me when she cut off her eyelashes. Anne told me when she drank the cherry wine. They both told me when they took the candy out of the ten-cent store. Perhaps they each told me what the other did, but anyway I got the truth one way or another, most of the time.

Then came adolescence and the birth of the wilful, deliberate, bold-faced lie. The lie, told, I finally decided, to test parents out, to see what kind of fools they really were.

It began with the lost wallet. Anne and Joan were each given five dollars a week allowance. This was to cover car-fare, school lunches, Saturday movies and occasional shopping trips. One Saturday Anne told me that she had lost her wallet with her "whole allowance in it." She cried a little when she told me and I felt niggardly and probing when I asked her for details. She was remarkably definite.

"It was in Frederick and Nelson's at the hat bar on the first floor at eleven in the morning last Saturday. I put the wallet on the counter right beside me while I tried on a hat and when I looked for it, it was gone. Probably taken by a shoplifter." While she was telling her story, Anne and Joan both fixed me with large innocent guileless blue eyes. Of course I believed them and gave Anne another five dollars. She snatched it eagerly but I was not suspicious.

The next Saturday the same thing happened. Almost the same story only this time it was Joan and the Vashon drugstore and the culprit probably "some poor starving farmer who needed the money."

I shelled out another five dollars.

Monday morning Velma, my cleaning woman, brought me Anne's green wallet which she had found behind the bed. In it were two one-dollar bills and the stubs of four loge seats in the Fifth Avenue Theatre.

When Anne came home from school I showed her the wallet and the theatre tickets and said sorrowfully, "You lied to me."

"I know it," Anne said cheerfully.

"Why?" I asked, my voice hoarse with emotion.

"I don't know," Anne said. "I guess I just wanted to see if I could. All the kids lie to their mothers."

"Very well," I said. "You owe me five dollars. You can pay me back two dollars a month. Did you lie to me too, Joan?"

Joan, who had her mouth full of apple, nodded brightly, vigorously.

"I'm very very disappointed in you," I said.

"Well, my gosh," Joan said, "Carol's been lying to *her* mother for months and months—she *never* catches on." She made it sound as if I had taken unfair advantage.

"Then why does Carol always borrow money from me?" Anne said furiously. "She owes me about a million dollars."

I said, "You can pay me back two dollars a month too, Joan."

Anne said, "I'm going to get my money back from Carol if I have to choke her to death."

A few nights later, at dinner, Anne announced, "Gosh, we had a hard geometry test today."

"We had an algebra test," Joan said, taking a tiny uninteresting sip of her milk.

"The geometry test was hard but I think I got an awfully good grade," Anne said, as she pushed her peas into a string of green beads encircling her mashed potatoes.

"How do you think you did in algebra, Joanie?" I asked.

"All right, I guess," Joan said. "I despise Miss Gantron but she's so senile she can't think up very hard tests."

"What did they have for lunch at school?" I asked conversationally.

Anne and Joan glanced at each other quickly, then said together, "Spaghetti—macaroni and cheese."

"Make up your minds," I said levelly. "Which was it—spaghetti or macaroni and cheese—surely they wouldn't have both?"

"The food at school gets more revolting every day," Anne said, taking a tiny bite of avocado. "Absolutely tasteless and always cold."

"The macaroni and cheese tastes just like Kem-Tone," Joan said.

"It's better than their vegetable soup," Anne said. "It tastes just like perspiration."

I said, "Speaking of perspiration, Aunty Mary saw you coming out of the Paramount Theatre this afternoon."

Ruthie said, "Oh, it couldn't have been us, Mrs. Mac-Donald. We were all at school. Weren't we, Jeanie?"

Jeanie said, "Sure they were, Mrs. MacDonald. Ask Kathy."

I said, "I don't have to ask anybody. I *know* you weren't

238

at school and I *know* you aren't hungry for dinner because you have spent the day stuffing down popcorn and ice cream and candy and Cokes. Now CLEAR THE TABLE, WASH THE DISHES, DO YOUR STUDYING AND GO TO BED!"

Later on when Don and I were lying in bed reading and trying to take our minds off adolescence, I heard Ruthie say to Anne, who was of course taking her bath in our bathroom, "Gee, Anne, your mom's sure sweet. I wouldn't dare tell my mom I skipped school. She'd kill me."

Anne said, "Oh, *she's* all right, I guess. Do you think Bill really likes me?"

There was also the music—the loud, blatting, tuneless music that boomed out of the record player from the minute the girls opened their eyes in the morning until they closed them at night. Boops Bigwig, Doggo Conray, Morks Ogle—or whatever their names were—all sounded exactly alike to me and made "Walkin' My Baby Back Home" indistinguishable from "Paper Moon" or Don's chain saw. To Boops, Doggo, etc., Anne and Joan and their friends danced the Avalon, a sort of crippled drag performed with the fanny stuck out and a pained expression on the face. They listened to Frank Sinatra, Frankie Laine, Billie Holliday and King Cole. Listening required that they be draped over some piece of furniture surrounded by a litter of Coke bottles, apple cores, candy wrappers, cigarette stubs, cookie crumbs and shoes. Nobody ever wore shoes except outside. Even at formal dances the girls kicked off their shoes and got holes in *my* nylons.

And perfume with names such as Aphrodisia, Quick Passion, Come Hither, Lots of Sin—all with a heavy musk base. I am not at all partial to heavy perfume, preferring light flowery scents, but I'm particularly not partial to heavy perfume slopped on by the handful at seven o'clock in the morning when I'm tentatively taking my first sip of coffee. Anne would come downstairs immaculate, pressed and perfect to the last hair but with the husky scent of Quick Passion hovering over her like smoke over a genie. Once or twice I remarked mildly, "Andy, darling, don't you think that perfume is awfully, uh, well, penetrating for school?" She and Joan, who by that time had also made an appearance quite obviously pinned in many places but drenched in Aphrodisia, exchanged long-suffering looks and sighed heavily. Any further mention of the stench in the kitchen I knew would bring forth a torrent of "You don't *want* us to smell nice. You'd like it if we had *B.O.* or used Lysol perfume. *Everything* we do is wrong. *All* you do is criticize." Keeping as far away from them as I could and drawing heavily on cigarettes, I put their breakfast on the table and thought with pity of the teachers who had to put up with perhaps thirty-five, all smelling like that.

Of course Anne and Joan treated Don and me as if we were tottering on the edge of senility. We weren't even thirty-five but if we danced (never exactly a spontaneous outburst of animal spirits on Don's part) we became the immediate objects of a great deal of humorous comment. "Oh, look at them! Do you mean to say they really used to dance like *that*? He, he, he, ha, ha, ha, you look so funny!" If I occasionally came back at them and reminded them how funny *they* looked when *they* danced they wailed, "You're so crabby all the time. You're never any fun any more."

I don't know how or when Anne and Joan learned to drive, but I do know that each one, on the day of her sixteenth birthday, demanded to be taken to town so she could go through the ridiculous routine of a driving test and be given a license to drive her steady's father's car and to lend our car to any bonehead friend who wished to back it onto a busy street without looking, run it into a tree, turn a corner without seeing "that dumb truck," or put it in reverse by mistake when going very fast. After a time I became rather accustomed to answering the phone and having a small quavering voice say, "Mrs. MacDonald, this is Joanne and I've had a little trouble with the car, your car I mean, and there's a policeman who wants to speak to you."

Once when we had been up very late listening to "then I said to Ted and Ted said to me" and then were kept awake further by the music of Morks and Doggo and further still by the pattering of big bare feet and shrieks and giggles and the thump of the refrigerator door and finally by my bedside light being switched on and Joan demanding, "Where have you put my down quilt? We're making up a bed for Evelyn and Ruthie on the porch," Don remarked with feeling, "What are we running here, a youth hostel? That Ruthie hasn't been home for two years. How come nobody wants to go anywhere but here? Why should we be the only ones with Coke bottles and shoes on the mantel? Where are the other parents? What are they doing?"

Yawning, I said, "Probably sitting around in their uncluttered houses saying, 'What is all this talk about the problems of adolescents? I don't find them any trouble at all.'"

Anne burst in and said, "Do you care if Carol smokes?"

"I don't care if she bursts into flame," Don said.

"Very funny," Anne said witheringly, "and *very old*." Taking our only package of cigarettes she went out, slamming the door.

"Never mind," I said to Don, "someday they will marry and leave home."

"Are you sure?" Don said, as he sadly sorted over the butts on his ashtray, finally selecting a pretty long one. He examined it critically for a minute or two then, with a sigh, struck a match and lit it.

CHAPTER XVI

ONIONS IN THE STEW

I DON'T know why I ever entertained such a ridiculous idea, but it was undoubtedly the fruit of misery and desperation—could even have been nature's way of keeping me from becoming an alcoholic or cutting a main artery or taking any other coward's way out. As I remember, the dream came to light first, the time I was called to school to learn that Anne, who had almost finished three years of high school, had accumulated exactly six and one third credits in required subjects. All the others were cooking, sewing, basket weaving, leather punching, mural painting and so on. I didn't even know they had so many courses for those "better with their hands," as the principal explained kindly. I told him again about Anne's very high I.Q. and he said without enthusiasm, "Yes, I've checked with her junior high school principal, but the problem is that unless you want her to graduate with a *certificate* instead of a *diploma* she will have to buckle down." That night after dinner when we were having a discussion of Anne's buckling down and Anne wasn't, Joan said finally, "Oh, why don't you just send her to Opportunity School" (a local school for the retarded) "that's where she belongs."

Anne said calmly, "I hate school. I've always hated school. I always will hate school. You'll never change me, so you might as well not upset yourself trying."

242

"But, Andy," I said, "you won't be able to get into any college unless you take science and languages and math."

"College!" Anne laughed derisively. "I wouldn't go to college if you slashed my wrists and beat me with a steel cable and cut off my allowance. I loathe school and I loathe all teachers."

"The feeling appears to be mutual," Don remarked dryly from behind *Time* magazine.

I said, "But, Andy, you don't know how different college is from high school. In college you're treated as an adult and the professors are brilliant and stimulating and you realize for the first time the importance of knowledge—the reason for studying."

Yawning elaborately, then inspecting her long red nails, Anne said, "I'm sorry, Betty, but you are just wasting your time. Anyway you seem to forget that I've seen some college students. Look at Evelyn Olwell. She's a sophomore in college and she thinks Villa Lobos is a sport like handball. And Martha Jones—she's a junior in college and last summer she told me her mother was 'alternating' her dress. And Catherine Morton—she's never read a book—not a single one—her family doesn't even own a book and her mother and father are both college graduates."

After a time we reached a sort of agreement, or hard-eyed, shouted compromise. Anne would change her courses, go to summer school and graduate with a *diploma,* but whether or not she went to college would be her decision.

I had the dream next when Joan, who for two or three Sundays had been singing at a local USO, suddenly decided that she was going to leave school and sing with a band. The first inkling Don and I had of this splendid plan was when we went in to check on Anne and Joan who were in town weekend baby-sitting with the two small children of a friend of ours. It was Sunday afternoon and we dropped by to see what time they expected the parents and what time they wanted us to pick them up.

I remember the nice feeling of pride I had as I ran up

the steps of the Morrisons' house. "Anne and Joan solicited this baby-sitting job all by themselves," I told Don, who was morosely inspecting a broken downspout. "And I think it shows encouraging signs of maturity for them to take care of two little children and stay in a house all by themselves from Friday afternoon to Sunday night."

Stepping up on the porch railing so he could take a look at the eaves trough, Don said, "We'll probably get a blast from Jim and Mary when they get the grocery bill."

"The trouble with you is that you don't want to see any improvement in the girls," I said crossly.

"Not at all," Don said, his chin on the roof. "I just like to face facts. I'd better tell Jim this eaves trough is rotten."

I rang the doorbell. There was no answer, but I thought I detected giggling and scuffling from somewhere in the house. Then Anne came to the door, wearing a dishtowel tied low over her forehead like an Arab's headdress. She was flushed and nervous. "How come you're so early?" she asked, ungraciously barring the door.

"We came to visit," I said cheerfully. "To see how you are getting along."

"We're getting along all right," Anne said, trying to shut the door.

"Where's Joanie?" I asked.

"Oh, she's around," Anne said evasively.

"What do you mean," I said firmly, moving her out of the way and going into the house.

"She's upstairs."

"Joanie," I called loudly. "It's Mommy. Where are you?"

"I'm up here," answered a muffled voice.

"You'd better not yell," Anne said. "The baby's asleep. Come out in the kitchen and I'll make you a cup of coffee."

Patty, the Morrisons' four year old, came down the stairs, slowly one step at a time. The front of her dress was quite wet.

We all went out to the kitchen. Patty settled herself in

244

a chair by the kitchen table with crayons and a coloring book. Carefully choosing a white crayon she announced companionably, "This is just the color Joanie's hair is going to be when she finishes bleaching it!"

"You be quiet," Anne hissed at her.

"Why?" asked Patty, whose shoes were on the wrong feet.

"Because you promised," Anne said.

"I promised not to tell about *your* hair," Patty said. "I didn't promise about Joan's."

I got up, walked over to Anne and jerked the dishtowel off her hair. She stood paralyzed, the coffee pot in one hand, the can of coffee in the other. Her hair exploded from under the dishtowel like a deep old rose chrysanthemum.

"Anne MacDonald," I shrieked. "What have you done?"

She began to cry, using the dishtowel as a handkerchief. Through her tears and the dishtowel, she said finally, "Well, Joan thought that her hair would look better platinum if she was going to sing with a band and so she bought a bottle of triple-strength peroxide and we both tried it and if you think I look awful just wait till you see Joan."

Then Joan appeared pale and trembling. Her head was swathed in a bathtowel. I told her the jig was up and jerked off the towel. Her normally ash-blond hair was the bright egg-yolk yellow of highway signs.

"We don't know what to do?" Anne sobbed. "We can't go to school like this."

"You could have your heads shaved," Don suggested helpfully.

"Or you can let it grow out," I added heartlessly. "It will take at least six months."

"It's all Joan's fault," Anne said. "She's the one that wanted to sing with a band."

"You're a double-crosser," Joan yelled. "You're the very one that told me to bleach my hair."

"But you bought the peroxide," Anne screamed.

"Only because you didn't have any money," Joan shrieked.

Don and I tiptoed out. The girls were so busy fighting they didn't even notice. When we got out to the car we found Patty with us. She said, "I'm going for a ride with you."

I said, "No, dear, you're going to stay with Anne and Joan. Run in the house and tell them we'll pick them up at six o'clock." We waited until we heard the front door close.

When we retrieved the girls about six, Anne's hair was a pinkish brown and Joan's a yellowish brown. "Don't we look keen?" Joan asked cheerfully as she squeezed past me into the back seat.

"Watch what you're doing with that suitcase," I said irritably as she dragged it past my ear and clunked it down on Anne's foot.

"Ouch," Anne shrieked. "You clumsy dope!"

"Don't call me a dope," Joan said calmly. "Remember I'm the one that figured out how to fix our hair."

"What did you do?" I asked, turning around and taking a closer look at their dusty rose and ochre heads.

"I went up to the drugstore and bought a bottle of light brown dye," Joan said proudly. "I dyed Anne's hair and she did mine. Don't we look keen?"

I said, "You don't look keen, but you don't look quite as awful as you did."

Joan said, "Gosh, you're crabby. I'll certainly be glad when I leave home. Everybody in this family is a big crab."

"Where are you going and when?" Don asked.

"Joe Charteris told me that if I quit school I could travel with his band and I'm going to," Joan said.

I said firmly, loudly, "You're not going *anywhere* and you are *not* going to sing at that USO any more."

"Okay," Joan said cheerfully, "but you don't have to get so worked up. Let's get Chinese food."

"Oh, please, Mommy," Anne said. "Let's go to Won Ton's."

"What about your hair?" Don asked.

"Oh, the Chinese don't care about our hair, anyway we brought our dishtowels," Anne said.

"I won't take you any place in those hideous dishtowels," I said.

"Oh, Betty, do you have to be so disagreeable *all* the time," both girls said, sighing. "You never say a civil word any more."

So we went to Won Ton's and while the girls argued about what they were going to have and Don intently studied the Chinese side of the menu, I lapsed into this familiar soothing daydream. It was Anne's eighteenth birthday and her presents were heaped by her place at the breakfast table, and Don and Joan and I were in the kitchen waiting for her to come downstairs. Then she appeared, my little girl, my own dear little serious-eyed Anne, all soft and sweet and loving, kissed us all, including Joan (this part of the picture was really far-fetched), and said, an amused smile tugging at the corners of her mouth, "Well, Betty and Don, you can start living again. One of us is out of adolescence." The dream faded as Don announced happily, as he always does, that he thought he'd just have the pressed duck and the waiter said as he always does, "Press dock take two day. Have to odah day befoh."

It was the night before Anne's nineteenth (I had adjusted my dream a little—after all there is no point in being just plain ridiculous) birthday, but as I sat on our bed wrapping her presents, a white cashmere cardigan, an album of Bidu Sayao and a triple strand of pearls (Japanese), I had an unhappy presentiment, bordering on certain knowledge that there wasn't going to be any Santa Claus. The morning of the birthday confirmed it. Anne and Joan had a furious quarrel over who was going to get the car before they even got out of bed. When she finally came shuffling down to breakfast with a bad case of hay fever, Anne tripped over Tudor who was lying in the kitchen doorway and when she kicked him "with only my soft old bedroom slipper" he nipped her ankle and Don heartlessly refused to drive her into Seattle for rabies shots and so she stamped upstairs without opening her presents.

Oh, well, she had graduated from high school and she did have a job in the advertising department of a large department store, even if the only apparent changes wrought by her new adult status were that she wore what she termed "high style" clothes (Don said she could call them what she liked but they looked to him like Halloween costumes), more and heavier perfume and eyeshadow in the daytime. However, she didn't seem to actively dislike Don and me as much as formerly. She still treated us like lepers, but good old lepers. The faithful non-irritating kind, who are so dumb they don't know they don't know *anything*. Her attitude toward Joan was that of a high caste Hindu forced to associate with an untouchable. Her friends were all models. She went steady with a boy Don referred to as "that sneaky Bradley."

Joan was a senior in high school. When she wasn't fighting with Anne over clothes or the car, she was going to sorority meetings which were every night in the week at our house, and going steady. Going steady meant that there were always two pairs of shoes on the mantel and twice as many Coke bottles under the couch. Joan didn't treat Don and me like anything, because we still weren't anything—just "she" and "oh him."

Then it was Joan's eighteenth birthday and I was sitting on my bed wrapping presents—a pink cashmere cardigan, two new petticoats and a single strand of pearls (Japanese). (*Nobody* wears triple strands of pearls any more—because they're corny that's why.) It was July and Joan had her steady spending the summer with us because she felt so sorry for him because she didn't love him, I was taking care of my sister Alison's three- and five-year-old boys because she was expecting a baby and Anne was in Seattle sharing an apartment with another girl and "living my own life at last" which seemed to us lepers to consist of drinking beer and not paying her bills. The morning of Joanie's birthday was cool and gray with rolls of dark clouds billowing in from the south, like smoke from a locomotive.

Joan was glum when she came downstairs. Before she

opened her presents she looked morbidly out the window and sighed, "Rain again. What a horrible summer." Darsie and Bard, very excited about the birthday and the presents they had "choosed" and wrapped at five-forty-five that morning using one whole roll of Scotch tape and all my meagre supply of self-control, hopped around her saying, "Open your presents, Joanie. Mine smells good. That's it, there—open it." Joanie opened her presents one by one, kissing Don, the children, me and Steady who unfortunately had also bought pearls, then she took the cap off a Coke, grabbed a handful of fudge and shuffled sadly off to the living room to exercise her birthday prerogative of no work.

Then Joan was in college living at her sorority house but coming home quite often because she was "starving to death." College had wrought no appreciable change in anything except her laugh which was now a bleat accompanied by a wide open mouth and tightly squinted eyes. Her best friends all laughed the same way. It seemed to be something they were teaching at the university that year. Don and I thought the new laugh very unattractive and one day I tactlessly said so. Joan blew up like a defective hot water tank. "I can't do *anything* right," she shrieked. "You don't like my hair, you don't like my clothes, you don't like my friends, you don't like the way I drive. The real trouble of course is that you haven't any sense of humor and you're terribly neurotic." She and her friends slammed out of the house—then slammed back in for two quarts of garlic dill pickles and a large bundle of ham sandwiches they had made earlier.

Stifling a strong unmotherly desire to pick up the refrigerator and hurl it after them, I poured myself a cup of coffee, sat down at the kitchen table and lit a cigarette. What was wrong? Where had I failed? Were all adolescents like Anne and Joan? What had happened to our happy home? Who had erected this great big spiky impenetrable wall between us and our children? Would it always be like this? Would things be like this if we hadn't moved to the country? It was Saturday and I hadn't vacuumed the living room or thrown out the dead flowers or changed the sheets on the bunkroom beds and I didn't care. All I wanted to do was to throw myself face down on the brick floor, beat my heels and scream. After two cigarettes I reached down beside me and listlessly picked up the eighty-third book I had bought on Handling the Adolescent. Without any enthusiasm at all I opened it. It would probably be written in the usual, "I'm reaching way down there from clear up here to hand you this crumb" vein and would undoubtedly go on and on and on about the glandular change in the pitiful body of the poor little misunderstood, maladjusted adolescent. I knew all this and I was tired of it. What I wanted was a magic formula, a charm, or a voodoo chant to help me cast out devils and restore my daughters to normal.

Then something caught my eye—something about this doctor's sympathies being with the *parents*. I put on my glasses. An hour later I still hadn't vacuumed or thrown out the dead flowers, but I had certainly cheered up. This Dr. Wilburforce was wonderful! He sounded as if he had had adolescent children. He said that adolescence was a difficult period but entirely normal and his sympathies were with the parents, not the adolescent. He said that there was entirely too much "understanding," actually excusing of the adolescent, his lack of manners, selfishness, tantrums and so on. He thought that the most intelligent approach to the problem was to understand that the adolescent, just by the nature of the beast, is going to chafe and rebel and *he needs something specific to chafe and rebel against*. Lay down strict rules of behavior and enforce them. Rebelling against nothing is very frustrating. Demand that the adolescent go along with the family routine. Do not allow him to keep the household in a continual uproar. If he were away at school such actions would not be tolerated. Why are they at home? He said there was entirely too much talk about "giving an adolescent his head." He said that this was actually merely the shifting of the responsibility from the parent to the child, because anybody knows that giving a sixteen year old his head is like handing him a squash. Instead of giving your child too much freedom, too much money and all the responsibility for his actions, try giving him limited freedom and money, a strict code of behavior and oceans and gallons and mountains of love. Not the deep-hidden-river I-bore-you-so-I-will-have-to-like-you type of love, but the visible, hug-and-kiss, lavish-compliment, interested-audience kind. Tell your adolescent he is brilliant, handsome, charming, witty and lovable. Tell him every day. Tell him even when you are taking away the keys of the car and would like to kick him. Assure him and reassure him and re-reassure him. Love is the *most important* element in human relationships. You can never give a child too much love.

I began to hum a little. After a time I heard a car door slam. I jumped up guiltily. I had almost forgotten that Anne and a model friend were coming for the weekend. I put the kettle on for a fresh pot of coffee, brushed some toast crumbs off the table with Dr. Wilburforce and went out to give Anne love.

Her appearance set me back just a little. From the tone of his book I was quite sure that Dr. Wilburforce had been speaking of ordinary adolescents. Girls in sweaters and skirts and saddle shoes. Anne was wearing a charcoal-gray *costume,* spats, a black-and-white-checked man's cap and about twenty pounds of pearls. I could smell her perfume clear from the kitchen door to the wild cherry tree. The model, who had such little hips I didn't see how she was going to sit on them, was all in black and heavy gold jewelry. I was pretty sure I was going to catch hell about my blue jeans (Vashon grocery store) and white blouse (Sears, Roebuck). "Really, Betty, you *are* getting older—you do have other clothes," and so on, and so on, and so on. I could feel the old familiar defensive wariness take over as I kissed Anne and said, "I'm just going to make fresh coffee."

Anne said, "It's wonderful to be home. It smells so good over here on the island."

The model said, "No wonder you rave about this house so much, it's dreamy."

Putting down her suitcase, taking off her man's cap and getting out a long black cigarette holder into which she carefully inserted one of my cigarettes, Anne said, "I love it here on the island. Being here gives me a different perspective. The right things are important over here." She smiled at me and then said briskly, to hide her moment of weakness, "Here, you sit down and I'll make the coffee."

I did sit down, with a thump of astonishment, opposite the model who smiled at me with her lips pulled out at the corners and her teeth all touching each other. She was very very pretty with the impersonal perfection of a Swedish crystal pitcher. I said, "You are certainly pretty, Renée."

She said, "Thanks, but I don't think black does much for me. I like black, I think it's real chic, but white's really my color."

Anne, who was pouring the coffee, said, "As soon as we drink our coffee, let's put on our jeans."

Renée said, "I didn't bring jeans, honey, I can't get them small enough around the waist, my waist is only nineteen inches, but I brought my leopard skin slacks. Gee, they're dreamy. Shall I go put them on now?"

"Yes, do," Anne said, winking at me. "They sound terribly smart."

After Renée had taken her suitcase upstairs, Anne said, "I realize that Renée's brain is the size of a proton, but I feel sorry for her—she's really very sweet and her husband beats her to a pulp practically every half hour. She is always coming to work in dark glasses to cover a black eye or in high collars to cover finger marks on her neck."

"Why does he beat her—is he insane?"

"Oh, no, just jealous and a drunk. Last week he blacked both her eyes and cracked a couple of ribs so she moved in with Janet and me. As she brought at least $150,000 worth of clothes, her husband may have some reason for his jealousy. Anyway she lets me borrow anything I want and she's a wonderful cook."

As we drank our coffee Anne asked me about Joan and I told her and even though I was all braced and ready for the usual "*Why* won't you realize Joan and I are grown up, *why* do you always nag?" it wasn't forthcoming. Instead, Anne said, "Poor Mommy. Never mind, she'll grow out of it. I did and nobody in the entire universe was ever such a revolting adolescent." I guess I must have lost consciousness for a moment or two because, when I came to, Anne and Renée in her leopard skin slacks were saying, "We've got to do something about your hair, Betty. The way you're wearing it isn't smart at all." They both had their hair peeled back from their faces and pinned with huge gold barrettes. I wore my hair in a medium bob with bangs. After surveying me for a while from all angles through squinted eyes and a cloud of cigarette smoke, they decided I should wear my hair skinned up into a sort of whale spout on top of my head, secured with the red elastic band from the stalk of celery on the drainboard. When they had finished with me and I was very wet around the shoulders and felt as though my eyebrows were up by my hairline, Anne said, "Now, you look smart." Renée said, "God, you're a doll, Mrs. MacDonald."

I went into the lavatory off the kitchen and looked in the spattered mirror of the medicine cabinet. I finally decided that the light must be wrong. When I came back into the kitchen, Anne said, "You don't like it, I can tell." She laughed, took off the elastic and combed my hair back into its normal do. Sunday night, as I kissed Anne goodbye, I realized that her adolescence really was over, that she was an adult. What is more important I felt I had a new friend. One who was witty, intelligent, loving, beautiful and *liked* me. My little Anne, my serious-eyed little girl whom I had mourned and longed to bring back, was gone as surely as yesterday's rainbow, but I was really happier with my new friend. The heavy perfume, high style clothes, eyeshadow in the daytime that had been major irritations in my little girl, were now just the small lovable eccentricities of a friend.

The following summer Joan got a job as a saleslady in an exclusive dress shop. The sorority laugh was gone, but she began wearing high style clothes and the haunted look of the bill-ower. However, she was a tiny bit of fun sometimes and, anyway, Don and I had Anne to help us understand her. In January Anne was married—not to Sneaky Bradley—and during the hectic preparations for the wedding, Joan suddenly emerged as an easygoing witty slapdash affectionate sympathetic adult. Now they are both married and each has three babies. They are loving wives, marvelous mothers, divine cooks and excellent housekeepers. Don and I are very proud of them, but, more important, they *like* us. Their husbands *like* us. We are *friends*. Sometimes we are such good friends I get all six of the babies—the oldest is four—but I love it and it is awfully good for my figure. You see, I wear the high style clothes now. Maternity clothes are about the lowest style there is.

Some lines from Vachel Lindsay keep coming back to me:

Gone were the skull-faced witch men lean . . . .
'Twas a land transfigured, 'twas a new creation . . . .
And on through the blackwoods clearing flew:
  "Mumbo-Jumbo is dead in the jungle,
Never again will he hoo-doo you. Never again will he hoo-
  doo you."

Though Anne and Joan are grown up and Don and I are in our forties and grandparents six times over, Vashon Island hasn't changed a great deal. There are a few more Halvorsen Houses, a few roadside signs (supposedly not allowed), quite a few Cadillacs and foreign cars in town on Saturdays, the movie theatre has changed hands three or four times, the Falcon's Nest burned down, there were two houses for rent on this beach this summer, there is talk of a floating bridge to the mainland, the telephone service is a tiny bit better even though we still have fourteen people on our line, and the electricity rates are much higher with only about five minutes between the first bill and the shutoff notice. Ordinary living—eating, sleeping, keeping warm—is somewhat easier than it used to be, but still has little in common with urban life. We continue to have summers that can be distinguished from winter only by looking at the calendar.

Life is always a struggle, but on an island you at least have a feeling of having entered into personal, physical combat with it. Today for instance. Every once in a while I put on my old beach coat and slog down the path to look at our sea wall being so mercilessly hammered by the waves, many of them unfairly armed with logs which they use like battering rams. I can't do anything but pick up an occasional clam tossed into the geraniums near the greenhouse, watch the spray being flung fifty feet into the air and move the picnic table and benches a little farther back from the edge. But if the sea wall does come through this storm unscathed, and I'm sure it will, I will experience a great feeling of personal accomplishment, of having won another round in our battle with the elements. This is not just a peculiarity of mine. Don has it, too, and I have heard other island-dwellers speak of "bringing her through another winter" as if they had stood in front of their houses and personally defended them from the rain, the logs, the forests and the waves.

Perhaps this is one of the reasons why people, even ones who have had their houses pushed into the Sound by slides, remain here on Vashon, to take the same chance again. Of course another reason is the feeling we islanders have that living in a hot apartment taking vitamin pills instead of sunshine is pitifully like a broiler chicken in a battery. There is also our dismay at the tenor of city life where parties are business obligations and most of the people on the street look as if they were wearing shoulder holsters. Then of course we island-dwellers get our papers a day late and when we snap open our morning *Post-Intelligencers* the droughts, killings, floods, lynchings, rapes, dope smuggling to teen-agers, and avalanches are a day old. A day-old avalanche is still an avalanche but it isn't as bad as a fresh one—at least we Vashon islanders are already a little used to it. Even communism can't hold its own on Vashon because practically everything over here is subversive, i.e., "having a tendency to overthrow, upset or destroy." Puget Sound spends every winter trying to batter down our sea walls and reclaim the land. The rain tries to push us down where the Sound can get at us easier. Old logs lie hidden like unexploded bombs on the hills above us waiting for enough rain so they can come charging down and flick our houses off the beach like ashes off a cigarette. The ferry crews go on strike. The ferries run aground, leave five minutes early or knock down the dolphins. Even our rats, brought in years ago by a grocery boat, have become so dedicated to the cause of overthrowing, upsetting and destroying that when gnawing from within seems to be getting them nowhere, instead of being sensible and writing a book or going to the FBI with a list of all the other rats who have been gnawing with them, they crawl into the walls and die.

Of course there have been times when I have wondered if we did do the right thing in moving to an island. If it was fair to Anne and Joan. If it was fair to me. Once I asked Don and he said:

"Guiding children through adolescence is no joyride no matter where you live. At least here on Vashon we had something to take our minds off it. Fun things such as sawing wood or cleaning out the storm sewers."

Then I foolishly said, "And how do you think it has been for us? For instance, how do you think I compare to other women my age?"

Giving me a long, fond husbandly look, Don said, "Well, you don't look as tired as you did yesterday."

About the Author

BETTY MACDONALD was born Anne Elizabeth Campbell Bard in Boulder, Colorado, on 26 March 1908. She married Robert Heskett in 1927 and settled on a forty-acre chicken farm near Chimacum, Washington. Her experiences on the farm became the subject of her first book, *The Egg and I* (1945), which sold over a million copies in the year following publication, was made into a film starring Claudette Colbert and Fred MacMurray, and spawned the successful series of "Ma and Pa Kettle" films. In addition to *Onions in the Stew*, which was originally published in 1954, her other books include *The Plague and I* (1948) and *Anybody Can Do Anything* (1950). She died in Seattle on 7 February 1958.